Black Theology
USA and South Africa

The Bishop Henry McNeal Turner Studies
in North American Black Religion

Vol. 1 *For My People*
by James H. Cone

Vol. 2 *Black and African Theologies*
by Josiah U. Young

Vol. 3 *Troubling Biblical Waters*
by Cain Hope Felder

Editor:

James H. Cone,
Union Theological Seminary, New York

Associate Editors:

Charles H. Long,
Syracuse University

C. Shelby Rooks,
United Church Board of Homeland Ministries

Gayraud S. Wilmore,
Interdenominational Theological Seminary, Atlanta

The purpose of this series is to encourage the development of biblical, historical, theological, and pastoral works that analyze the role of the churches and other religious movements in the liberation struggles of blacks in the United States and the Third World. What is the relationship between black religion and black peoples' fight for justice in the U.S.? What is the relationship between the black struggle for justice in the U.S. and the liberation struggles of the poor in Asia, Africa, Latin America, and the Caribbean? A critical investigation of these and related questions will define the focus of this series.

This series is named after Bishop Henry McNeal Turner (1834–1915), whose life and work symbolize the black struggle for liberation in the U.S. and the Third World. Bishop Turner was a churchman, a political figure, a missionary, a pan-Africanist – a champion of black freedom and the cultural creativity of black peoples under God.

The Bishop Henry McNeal Turner Studies
in North American Black Religion, Vol. IV

Dwight N. Hopkins

Black Theology
USA and South Africa

Politics, Culture, and Liberation

ORBIS BOOKS

Maryknoll, New York 10545

Second Printing, January 1990

The Catholic Foreign Mission Society of America (Maryknoll) recruits and trains people for overseas missionary service. Through Orbis Books, Maryknoll aims to foster the international dialogue that is essential to mission. The books published, however, reflect the opinions of their authors and are not meant to represent the official position of the society.

Library of Congress Cataloging-in-Publication Data

Hopkins, Dwight N.
    Black theology USA and South Africa : politics, culture, and
liberation / Dwight N. Hopkins.
        p.   cm. — (The Bishop Henry McNeal Turner studies in North
American Black religion; vol. 4)
    Includes bibliographical references.
    ISBN 0-88344-639-1
    1. Black theology.   2. Theology, Doctrinal — United States —
History — 20th century.   3. Theology, Doctrinal — South Africa —
History — 20th century.   I. Title.   II. Series.
BT82.7.H66   1989
230'.089'96 — dc20   89-36831
                                                                CIP

In memory of my mother
Dora H. Hopkins

and

for my father
Robert R. Hopkins, Sr.

Contents

PART III
BLACK THEOLOGY SOUTH AFRICA

PART IV
DIALOGUE AND THE FUTURE

Chapter Six
Black Theology in the USA and South Africa:
   What Can They Say to Each Other?   *147*

Chapter Seven
Black Theology: The Culture of Politics and the Politics of Culture   *167*

Notes   *181*

Bibliography   *209*

Index   *245*

Acknowledgments

Without the support of Nancy Diao and James H. Cone, this book would not have been written.

My wife, Nancy Diao, discussed and debated the ideas in this book with me from beginning to end. It is the broadness of her political vision for the poor, her cultural sensitivity to people of color, the depths of her spirituality for all humanity, her warm love for our family, and her role as my intellectual comrade that have helped to sustain me.

James H. Cone suggested the topic for this book. It is difficult to express sufficient appreciation for his contributions to my intellectual growth. Cone was my graduate advisor and chaired my dissertation committee. I was also his research assistant and student. But most importantly, Cone consistently pressed his graduate students to remember that African-American *poor* people have the right to *think* and to *publish*. In fact one of the greatest sins committed by those with racial, class, and gender privileges is the assumption that their theology is normative. One day history will record more fully the importance of Cone's doing theology from below, from the perspective of the poor.

Christopher Morse and Cornel West were my professors. Along with Henry Mottu (from Geneva), they sat on my dissertation committee, giving of their valuable time, patience and creative theological insights.

Others who read parts of my manuscript or helped me in my studies were Kelly Brown, Hyun Kyung Chung, Willie Coleman, George Cummings, Alonzo Johnson, Marilyn Legge, Lillie McLaughlin, Dennis Wiley, and Josiah Young. Union Theological Seminary was the supportive "space" where I honed my theological skills. Mention must be made of president Donald Shriver, dean Milton McC. Gatch, James Washington, James Forbes, Kosuke Koyama, Beverly Harrison, and the U.T.S. library staff.

I would also like to thank the black religious scholars who altered their schedules so I could interview them; all those in South Africa who made my trip there a success; and pastor William A. Jones and the Bethany Baptist Church of Brooklyn, New York, where I served as associate minister during my graduate work.

Although physically distant, my sisters (Shirley and Brenda), brothers (Robert, Calvin, Leroy, Charles, James), and parents have been with me spiritually throughout this project. Lastly, I want to acknowledge the new generation—my son, Willie, and daughter, little Eva Shirley.

xi

Black Theology
USA and South Africa

Introduction

Blacks in the United States of America and in South Africa are brothers and sisters of the African diaspora. They share a specific and similar relation to the gospel — the good news of holistic liberation, systemic and individual, political and cultural. Such faith and theological claims in both communities, coupled with demonic and heretical white racist confrontations, provide the basis for a comparative theological study. Moreover, a Christian commitment to the genuine practice of all churches requires one to engage in "God-talk," theological dialogue, in order to confess faith and non-faith. Whether black or white, one enters the Christian tradition to "prepare the way of the Lord." Thus the joining of black theology in its United States' and South African counterparts results from common life experiences with the gospel and a need to witness before all Christians.

The emergence of black theology in the late 1960s marked a new level in theological discourse. At stake was the legitimacy of the connection between the gospel message of liberation and the movement for political and cultural liberation on the part of black people. In theological academies both black theologies challenged the false European-North American presupposition of the universality of God-talk. On the contrary, black theology argued the specificity of all theologies and, thus, the authenticity of black theology. Black theology lambasted the white church as the gathering of the Anti-Christ. In the black church black theology attacked the cultural mimicking of white ecclesiology and chastised the black church for the betrayal of its own radical political tradition. In larger society black theology maintained the seemingly heretical declaration that the Black Power Movement and Black Consciousness Movement revealed God's presence.

Today the stakes remain high. The gospel message has become a justification for an ideological shift in society toward conservatism, racist violence and a perpetual "state of emergency." The white church has split the gospel between a charismatic fundamentalism and entrenched *laager*[1] ecclesiology, on the one hand, and a retreating liberalism, on the other. In theological academies black theology runs the risk of becoming institutionalized "liberation theology" liberalism. And suffering historical amnesia since the assassinations of Malcom X and Martin Luther King, Jr., the American black church has flirted with a passive form of survivalism.

For Christians today black theology continues to pose the challenge to our witnessing and faith. For Christians black theology is important because

1

of our faith in Jesus Christ's mission (Lk 4:18ff.) and commission to his followers (Mt 25:31ff.). Christ's inaugural proclamation in Luke and judgment day court session in Matthew both reflect the essence of the gospel—justice for the poor. Christians must judge everything—culture, politics and theology—from the perspective of the "least of these" in society. If one does not side with the poor, then one is not a true Christian. In the United States and South Africa the poorest of the poor are the black poor.

Theologically, blacks in both the United States and South Africa are created in the image of God; they are black people. Consequently they have a right to think, to reflect on their unique black existence with the God of their liberation. Both black theologies continue to grapple with a common theodicy, the specific face of the demonic—the white racism of the white power structure. Both have been, generally speaking, developing a black theology independent of one another. This present study follows international dialogue between black theologians from both countries.[2]

My purpose in this work is to interpret black theology in the United States of America (BTUSA) and black theology in South Africa (BTSA). It poses and seeks to answer this major question: What is the common denominator between the two black theologies? It develops one basic claim: *Both theologies understand political and cultural liberation as the heart of the gospel message.* For black Christians in particular and the black community in general, this core message translates into the gospel of liberation against racism and other forms of oppression.

By black theology in the United States (BTUSA), I signify theology done by black people of African descent on the North American continent (excluding Canada) in their attempt to understand what the Christian gospel means for them and their community as the minority population in a situation of illegal white racism. By contemporary BTUSA I mean North American black theology that began with the *New York Times* publication of the 31 July 1966 Black Power statement by the ad hoc National Committee of Negro Churchmen.

By black theology in South Africa I mean theology done by black South Africans (including Indians and so-called Coloureds) in their effort to decipher the Christian gospel's meaning for them and their community as the majority population in a situation of legal white racism under apartheid. By contemporary BTSA I refer to South African black theology that commenced with the theological discussions of the University Christian Movement and the South African Students Organization in late 1969 and early 1970.

The common denominator between these two theologies is their stress on both political liberation and cultural liberation, that is, the common denominator between BTUSA and BTSA is the gospel of cultural and political liberation against white racism and other forms of oppression. This gospel, for one group of black theologians, focuses more on political liberation, and for another group more on cultural liberation. I emphasize the word more because both trends overlap in their cultural and political concerns. Each theologian, whether in the United States or South Africa, wrestles with both cultural and political questions.

I hope this study will make several contributions to the theological enterprise. No one has accomplished a major book-length study comparing black theology in the United States with black theology in South Africa, yet there is a need to examine the two theologies as they grapple with very similar existential questions. Although differences in social terrain and specific shadings of theological thought emerge, both theologies begin with the basic question of the relevance of the gospel message to the black situation. Perhaps by examining the birth of black theology, its original intent and goals, its theological import today and its connection to the black freedom movement, the black church and black theologians can further strengthen their relation to Jesus Christ's primary call of liberation for the black poor in the United States and South Africa. This book, in turn, will join the slow but steady column of liberation theologies marching to the tune of Jesus Christ Liberator in Africa, Asia and Latin America. Finally, this study seeks to contribute to European-North American theologies. By viewing one slice of the theologies of the poor, white theology might learn that its future and that of white humanity lie with Jesus Christ's option for poor people of color.

Chapter 1 sets the historical, political, cultural and theological contexts for the interpretation of both black theologies. In fact, by looking at the central aims of both settings, we obtain a clue about the common denominator for both theologies. Chapter 1 examines the distinctiveness of each country, what gave rise to each black theology, what theological issues theologians struggled with, and why black theology emerged.

In my review of the black theological movements I have chosen representatives of the political bent and of the cultural bent. The political black theologians incline their black theology more toward black political liberation. In their struggle against white racist theology in their black theology of liberation these theologians show concern more toward change of political systems, governments, power relations and, in the South African case, the establishment of non-racial political movements. These theologians also see the worth of black culture in the doing of their theology.

The other representative theologians lean slightly more toward black culture being the dominant source in the doing of their black theology of liberation. They inevitably suspect the more politically inclined spokesperson of downplaying the centrality of self-reliance on black cultural resources and sources in the development of a black theology of liberation. Nevertheless, both black theologies share, in my opinion, the commonality of the gospel of liberation but expressed in two accents—political and cultural.

Accordingly, Chapters 2 through 5 engage in a process of examining case studies within the black political theological trend and the black cultural theological trend. Both trends present theological positions on theology, liberation, Christology, reconciliation and black cultural sources. More specifically, the United States' political vein in Chapter 2 will be contrasted with the United States' cultural vein in Chapter 3; the South African political trend (Chapter 4) will be viewed in relation to the South African cultural trend (Chapter 5). Not all the black theological representatives in these chapters are trained academically in systematic theology. Yet in their own contexts they have all contributed and/or continue to add to black theology's developments. I will *interpret* their religious thought from a theological perspective.

Chapter 6 draws on earlier chapters and places BTUSA and BTSA in dialogue. We will discover the history of the dialogue between the countries and the theological issues emerging from the discussion; I will also pose a critical assessment of both theologies, stating more systematically and clearly the hints of the theological interpretations suggested by various lines in the preceding chapters. By comparing both theologies' strengths and weaknesses, similarities and disunities, and what they can learn from each other, I will highlight the common denominator between BTUSA and BTSA: They both claim the Christian gospel as the gospel of liberation for black people struggling against racism and for a holistic humanity—physically and spiritually, politically and culturally.

The final chapter advances my beginning effort at developing a black theology of liberation today. It presents what I perceive as the necessary issues and sources for the emergence of a black theology of political and cultural liberation. Its purpose is to suggest to both BTUSA and BTSA some theological relationships between the political and cultural trends as two tributaries within the same current of the black theology of liberation.

Part I

HISTORICAL CONTEXT

CHAPTER ONE

Black Power and Black Consciousness: The Contextual Backdrop

This is 1966. It's time out for beautiful words. It's time out for eu-
phemistic statements. And it's time out for singing "We Shall Overcome." It's time to get some Black Power. . . . It's time to get some
Black Power.

Stokely Carmichael, 1966

As long as blacks are suffering from inferiority complex — a result of
300 years of deliberate oppression, denigration and derision — they
will be useless as co-architects of a normal society where man is nothing else but man for his own sake. Hence what is necessary as a
prelude to anything else that may come is a very strong grass-roots
build-up of black consciousness such that blacks can learn to assert
themselves and stake their rightful claim.

Steve Bantu Biko, 1970

It is impossible to appreciate black theology in the United States
(BTUSA) and black theology in South Africa (BTSA) without exploring
their contexts. All theologies germinate from humanity's questioning the
relation of its existential predicament to ultimate concerns. The existential
situation provides the type of questions posed and colors the answers received. Similarly, one can only grasp the contours of black theology on both
sides of the Atlantic by unraveling the contextual backdrop. Chapter 1
fleshes out this contextual backdrop by describing (a) the contemporary
history, (b) the political trend, (c) the cultural trend and (d) the theological
emphases that evolved during the Black Power and Black Consciousness
movements. By connecting the social ideas of these two movements (the
fight against white racism and for black liberation) with the gospel (the call
for liberation of the poor), theologians forged BTUSA and BTSA.

BLACK THEOLOGY IN THE UNITED STATES

In the United States black theology developed out of the Civil Rights and Black Power movements.[1]

Civil Rights

December 1, 1955, began the contemporary Civil Rights Movement. On that day a black female worker, Rosa Parks, sat down in a Montgomery, Alabama, bus and refused to give her seat to a demanding white man. Her act of radical defiance of southern segregation laws sparked a new generation of black civil rights protest. Because she was tired from a day's work and because she felt mistreated, Mrs. Parks began a movement that propelled Dr. Martin Luther King, Jr., and the North American blacks' struggle for justice into the national and international arenas. For the next 382 days King and the Montgomery blacks successfully boycotted the city buses to protest segregation and to walk for freedom. One old black woman captured the determined spirit of protest. When asked about the weariness of walking to and from work, she replied: "My feets is tired, but my soul is rested."

It was these tired feet marching for freedom that symbolized the historic resistance of black Americans since slavery. Just as the "invisible" slave church and the independent African Baptist and African Methodist churches had initiated and led the antebellum movement against chattel slavery, the black church of the 1950s and the early 1960s, under King's leadership, played a vanguard role in breaking down legal segregation, primarily in the South. The black church knew that the Christian gospel contradicted the discriminating laws of white supremacy. Meeting, organizing, worshipping and singing in the church, the southern black community was empowered by the spirit of freedom. Indeed, King described Mrs. Parks' solitary act and the entire eruption of the Civil Rights Movement as being tracked down by the *Zeitgeist* — the spirit of the times.

The Civil Rights Movement ushered in a new time in response to God's kairos. Building on the persistent legal battles of the National Association for the Advancement of Colored People (NAACP) in the 1940s and early 1950s, the Civil Rights Movement ushered in a new form of protest. Blacks moved from the court chambers into the streets and backwoods of the southern states. Massive boycotts, sit-ins, kneel-ins and acts of civil disobedience undermined Jim Crow practices and segregation ordinances. On the social level the Civil Rights Movement demanded full equality for all Americans within the dictates of the United States Constitution. But the religion of freedom, the historical religion of black faith, fueled the movement against Ku Klux Klan terrorism, racist politicians and a general "white backlash."

Black theology arose from black pastors who had participated in King's Civil Rights Movement. These ministers were veterans of civil rights resistance in the South and desegregation activities of the North. They were familiar with water hoses and cattle prods. They had religiously exhorted white officials to abide by Christian love and nonviolence. They had also preached funerals for civil rights workers. And they had experienced the pain of having their churches "mysteriously" dynamited in the early morning hours. Interpreted by King, the Christian gospel called for loving one's enemy and pricking the moral consciousness of white supremacists. But by 1966 a growing group of black ministers who had faithfully followed King found themselves at a crossroads between King's nonviolent Christian philosophy and Black Power, urban rebellions and Malcolm X's black nationalist philosophy. Thus black theology came from a synthesis of King's Christian gospel of racial justice and Black Power's black liberation nationalism. Black religious leaders began to conclude that the God of Moses and Jesus did not condone slavery and segregation. Quite the opposite, authentic Christianity meant racial justice and black liberation by any means necessary.[2]

Black Power

The Black Power Movement, which grew out of the Civil Rights Movement, resulted from several strands. First, despite the 1954 Supreme Court decision that separate was not equal and white liberals hailing 1955 to 1965 as the decade of Negro progress, the masses of black people suffered. Between the successful 1955–56 Montgomery bus boycott and the signing of the Voting Rights Act in 1965, the gap between black and white in every sphere of American society had widened.[3] Despite the passage of the Civil Rights acts of 1957, 1960 and 1964, and the Voting Rights Act of 1965, the myth of the decade of Negro progress applied only to a minute sector of the black community. In particular, the black middle class reaped whatever meager benefits resulted from the struggle for civil rights. But the black poor—the overwhelming majority—languished in poverty and lack of significant societal gains.

Second, increasing numbers of youth in the Civil Rights Movement voiced a growing disdain toward the hypocrisy of white liberalism. The Student Non-Violent Coordinating Committee (SNCC) mirrored this changing mood. In opposition to the local segregated Democratic Party, SNCC played a leading role in instituting the Mississippi Freedom Democratic Party (MFDP) as a representative of the state's loyal (black) majority for the presidential ticket of Lyndon Johnson. However, at the 1964 Democratic National Convention in Atlantic City, Lyndon Johnson, Hubert Humphrey, Walter Mondale and other white liberals on the convention's credentials committee, as well as black civil rights establishment leadership, supported the illegal, white, segregationist delegation from Mississippi.

Suffering "betrayal at the hands of the white liberals," SNCC analyzed the defeat inflicted by the liberal-segregationist maneuvering at the 1964 Democratic Convention. By the convention's conclusion the youth group "was convinced that membership in the Democratic coalition held little hope for Southern blacks and that, lacking power, they would always be sold out by the liberals."[4]

Third, in addition to the hypocrisy of liberal Democrats, the failure of federal government support for voter registration continued the disillusioning process for SNCC. In 1961 the John F. Kennedy administration sought to redirect the growing militant energy of SNCC into voter registration in the deep south. The president volunteered federal protection if the youth agreed to the proposed refocus. One wing of SNCC accepted the opportunity. But as early as the 1962 voter registration organizing, SNCC workers underwent bloody beatings from local segregationists as federal agents of Robert Kennedy's Justice Department stood nearby, watched and took notes. Extending sympathy without substance, Attorney General Robert Kennedy admitted that "careful explanations of the historic limitations on the federal government's police powers [were] not satisfactory to the parents of students who have vanished in Mississippi."[5]

Fourth, Black Power arose in reaction to white segregationist terrorism in the South. The stakes for registering to vote proved dear. SNCC activists and local black residents experienced dynamite bombings, beatings, shootings, burnings, maimings, kidnappings, sabotaging of cars and murders. And, legally, "gangsterlike" sheriffs jailed "outside agitators," who disrupted the normal ties between whites and blacks. Legally, banks and insurance companies conveniently cancelled loans and policies, thereby intimidating powerless, black sharecroppers and farm workers. Legally, from state governors down to city council members, politicians simply ignored federal mandates by upholding the doctrine of "interposition and nullification" (states' rights).

Black youth began to question whether the turn-the-other-cheek philosophy was merely another form of the bowing and scraping their grandparents had gone through in order to get something from the white man. Why did they have to wear suits and ties, "sit-in" and calmly have their bodies beaten to a bloody pulp for rights supposedly guaranteed by the Constitution? Why wouldn't America give black people rights other citizens enjoyed by birthright?[6]

Finally, Black Power revealed the resurrection of the spirit of Malcolm X, the contemporary father of black nationalism. More than any other public figure in the late 1950s and early 1960s, Malcolm grasped the profound sense of psychological self-hatred and self-denigration internalized by black America. With trenchant clarity he declared, "The worst crime the white man has committed has been to teach us to hate ourselves."[7] Malcolm X comprehended the true meaning of integration—white people banding together in their white ethnic groups and using power while calling on blacks to appeal to the moral consciousness of whites (even as the latter beat black people physically) through use of an integrated coalition. Malcolm sought to shatter the myth in the black person's mind that equated value and the norm with whiteness and defined blackness as derivative of white. Before Black Power, white people stood for cleanliness, beauty, and saintliness. Black people were synonymous with nastiness, ugliness, and evil. Describing the effect of having white northern liberals involved in the 1964 voter registration campaign conducted by SNCC in Mississippi, black activist Julius Lester wrote:

> A Negro would follow a white person to the courthouse, not because he'd been convinced he should register and vote, but simply because he had been trained to say Yes to whatever a white person wanted.[8]

Like a tireless prophet wielding the flaming sword of truth against "principalities and powers," Malcolm X demanded black liberation "by any means necessary." Politically he articulated black solidarity and the right of self-determination. Culturally he lifted up black pride and pan-Africanism. And theologically he defined the white man as "the devil." Describing SNCC's turn toward Black Power, James Foreman cites the influence of the ideas of Malcolm X as a definite factor.[9]

The stage was set for Stokely Carmichael, newly elected chairman of SNCC. In June 1966, on the Meredith March Against Fear, Carmichael hurled the thunderbolt of Black Power from the backwoods of Greenwood, Mississippi. Carmichael received one graphic response to his declaration in October 1966. During that month a group of black, urban militants donned black outfits and patrolled the streets of Oakland, California, with carbines, rifles and shotguns. The Black Panther Party for Self-Defense was born. Further responses burned like prairie fire. Between 1965 and 1968 nearly three hundred urban rebellions exploded across America and thrust a new term into the national lexicon—*the long hot summer*. The entire political and cultural scenery in black America underwent rapid alteration. The young, black revolutionary generation, whom Julius Lester knighted "the angry children of Malcolm X," had taken center stage.

Political Themes

As a movement in the 1960s and 1970s, Black Power comprised scores of local and national groups. Not being one organization, it could never present one political program. Yet all sympathizers in the Black Power Movement agreed on one point—to oppose white racism and enhance black advancement. From that point the political platforms of Black Power diverged from building socialism to operating within the Democratic and Republican parties, and from conducting violent warfare against the United

States government to seeking funding from United States monopoly capitalist foundations.

One black political scientist devised a four-part approach in categorizing Black Power. He classified the Black Power advocate as a "political bargainer," struggling for goods and services within the two-party system; a "moral crusader," seeking to transform the soul of society; an "alienated reformer," concentrating on local black community control; or an "alienated revolutionary," calculating violence.[10]

Despite the lack of consensus around the political definition of Black Power, two of its proponents had a major impact in the media and movement at that time. They were Stokely Carmichael, the father of Black Power, and the Black Panther Party. Carmichael's experience in Mississippi as a SNCC organizer shaped his political definition of Black Power. He concluded that black Americans faced two fundamental problems—being black and poor. All other problems arose from this dual reality. As a result, Carmichael's and SNCC's basic program endeavored to win political power for poor southern blacks. Even when Carmichael targeted the psychological inferiority complex among blacks, he believed that the way to realize black consciousness was through blacks politically organizing their own community.

Carmichael also called for ownership and control of the black community by black people. Blacks should own and control ghetto schools, stores, recreation and sports activities, housing and the flow of money in their own neighborhoods. Summing up his experience in the rural black belt counties of the South, he projected black community control as a panacea for northern and southern urban areas.

Representing the fluidity of definitions during the Black Power era, Carmichael, at times, seemed to contradict his political definition of black power. At one point he justified the movement by comparing it to other ethnic groups' history in the United States. Polish, Irish and Jewish immigrants had formed ghettoes—basically ethnic power blocks. By organizing their own institutions, they had successfully integrated into the over-all pluralistic society. However, in another context Carmichael called for black revolution, armed struggle and guerrilla warfare. Politically he threatened, "the only solution is black revolution. . . . Armed struggle . . . is the only way. . . . People who talk about peaceful coexistence are talking about maintaining the status quo. . . . We are going to develop urban guerrilla warfare."

Internationally Carmichael's politics of Black Power meant black Americans supporting black South Africans by advising the latter on the necessity of black power. Black South Africans needed to control South Africa by expelling Chase Manhattan Bank, Standard Oil and missionaries along with their Bibles.[11]

Like Carmichael, the Black Panther Party expounded Black Power politically. Huey Newton (minister of defense of the party) attributed the lack of freedom for black America to the lack of political power. Even black political representatives, Newton contended, were impotent because the black community possessed no land or industries. In short, blacks owned no means of production. As a result, they had to turn toward armed self-defense — military power — to realize political power. From a position of military strength blacks could negotiate politically. If the white power structure failed to meet the community's demands, exhorted Newton, the power structure would suffer a loss in its profits. Military power facilitated an equality in negotiations between the community and the power structure. For the Black Panther Party, politics was war without bloodshed and war was politics with bloodshed.

Newton called for black people to rule and determine their own destiny. As an internal colony oppressed by United States imperialism, black people had only one long-range political goal. Black Power stood for people's power. And people's power equaled socialism.

Thus, within the political trend of Black Power common agreement focused on redistribution of political power in the sense of control of political offices and economics within the black community. However, this trend ranged from the reformist attempt by the black middle class to advance its own political and economic status within existing society to the radical solution of transforming the monopoly capitalist system into some form of socialism.

Newton divided the Black Power Movement into the Revolutionary Nationalist wing and the Cultural Nationalist wing.[12] Revolutionary nationalism, for him, was dependent on a people's revolution, the goal of which was to put "the people in power." Once in power, the leaders of the people would forego the profit motive as a means of exploitation. Instead, the political economy of the new society would revolve around communalism in ownership and participation. Black liberation and the right of self-determination would evolve from the establishment of political freedom.

From Newton's perspective the Cultural Nationalist wing incorrectly looked backward to its African roots. Somehow "returning to the old African culture" would satisfy the demands for "identity and freedom." However, African culture itself did not inherently stand for reaction. Newton's critique assailed cultural nationalists for grabbing on to past culture in such a way that "Africa" and "blackness" became posturings to cover up the black intellectuals' and black middle class' support for capitalism. The Revolutionary Nationalist, that is, the political trend emphasis, asked one question of the Cultural Nationalist, that is, the cultural trend emphasis: How does returning to African culture and focusing on blackness as identity alleviate the political (and economic) suffering of the majority of the black community, the poor? Speaking for the political trend, Newton wrote: "We believe that culture itself will not liberate us."[13]

Cultural Themes

Representatives of the cultural trend in the Black Power Movement attempted to connect identity and power as the means of black liberation and self-determination. They took seriously Malcolm X's caustic focus on the brainwashing of black America. They struggled with the black ontological duality, what W.E.B. DuBois termed the "peculiar sensation, this double consciousness." What sort of hybrid concoction were blacks in the United States? They were not fully African, nor were they fully American. Lack of resolution of this identity question tore at the soul and very being of blacks. In fact, it stood as the major factor for black subservience to white supremacy.

Ron Karenga and LeRoi Jones[14] represent the chief spokespersons for this conviction. Karenga codified his cultural ideas in a pamphlet called "The Quotable Karenga."[15] He dealt with four areas. First, Karenga designated the ultimate reality as blackness. "The fact that we are Black is our ultimate reality. We were Black before we were born." The fundamental task of the black nationalist was to pursue blackness — "to Think Black, Talk Black, Act Black, Create Black, Buy Black, Vote Black, and Live Black." What is black? For Karenga, like most cultural trend advocates, black denoted color, culture and consciousness. Culture was stressed because it provided identity, purpose and direction. Culture explained who black people were, what they had to do, and how they had to do it. Culture dictated the study of black art and black history as means of self-definition. In brief, black power was black culture.

Second, Karenga emphasized self-love. White culture had bombarded blacks with the saintliness and purity of whiteness. Therefore black people needed to comprehend black as beautiful. Part of the pursuit of blackness was race pride. Drawing on the historical currents of Marcus Garvey, Karenga decreed a new black self-image. White pride displayed itself by white people's monopoly in media, culture and positions of power. To combat the mental slavery of blacks, race pride created new pictures of black people in place of white faces.

Third, to facilitate race pride black people needed to return to their African roots and heritage. Indeed, Karenga proclaimed, "to go back to tradition is the first step forward." Proud people who controlled their history could win their liberation. Part of reclaiming history involved wearing African headdress, shirts, robes, jewelry and sandals. To further remove themselves from "white" conditioning, black people had to adopt African or Arabic names. All black Americans possessed "slave names," that is, the surnames of their masters under slavery. The return to the African roots demarcated one of the major features of the Black Power cultural trend. Somehow a reconnection with Africa would end the warring contradiction in black identity, the incongruity between one's America-ness and one's Africa-ness, the unyielding need for role playing and duplicity before the larger American society. Africa could provide a homeland identity to which to return, and it could assist the building up of the "black nation" in the United States.

Fourth, Karenga presented a direct challenge to the Black Power political trend. In his opinion, because the first half of the black liberation movement was for the minds of black people, "we must free ourselves culturally before we succeed politically." Politics flows from culture and not the reverse. There had to be a cultural revolution before the violent revolution. Why the initial struggle for culture? "Racist minds created racist institutions. Therefore we must move against racism, not institutions. For even if we tear down the institutions, that same mind will build them up again."

LeRoi Jones echoed Karenga. Writing in his poetic style, Jones ferreted out pseudo-Black Power advocates on the basis of culture:

> There are people who might cry BlackPower, who are representatives, extensions of white culture. So-called BlackPower advocates who are mozartfreaks or Rolling Stones, or hypnotized by Joyce or Hemingway or Frank Sinatra, are representatives, extensions, of white culture, and can never therefore signify black power.[16]

He criticized Black Power and civil rights organizations that collected "memberships on strictly socio-political grounds." In his view an inability to translate their political ideas into the language of the people caused their membership to decline. In other words, they made "little reference to the totality of black culture." As an artist Jones felt the imperative for cultural language, images, emotions and moods. The propagation of black art was "centrally" the commitment of Black Power.

One of the fundamental accusations the cultural trend cast against the political trend in Black Power was the latter's apparent usage of white epistemological categories. For Jones, black people's own creativity acted as sufficient resource and source for black liberation. White European-North American mental constructs only delayed freedom into blackness. Jones exclaimed:

> A culturally aware black politics would use all the symbols of the culture, all the keys and images out of the black past, out of the black present, to gather the people to it, and energize itself with their strivings at conscious blackness. . . . The politics and the art and the religion all must be black.

Hence the cultural proponents derided class analysis as a European category and a foreign thought imposed on the black community. Applied to the black community, class analysis, over against cultural analysis, divided blacks and deflected focus away from the main enemy. The continued utilization of "white" worldviews, for example, Marx's class analysis, merely verified the cultural trend's claim that the political trend adherents were so damaged by the disease of psychological inferiority they did not realize they could only find white tools of analysis for black freedom. In the cogency of the cultural trend perspective LeRoi Jones wrote, "Black power movements not grounded in Black culture cannot move beyond the boundaries of Western thought."

The cultural trend exponents demanded a response to one major question: How does the usage of "white thought" for change in political (and economic) structures alter racism in the minds of whites and also improve (the mental) self-identity, self-reliance and culture of blacks?

Theological Themes

In the midst of Carmichael's Black Power cry, urban rebellions and political-cultural trends in the black liberation movement, black theology burst forth. Black American pastors and laypersons found themselves caught with a theology suitable for the "We Shall Overcome" era of integrationism and liberalism, but apparently insufficient and irrelevant to the needs of the black community in the era of "I'm Black and I'm Proud!" In the hurricane eye of a black revolution, the ad hoc National Committee of Negro Churchmen (NCNC) coalesced. In the fall of 1968 Gayraud Wilmore, first chairman of the NCNC theological commission, described "the rising crescendo of voices from both the pulpit and pew demanding that black churchmen reexamine their beliefs; that unless they begin to speak and act relevantly in the present crisis they must prepare to die." The black revolution presented an ultimatum: Unless black pastors " 'do their thing' in some kind of symbolic and actual disengagement from the opprobrium of a white racist Christianity, they have no right to exist in the black community."[17]

The voices and protests of black people forced the issue of the role of Christianity in the black community. "Negro" pastors had to become relevant and "black" or "prepare to die"! They were challenged to "reexamine their beliefs" and conduct a "disengagement from the opprobruim of a white racist Christianity." Thus black theology arose as an answer to the reality of black liberation moving against white racism. What did it mean to be black and Christian? Where was God and Jesus Christ in the urban rebellions? Was the black church simply serving an Uncle Tom, otherworldly role, or was it aiding in black control of the community and black people's destiny? Could blacks continue to uphold the theology of integrationism and liberalism — a theology where all power remained in the hands of white people? When stripped of its "whiteness," what did Christianity say to black Americans? Could black identity, culture, history and language become authentic sources for the doing of theology? What did a blue-eyed, blond-haired, "hippie-looking" Jesus have to do with Black Power and black liberation?

Contemporary black theology in the United States grew out of the National Committee of Negro Churchmen (NCNC). Therefore it is important to take an in-depth look at NCNC's origin.[18] NCNC was comprised of black

pastors and church executives, the majority in predominantly white denominations, who united to respond favorably to Black Power. The Rev. Leon
W. Watts, II, one of the founders of NCNC, depicted the volatile environment at that time.

> In 1966 . . . everybody, including Martin Luther King Jr., came out
> with a negative statement about Black Power. It was as if Stokely
> Carmichael had loosed some monster upon the country that was going
> to devour it, the way in which both black political leaders and the
> press came out in an almost unanimous voice opposing the concept
> of Black Power.[19]

Thus when NCNC published its full-page, Black Power apologia in the
31 July 1966 edition of the *New York Times*, the National Committee swam
against the ecclesiological and societal tidal wave of anti-Black Power hys-
teria. In fact, the NCNC would not have formed were it not for the nationwide negative response to Black Power. Leon Watts explains: "The
National Committee of Negro Churchmen . . . had its beginnings in response to the way in which the press responded [rabidly] to Stokely Carmichael's call for Black Power on the Meredith March." By focusing on
black liberation over against integration, the Committee broke with King
and the Civil Rights Movement.

The Rev. Dr. Calvin B. Marshall, another NCNC founder, states that
black churchpeople "found ourselves in a vacuum" and thus formed the
Committee. The turbulence in the black community had caused black
churchpeople to choose between the "vacuum" of integrationism and the
relevancy of black liberation. Marshall continues: "We had gotten to the
point where we had to hear God speaking through what we [the black
church and the black community] were going through." And where did the
Committee hear the word of God? Previously the white church power structure had condoned only the formally educated and "reasonable" black
church leaders such as Martin Luther King, Jr. No matter how many
marches civil rights churches and organizations undertook against racism,
the white church suspected that it shared the same *theology* with the black
church. The white church could draw on a common theological framework
and speak a common theological language.

In complete contradiction to this integrationist, theological contract,
NCNC began to radically hear the word of God elsewhere. Watts recounts
how the Committee

> began to talk about what would be the response of the black church,
> not simply to what Martin Luther King, Jr., was doing, because many
> people were participating in [the Civil Rights Movement] as churches,
> but also to take some account of the more militant groups such as

the Black Muslims . . . Black Panthers, Ron Karenga's group . . .
Stokely Carmichael.

The Committee had turned to the militant currents among the black
poor to hear a "message from the Lord."

In 1967 in Dallas, Texas, NCNC held its first national convocation and
formally established its theological commission. The Committee charged
the commission to explore the uniqueness and profundity of the black religious experience in America. The commission had to articulate in clear
theological terms the "differences and distinctions" between how black
people and white people saw themselves as Christians. The black liberation
movement required a theological response to the juxtaposition of "black"
and "power." In short, the black churchmen turned to God to answer how
black Christians could remain authentic witnesses of the gospel and not be
either integrationists or segregationists.

In 1967 Dr. Nathan Wright, Jr., surfaced some of the major theological
themes and began to address the theological roadblocks facing a nascent
black theology. Wright claimed:

> To the precise extent that Black Power affirms and extends God's
> truth and purposes, it is in that same degree possessed of a sacred
> and eternal nature. It is partially thus a sign of the presence of God's
> rule, which is what is meant by the term "the kingdom of God."[20]

Wright had pinpointed foundational, black theological issues—the positive relation of God to Black Power, the divine presence in Black Power,
and Black Power as a revelation of God's rule. A year later at the 1968
second convocation of NCBC (*Negro* had been changed to *Black*) in St.
Louis, the Committee had begun to use the phrase *black theology* to describe
the encounter of God with the black experience. A 15 November 1968 *Time*
magazine article reported on the gathering and described how "a number
of speakers suggested that a major goal should be the creation of a fully
developed black theology."[21]

The seeds of black theology in the United States sprouted with the
formation of NCNC in 1966. However, not until the spring of 1969 would
a little-known theologian bring those seeds to fruition. James H. Cone's
Black Theology and Black Power appeared in March 1969. NCBC and the
black church had finally received a scholarly work, which sharply presented
the black religious experience, not merely as a challenge to the sociological
practice of the white church, but as a devastating critique of the white
theology dominant in white and black churches. Cone dropped a bombshell.
Theologically he argued that black power *was* the gospel of Jesus Christ![22]

The work of black theology in the United States also chastened racism
in South Africa. "Back in the '60s," in the words of Rev. Watts, "the
National Committee of Negro Churchmen was speaking out against apart-

heid. [The Committee] had written several documents" condemning white racism in South Africa. The statements of the NCBC and, primarily, the works of James Cone found a ready theological audience among blacks struggling to make sense out of God's relation to apartheid and the Black Consciousness Movement. In its own evolution black theology in South Africa followed a course similar to the dynamics of black theology in the United States. Thus it is helpful to examine the historical backdrop and the political and cultural themes in South African society as preconditions to the theological themes in black theology in South Africa.

BLACK THEOLOGY IN SOUTH AFRICA

Similar to the Civil Rights Movement's and Black Power's relation to black theology in the United States, nonviolent civil disobedience protest and the Black Consciousness Movement (BCM) fostered the arrival of black theology in South Africa.

Civil Disobedience

At the beginning of the 1950s the African National Congress (the primary voice of black resistance) included both an older, liberal tendency and a younger more nationalist influence. The influx of younger leadership pushed ANC from passive petitioning and court battles to civil disobedience. No longer would ANC rely primarily on elite black delegations' attempts to prick the white government's sense of justice. Tactics shifted from appeals to white supremacists to massive mobilization of boycotts, strikes and marches in order to wrest away black rights from apartheid. Yet in the 1950s ANC still hoped to bring about black participation in the government nonviolently. ANC wanted to have apartheid laws repealed and blacks granted the franchise. In fact, they believed a more militant approach would woo whites from apartheid policies. In other words, a shift to militant tactics remained within a liberal democratic strategy.

Underneath the social movement toward liberal democracy, a liberal Christian worldview existed. Many of the ANC leaders were trained in white missionary schools. And many ANC rank and file were Christians. A missionary upbringing had taught older black activists of the 1950s that all protest movements were immoral and unethical unless whites and blacks worked together. The goal of nonracialism, then, had to determine that the means of struggle include multiracial participation. The inclusion of all races in nonviolently pressuring the apartheid government would show white supremacists, and the world community, that South African blacks were mature enough to deliberate in government.

However, by the end of the 1950s the young nationalists in ANC began to coalesce around an "Africanist" position. They sought "Africa for Africans," the return of stolen land to indigenous African ownership prior to white people's arrival, black psychological freedom from European thinking, and black self-determination toward a future black-ruled South Africa. This nationalist section of ANC saw no distinctions between radical whites and white liberals. They blamed all whites for enforcing blacks' cultural self-negation. In fact, white radicals in particular claimed blacks' yearning for self-reliance to be a racist and fascist immorality. In contrast, black nationalists argued that a true and healthy culture and morality forced oppressed black people to appreciate themselves, their history and their culture. Immorality and cultural enslavement came about through participation with any sectors of the white oppressor. Therefore black people had to go it alone to achieve black majority rule in post-apartheid South Africa. Lacking any minority privileges, whites would be absorbed into the black majority.

In 1959 ANC's Africanist wing formally broke away and established the Pan-Africanist Congress (PAC). Like the ANC, PAC leadership and membership experienced Christian influences. At the founding PAC congress in 1959 an address was given by a clergyman who headed the largest federation of African independent churches. Also, the PAC president, Robert Sobukwe, was a Methodist lay preacher.

PAC attempted to build on the growing impatience of younger blacks and the African urban population. The Afrikaner government had consolidated its policy of "separate development" in all walks of life. Laws prohibited mixed-race sexual relations, enforced segregated living, stipulated inferior "Bantu" education, codified black identity with mandatory, tribal pass books, and curtailed black employment and movement by influx control policies. Sensing a new mood for direct action, PAC focused on a campaign of massive civil disobedience against pass books. This campaign for "positive action" set March 21, 1960, as the time for direct confrontation with the state. At that time all Africans would refuse to carry passes, voluntarily go to jail and refuse any offer of bail.

At the Sharpeville demonstration police indiscriminately opened fire, killing sixty-seven blacks, the majority shot in the back. One hundred eighty-six were wounded. The response to the "Sharpeville massacre" was immediate. ANC, PAC and South African white liberals launched public rallies and protests. World opinion likewise centered on the apartheid government's unprovoked shootings. The government, facing an unprecedented crisis, swooped up the leadership of both the PAC and the ANC. Consequently some black leaders went underground. Others fled into exile. Without coherent internal leadership, black resistance ground to a standstill on the threshold of the 1960s.[23] Black resistance smoldered until the rise of black consciousness.

Black Consciousness

Like the birth of Black Power, the Black Consciousness Movement initially rallied against the hypocrisy of white liberalism, primarily English-speaking whites. By the mid-1960s the National Union of South African Students (NUSAS) played the leading role in white liberal defense of black rights. Due to the aftermath of the March 21, 1960, "Sharpeville Massacre," an immense political vacuum characterized the anti-apartheid scene of black South Africans. Fear gripped blacks to such a degree that the general population incorrectly believed political protest was illegal. NUSAS stepped in to fill this enormous void. Black students discovered that this liberal formation afforded one of the few remaining legal avenues for national dialogue among blacks. However, at a July 1967 NUSAS conference, black delegates were forced to live in appalling, segregated accommodations away from the conference site. This contradiction between liberal proclamation of multiracial equality, on the one hand, and NUSAS's persistent practical disregard for black student concerns, on the other, marked the beginning of the demise of a white-black, master-slave mentality in South Africa. A year later the South African Students Organization (SASO) formed; it held its inaugural conference in 1969.[24] Steve Bantu Biko, the father of Black Consciousness, chaired the youth organization. SASO's "Policy Manifesto" added weight to the deep pain inflicted on black students by the liberals. The Manifesto decried a scurrilous integration as a sham. "Integration does not mean an assimilation of Blacks into an already established set of norms drawn up and motivated by White society."[25]

In 1966 Biko attended Durban University and discovered an anomaly in black-white relations. He and his colleagues realized that "whites were in fact the main participants in [blacks'] oppression and at the same time the main participants in the opposition to that oppression." Biko referred to this situation as the "totality of white power." In particular, he pictured the white liberals as "playing their old game." They claimed a "monopoly on intelligence and moral judgement" and "set the pattern and pace" for black liberation. When the inevitable liberal backlash to black unity reared its ugly head, Biko retorted that white liberals "are the greatest racists for they refuse to credit us with any intelligence to know what we want."[26]

In addition to white liberal hypocrisy, BCM attacked the over-all apartheid system. Ownership of land ranked high among the grievances. Biko articulated the BCM position against bantustans — the Balkanization of the majority population into arid areas based on language groupings:

> Above all, we black people should all the time keep in mind that South Africa is our country and that all of it belongs to us. The arrogance that makes white people [today's Afrikaans-speaking whites] travel all the way from Holland to come and balkanise our country and shift us around has to be destroyed. Our kindness has been misused and our hospitality turned against us. Whereas whites were mere guests to us on their arrival in this country [in 1652] they have now pushed us out to a 13% corner of the land.[27]

The bantustan law proved to be a burning concern in the BCM. It expressed the continued process of forced removal of blacks from "white areas" and the black segregation onto non-fertile lands far away from cities, that is, away from the centers of power and commerce. It also employed the divide-and-conquer tactic of separating South Africans by their "tribal" languages and stripping all blacks of their common South African citizenship. And finally, it manifested the height of white arrogance. How dare the white minority of five million visit black people's home — South Africa — then expel those same people from their place of residence and legislate mandatory use of pass books on the majority of seventeen million? Reproaching the system, Biko exclaimed: "Nothing can justify the arrogant assumption that a clique of foreigners has the right to decide on the lives of a majority."[28]

Furthermore, the white liberals' refusal to allow the black majority to exercise the right of self-determination and the Afrikaners' entrenched apartheid laws had produced a sorrowful psychological existence for black South Africans.[29] The post-Sharpeville political void and the implementation of the bantustan policy in the early 1960s caused blacks to resemble shadows of men and women. Biko penned a graphic account of the black majority's deep inferiority complex. He echoed Malcolm X's repeated claim about black Americans' suffering from lethal self-hatred and brainwashing. The SASO president contended: "All in all the black has become a shell, a shadow of [personhood], completely defeated drowning in his own misery, a slave, an ox bearing the yoke of oppression with a sheepish timidity." Apartheid and white liberalism had beaten down black self-esteem to the level of sinful duplicity. Biko resumed his indictment against the ontological depravity of black South Africa: "In the privacy of his toilet his face twists in silent condemnation of white society but brightens up in sheepish obedience as he comes out hurrying in response to his master's impatient call."[30] Paralleling the pre-1966 black American quandary, the black South African threshed out the same questions — Why did blackness allude to everything bad and evil while whiteness conveyed God and beauty? Why was whiteness equivalent to value? Adam Small, a BCM poet, warned of the danger of self-denigration. Blacks' "equation of Whiteness with Valuableness," he wrote, "is foolish and indeed dangerous for them, as it will destroy them."[31]

Tom Lodge cites an additional source in the emergence of the BCM. He investigated the trends of black employment in industrial and white-collar jobs in urban areaᵤ in the 1960s and concluded that the social base of the township population had changed markedly. In other words, with a rise in the black clerical work force, one noted a sharp rise in black literacy and the concomitant openness to political ideas.[32]

Finally, the black South Africans attentively scrutinized the international experiences of blacks in Africa and the United States. Ghana had become the first politically independent African country below the Sahara in 1957.

Dozens of African countries had lowered colonial flags and hoisted their own native colors by the late 1960s. With independence came questions of cultural indigenization and political direction for postcolonialism. Therefore, black South Africans studied the words of Julius Nyerere, Kenneth Kaunda, Leopold Senghor, Franz Fanon and Aime Cesaire.

Similarly, black South Africans absorbed lessons from American developments. In the United States the 1955 to 1966 civil rights struggle and the 1966 Black Power Movement evidenced a political and cultural renaissance. Not since the era of Marcus Garvey had black activities had such an impact on the black community and the social fabric of the United States. Black South Africans diligently scoured the media for the latest news and shared works such as *The Autobiography of Malcolm X*, Stokely Carmichael's and Charles Hamilton's *Black Power*, Eldridge Cleaver's *Soul on Ice* and James H. Cone's *Black Theology and Black Power*.[33]

Unity of Politics and Culture

Having examined prominent sources in the conception of the Black Consciousness Movement, we can now probe its salient political and cultural themes.

As reviewed above, the political and cultural proponents in the Black Power Movement in the United States differed sharply in their definitions of Black Power. In the Black Consciousness Movement in South Africa, however, there was a closer intertwining of the political and cultural themes among most advocates of BCM. Since the Nazi-like apartheid government cracked down on all black resistance, political and cultural expressions were forced into one analysis. Therefore, though the political and cultural categories follow below as a framework, one has to keep in perspective the non-antagonistic stance of both themes in the actual practice of the South African Black Consciousness Movement.

For example, in its *Policy Manifesto* SASO defined Black Consciousness as "a way of life, an attitude of mind." This pursuit of "life" and "mind" would contribute to SASO's purpose of "working for the liberation of the Black man first from psychological oppression by themselves through inferiority complex and secondly from physical oppression accuring [sic] out of living in a White racist society." SASO, then, projected liberation in a bifurcated political-cultural approach, with an initial slant on cultural oppression. In a similar vein Biko succinctly delineated the relation of politics and culture in a paper presented at a SASO leadership training course in 1971:

The interrelationship between the consciousness of the self and the emancipatory programme is of paramount importance. Blacks no longer seek to reform the system because so doing implies acceptance of the major points around which the system revolves.[34]

Biko highlighted a concern for fundamental transformation of the political configuration in South Africa. He also exhibited the clear connection of culture to politics. In short, on the one hand the BCM had to realign the basic political power relation in South Africa, and on the other BCM had to attend to ameliorating the cultural values and perception of the black self.

At least two reasons occasioned the co-mingling of political and cultural themes in the BCM. First, the black South Africans were indigenous to the land prior to the arrival of whites. Therefore blacks maintained a reference point to their unified pre-colonial African cultural and political lineage. Thus, when BCM waged a campaign for psychological and physical liberation, it sought to reconnect to and build on how black foreparents had politically and culturally ruled black life. Simply put, blacks in the BCM wanted to reclaim a holistic self-determination which had been stolen from them. Second, black people could not speak of any type of movement against political oppression without simultaneously targeting the racial (and thereby the cultural) entanglement; the entire apartheid system rested on a relatively minute, white political-cultural minority subjugating the overwhelming population of the country on the basis of its blackness. Thus a move to correct white discrimination automatically raised systemic reformulations. Encompassing the political and cultural thrusts, Barney Pityana, a major BC interpreter with Biko, offered the common BCM adage: "Black man, you are on your own."[35]

Keeping in mind the above proviso regarding the intimate cohesion between political transformation and cultural self-consciousness and with some understanding of the reasons for that relation, we can now turn to an exploration of BCM political and cultural themes.

Political Themes

The crux of the BCM's political goals centered around radically transforming apartheid systemically and reconstructing an entirely new societal arrangement. Bennie A. Khoapa, then director of the BCM's Black Community Programmes, zeroed in on the major political theme. Khoapa steered clear of both the liberals' call for integration and the Afrikaners' objective of separation, and thereby reoriented the issue back to black power and authority in human associations. He styled BCM in the light of liberation. "Liberationists contend that integration is 'irrelevant' to a people who are powerless. For them the equitable distribution of decision-making power is far more important than physical proximity to white people." While both integration and separation evinced an inordinate dependence on the presence or absence of whites, liberation relegated integration and separation to subordinate status. Khoapa continues: "What the new black man is talking about is liberation by any means necessary and this does not depend on the question of whether blacks should integrate or separate."[36]

Specifically, liberation entailed a complete restructuring of the apartheid government and a transformation of the economic system. A mere alteration in the political sphere of the new society without a corresponding realignment in the economic sphere would render liberation meaningless. Even if black faces replaced white faces in government, the vast majority of blacks would remain poor while a few blacks acquired a niche in the "bourgeoisie." Therefore the lopsided, undemocratic distribution of wealth under capitalist South Africa mandated an equitable dispersal of control and ownership of the nation's wealth and natural resources.

In response to an inquiry about the exact nature of the egalitarian society in the new South Africa, Biko affirmed his intention for a socialist country. Likewise, the Constitution of the Black Peoples' Convention stated: "The principles of socialism are institutionalized into industry, trade and commerce."[37] The BPC's Constitution exemplified how widely a radical political economy had taken root in the BCM discourse, and also how a broad consensus had coalesced around the platform of socialism. Under a section titled "The BPC Economic Policy" in the Constitution, the Convention enumerated a thirty-point plan to realize socialist social relations in "a liberated Azania" (South Africa). This maturity in the specificity and elaboration of political, economic power relations pointed again to the particularity of the South African reality—effectively visualizing the destruction of racism required dismantling an exploitative politico-economic system.[38]

In addition to socialism the issue of land also occupied a high priority in the political themes of the BCM. The BPC's Constitution cited land under the first category of "Towards A Free Azania—Projection: Future State." Following the socialist prescription for post-apartheid South Africa, ownership of the land would be vested in the state, the latter reflecting the generic interests over against private social relations.[39] In contradistinction to the apartheid bantustan policy, the BCM promised equal ownership of the land by all the people in order to consummate the aim of "One Azania, One Nation." This latter policy cut the jugular vein in apartheid, which literally translates into "apartness." Only with a unified nation could socialist Azania be realized.

Non-racialism also occupied the BCM political platform and became an important point of demarcation. This issue contrasted with the white liberal demand for "multiracialism" as well as the Afrikaner stance on privileges for white minority "rights." BCM rejected the liberal and the conservative standpoints because these perspectives embraced the creation of racial distinctions in the new society. Commenting on the possibility of black-white equal relations in a non-apartheid South Africa, Biko elaborated:

We see a completely non-racial society. We don't believe, for instance, in the so-called guarantees for minority rights, because guaranteeing minority rights implies the recognition of portions of the community on a race basis. We believe that in our country there shall be no minority, there shall be no majority, just the people.[40]

For instance, the multiracial rubric deviously allowed for the divisive recognition of many races within one Azania and suggested adherence to a policy of racial privilege for the minority, the same white minority that had attempted genocide against the black majority by utilizing racial privilege! Nonracial, on the other hand, guaranteed equality to all citizens and legislated unified criteria upon which social relations would function.

How would the BCM bring about the non-racial, socialist Azania? The future nation would be constructed on the universal franchise of "one person, one vote." In the famous SASO/BPC Terrorism Trial of May 1976, Biko concisely pictured SASO's attitude toward the franchise once the anti-apartheid struggle ceased. "The attitude is a simple one," Biko retorted from the dock, "an open society, one man, one vote, no reference to colour." Motlhabi analyzed further the intention of "one person, one vote" and pinpointed BCM's actual aim: "Universal franchise, for [BCM], would necessarily lead to majority rule," Motlhabi surmises, "which meant a *predominantly* Black representation in government."[41]

Finally, in the political struggle BCM devised clear instructions on the role of whites in the black liberation movement. Motlhabi articulated the movement's exclusion of white liberals from black people's struggle for freedom:

> The specific, historical role of white liberals in Black organizations was rejected [by the BCM]. Total identification of a privileged group with an oppressed group in a system of government which forced one group to prey on the other was seen as inconceivable. No white person could escape being part of the oppressor camp.[42]

The BCM had learned from history how the white liberal had refused to surrender his/her privileges. In fact, the apartheid system disallowed this option. Being white, the liberal automatically enjoyed the benefits of whiteness.[43]

The political themes of non-racialism versus multiracialism and the role of whites in the black liberation movement foreshadow the tensions in the South African black theologians' dialogue in Chapters 4 and 5. At stake will be a theological understanding of self-reliance, self-determination, black liberation, and the nature of black-white cooperation. But first, we must attend to BCM's cultural thematic designations.

Cultural Themes

In 1971 the South African Students Organization coordinated a "Formation School" to explicate the meaning of SASO and Black Consciousness. In a position paper presented to enunciate this definitional clarification, one glimpses several cultural themes. SASO depicted the BCM as "an inward-looking movement calculated to make us look at ourselves ... with new eyes." This viewpoint marked a radical rupture with whiteness and a turn to the inherent worth of blackness. The inward-looking methodology revealed "the innate value in [black people], in our institutions, in our traditional outlook to life and in our own worth as people."[44] Here, SASO indicated three cultural themes: self-reliance, new values and black pride, and the centrality of traditional, indigenous culture.

Before we attempt a more detailed consideration of these three cultural features, a further look at the SASO position paper sheds more insight into the BCM cultural nuances. " 'Black Consciousness' is by no means a slogan driving people to think in a certain way politically," continues the paper. Rather, it "is a way of life that must permeate through the society and be adopted by all." In this instance the BCM branched out beyond politics and spotlighted a *cultural ontology* embracing and permeating the totality of a black way of life. Black Consciousness, then, was not a mere rejection or adoption of one or another political platform. More profoundly, it questioned the very being of blackness in a holistic manner.[45] Moreover, it confronted the *cultural anthropology* of the black South African by demanding a congruence between the questions of Who am I? (clarity of one's humanity) and "Where am I?" (particularity of existential locus). "The logic behind [Black Consciousness] is that if you see yourself as a person in your own right there are certain basic questions that you must ask about the conditions under which you live."[46] With this backdrop, we now return to the aforementioned cultural themes.

Above all else, the BCM rested on the cultural theme of self-reliance by way of black solidarity. Not only was self-reliance prescribed as a tactic in the political struggle, it also applied to every sphere of black life. More specifically, the BCM's Black Community Programmes persuaded the community to achieve an independent, non-appendage existence. Through these do-for-self community projects, black students, professionals and skilled persons worked together with unlettered folk to improve the community in the areas of literacy, health, community centers and physical projects in the rural area. This act of cross-class solidarity began to produce a veritable psychological transformation. Previously, black people had relied on the government and white liberal "trusteeship" (known as *baasskap*). Nengwekhulu capsulizes the importance of self-reliance:

The aim of our community development projects [was] to inculcate in our people a sense of self-reliance, initiative and solidarity that is essential in our struggle to free ourselves from white racism, capitalism, colonialism and psychological servitude instilled in us during all these centuries of colonial emasculation.[47]

Thus the first step in the cultural journey advanced with black people discovering they were absolutely on their own. And with one foot forward, they could then heed the cry of "Zimele!"—"stand on your own feet!"

New values and black pride were to substantiate the call for self-reliance and solidarity. Fortifying black pride, the New Black discarded the derivative term *non-white*. As Black Power militants had ridiculed sell-outs as "Negroes," BCM members heaped derision upon black bantustan collaborators as "nonwhites." "The philosophy of Black consciousness," Biko argued, ". . . expresses group pride." And this pride fostered the independence of blackness from whiteness. Consequently the BCM made black people perceive themselves as complete beings, "and not as an extension of a broom or additional leverage to some machine."[48]

Concomitantly, a renaming of self naturally gave rise to a redefinition of values. The SASO "Policy Manifesto" propagated the rejection of all value systems that construed blacks as visitors in their indigenous land. To counter such a demeaning and destructive approach, one that made blacks foreigners in the country of their birth, the BCM reclaimed its own norm, worth, outlook and worldview.[49]

To uphold self-reliance in light of black pride and values, the BCM turned to its own resource of traditional culture. Commenting on "Some African Cultural Concepts," Biko sifted out the ingredients of a veritable, indigenous cultural revolution. The "modern African culture," Biko avowed, had survived the colonial assault by Europeans. In this culture one detected basic expressions adequate for the BCM. Biko highlighted the African cultural anthropology (the human-centeredness of African society and, thus, the community-centeredness); the importance of song and rhythm as part and parcel of the African self; the proclivity toward "situation-experiencing" over against the Westerners' inability to *not* intervene in problem solving; the totality of religion in African, everyday life and the lack of hell as a place for punishment; the proximity to nature that nurtured a fuller emotional resonance with those who suffer; and the forging of a culture of resistance through group oppression.

In addition, Biko spoke to the traditional culture of communalism—the joint ownership by the community of the land and all resources.[50] Such an indigenous attempt at modifying a modern industrial society with traditional, African economics and social relations in opposition to economic schemes originating from externally based cultures, will feed into the nonracial and black theology debate among black South African theologians in Chapters 4 and 5 below.

This cultural themes section completes the background setting that black theology in South Africa encountered while discerning God's presence under apartheid. Theology arose out of the political movement for social transformation and the cultural effort at "Being-Black-In-The-World".[51]

Theological Themes

The Black Consciousness Movement (BCM) sharply focused a critical duplicity in faith faced by black South African Christians in general and black pastors in particular. On the one hand they mouthed the Christianity learned from white European missionaries centuries past and the same religious doctrine professed by whites in contemporary South Africa. But on the other hand blacks muffled the burning beat of their own visceral faith encounter with Christ. Bonganjalo Goba, a participant in early black theology in South Africa, relates theology, black identity and the black Christian dilemma:

> There was a feeling amongst those of us who were involved [in early black theology] that somehow we had experienced . . . a theological schizophrenia. We were split. . . . Part of our formation was terribly white, influenced by the western theology. . . . And there was another side to that in that we had our own [black] agenda which had never been addressed. So that the issue had to do with the identity crisis which we confronted.[52]

The BCM clashed head-on with black pastors' training and their avowed allegiance to an oppressive white theology and white Christianity. Like the political and cultural identity crises haunting BCM followers, the theological identity crisis gripped black church leaders. Goba comments further: "We were young pastors, most of us. The only academic theologian when black theology started was Dr. Manas Buthelezi. . . . Most of us were simply pastors who were part of the Black Consciousness Movement."

Sabelo Ntwasa, the first director of the Black Theology Project of the University Christian Movement, cited white Christianity's absolute negation of black peoples' value in the doing of Christian theology; and thus the need for a black theology. Ntwasa described how Europeans brought to South Africa a Christianity that positioned white men in ecclesiastical authority, demeaned indigenous black religion and culture as heathen and immoral, interpreted conversion to Christ as a demand to adopt white culture and fabricated a white God.[53]

In response to the racism of white Christianity, black theology in South Africa asserted its own theological agenda and incorporated the black reality of indigenous religious experience and struggle for liberation into the Christian hermeneutic. Manas Buthelezi, the father of contemporary black theology in South Africa, framed the essential ontological, existential and theological query: If the gospel means anything, it must answer the "basic existential question 'Why did God create me black?' "[54] Around this basic issue, a constellation of other matters crystallized. Was Christianity ever meant for black people? How authentic was the church in catering to black needs? Did the white, apartheid designation "non-white" allow for the unity of blackness and Christianity? Did the Christian God support black acceptance of apartheid? What was God doing in a situation where blackness brought legal disenfranchisement and death in one's own land? What was God saying to black people who defined their life as appendages to white people? Why did blacks suffer because God had made them "nonwhites"? Did Jesus Christ belong to the Afrikaner and white, English-speaking liberals, and blacks to the line of Ham? Did God reveal God's self in black people's political and cultural realities?

To resolve these questions blacks turned to themselves and found that the gospel message complemented their own lived circumstances. Instead of a white, other-worldly God, black Christians discovered a God of freedom who called black humanity into wholeness. Just as Black Consciousness announced the liberation of blacks, Yahweh's promise of liberation to the Hebrews constituted Christianity's core message of hope to blacks withering away under the yoke of apartheid. Black Christians reaffirmed and rejoiced in their God-given humanity, black pride, ability to decide for themselves and cultural aspirations.[55]

Contrary to the white, passive Christ, blacks embraced Christ, the "fighting God," in the words of Biko, who suffered with them under oppression and exemplifed a vocation of struggle for freedom against spiritual and physical (systemic) wickedness. Because Jesus was poor, discriminated against and exploited in his time, and because blacks agonized in poverty, discrimination and exploitation under apartheid, and because God incarnated in this particular oppressed Jesus, a meaningful contemporary symbol of God's presence in South Africa revealed a black Christ.[56]

Black theology in South Africa denounced the church's apartheid setup with a white hierarchical leadership (a manifestation of white Christian power and the absence of democracy), European liturgy, and discrepancy between the profession of "in Christ, neither Greek nor Jew" and the practice of "in Christ, separate development only." Black theology in South Africa argued against a turn-the-other-cheek, bureaucratic and white-valued church. As a substitute it proposed an ecclesiology where the followers of the Way reflected the quality of "Christ-in-his-struggle-against-human-bondage." In contrast, the white church affronted the body of Christ by adhering to a theology of the tower of Babel. In its bowing down before "ethnic and political gods," it proved itself a heresy.[57]

In addition, black theology in South Africa struggled with eradicating the sacrilegious notion that black people survived through the grace of whites and not the grace of God. The new hermeneutic had to force a break with the theological dependency on white authority. The authority question cut at the very substance of what it meant to be a Christian. How could black people claim faith in the lordship of Christ and the kingdom of God and, at the same time, desecrate their God-given humanity by kneeling before white apartheid? Biblically the issue of authority and derivation of grace challenged black Christians to undertake a radical exegesis and rereading of Romans 13 and Revelations 13.[58]

Finally, black theology in South Africa broached the theological theme of anthropology. Freedom in God was the "stirring call" within the black person. It summoned black uniqueness, a need for a community of human love, and an affirmation and glory in blackness. To theologically focus on blackness, one had to reassess black history, culture, traditions and African beliefs. In pre-colonial South Africa African traditional religion exhibited a sophisticated theological anthropology. There, Africans worshipped a good God, who bestowed goodness upon black people and, as a result, an inherent dignity in humanity. If stripped of this dignity, the African would sink to the level of beasts. Fortunately African traditional religion coincided with Christianity's call for human liberation. For in Christianity the black person had been created with dignity in the *imago dei* and had received infinite value through Christ's redeeming work.[59]

Though various Christian theological themes were debated wherever black people fathomed the relation of God and Christ to the black condition, the primary organizational vehicle for coordinating the discourse of black theology in South Africa was the Black Theology Project initiated by the University Christian Movement (UCM). Like NUSAS, UCM played the role of a liberal, white group that offered some legal space for black national dialogue and contact. UCM formed in 1967 and by the end of 1969 black seminarians and pastors were discussing black theology, particularly as expressed in James H. Cone's *Black Theology and Black Power*. Though SASO had created a theological commission, Motlhabi contends that the Black Theology Project "was the main black theological movement. SASO's commission was simply to ensure that the students discussed relevant theological issues." The project "came into being around 1970"[60] and sponsored a series of meetings and seminars on black theology during 1970 and 1971.

CONCLUSION

The contemporary history of black power, black consciousness and black theology in both the United States and South Africa has laid the groundwork for a more in-depth review of what I have termed the black political theology trend and the cultural theology trend. The challenge for black people to remain Christian in the face of the political and cultural revolutions in both countries during the 1960s and 1970s stood at the center of the whirlwind in which black Christians found themselves. Like the accents in the secular movement toward black liberation, the black theologies of liberation likewise tended toward the poles of politics and culture. In Chapter 2 we examine black political theology in the United States. As we move toward Chapter 5 we will discover that black theology in the United States and black theology in South Africa are, in fact, several black theological streamlets of liberation, all struggling to maintain their faith in, confession of and witness to the gospel of liberation from a black perspective.

Part II

BLACK THEOLOGY USA

CHAPTER TWO

Black Politics and Black Theology

> O Freedom! O Freedom!
> O Freedom! I love thee,
> And before I'll be a slave
> I be buried in my grave
> And go home to my Lord and be free.
>
> Slave Spiritual

> Any religion that professes to be concerned about the souls of [people] and is not concerned about the slums that damn them, the economic conditions that strangle them and the social conditions that cripple them is a spiritually moribund religion awaiting burial.
>
> Martin Luther King, Jr.

> I believe in a religion that believes in freedom. Any time I have to accept a religion that won't let me fight a battle for my people, I say to hell with that religion.
>
> Malcolm X

To foster dialogue between black theologians in the United States and South Africa, we need to involve ourselves in a critical and self-critical communication. Since contemporary black theology originated in the United States, the first voices we hear are North American black theologians. Chapters 2 and 3, therefore, initiate the discovery process of political and cultural theological shades internal to North America. This range of theological representatives will enhance the understanding of the South African dialogical partners.

In contrast to the cultural theologians of the next chapter, the political theologians in this chapter give more weight to opposing racism in the white American political system, church and theology. As a group they respond to Black Power's call for black Americans to fight the inhuman practices of white political power. They expose white people's use of religion and theology to justify the maintenance of white rule over black life. For them, black theology has to serve black people's daily struggle against the grip of a white power structure. They want to know how theology and the church aid in alleviating poor education, KKK terror, police brutality, insensitive and corrupt politicians, the hopeless job situation of black youth, rat infested ghettos, the lack of civil and human rights, and all situations in which whites control black humanity. To combat white supremacist power, the political theology group chooses theology as its area of resistance. Each theologian in the political trend acknowledges the contribution of his colleagues. But, at the same time, each builds on the existing state of black theology by contributing something new to the over-all political theological trend. Put differently, within the black political theological unit, the theologians complement and contrast one another as they jointly struggle against the main enemy—the racist politics of white theology. The political theologians believe that it is a God-ordained gift for black people to fight to alter the unjust and inhuman power relations in American society. And they want to discover how black theology can be involved in that fight.

In this chapter we expound on four representatives of the black political theology trend—Albert B. Cleage, James H. Cone, J. Deotis Roberts and William R. Jones. The theological categories of (a) black theology, (b) liberation, (c) Christology and (d) reconciliation will serve to probe each theologian's viewpoint on black theology and political power relations.

ALBERT B. CLEAGE

Black Nationalist Theology

Cleage was the first member of the black political theology trend to write a book in the Black Power era. In 1968 he published *The Black Messiah*, the first book on the religious roots of black power. His unique contribution to the political theologians was his challenge to the black church to lead the black community in building a black nation. Closely related was his insistence on the literal blackness of Jesus, the Messiah. In his opinion, just as a black Jesus had fought the racism of white Gentile Rome by struggling to build a separate black nation, Cleage argued that black people needed an independent political entity controlled by blacks (a Black Nation) to deal with the politics of white racism in America.

To understand Cleage's radical call for a separate black nation one has to grasp the motivating factors underlying his political theological project. Cleage was keenly aware of the physical assaults on southern civil rights workers. He knew the Klan had bombed innocent black girls in a Birmingham church in 1963. Like all of black America, he watched the open callousness of southern governors, sheriffs and the KKK against the nonviolent practice of Martin Luther King, Jr. As a pastor in a northern black community (Detroit) Cleage also knew that the 1960s civil rights bills and the southern Civil Rights Movement had not fundamentally changed the status of northern segregation and white racism. And more than likely, King's defiance of southern laws made northern blacks more impatient with their own situation of political impotence. In fact, Cleage saw black impatience explode in the July 1967 Detroit rebellion. The Detroit destruction focused on and targeted white property symbols of power and authority. Blacks did not primarily attempt to take white lives. In response to blacks' outburst against years of white control, the white political and military forces occupied the Detroit ghetto as if it were an oppressed colony. They bypassed constitutional and legal rights in order to protect white private property at the expense of black suffering and death. Thirty-three blacks were killed, over a thousand wounded, and seventy-two hundred arrested, all in four days. White power cordoned off the black community as the United States military had controlled South Vietnam.

Coupled with his direct experience with the Detroit rebellion, Cleage was deeply involved in the Black Power Movement. He was a close friend of Malcolm X. He sensed the radical shift from evolutionary to revolutionary change sweeping black America. Black Power and Malcolm X's nationalist philosophy had become familiar throughout the nation. Black caucuses mushroomed in predominantly white churches and annual professional meetings. Black Student Unions blanketed college campuses. Black communities, particularly in the North, were calling for community control of the ghettos, the dismantling of racist power and the establishment of black power over black lives. A strong sense filled black America that whites were attempting black genocide. As a result, separation became a viable alternative for many black grassroots and Black Power groups. Some believed the government should finance blacks' migration back to Africa. Others stated that the federal government should give black America several southern states. And still others wanted whites to leave the ghettos so that blacks could set up a loose confederation of politically autonomous enclaves throughout the United States. Blacks wanted political and economic power transferred from white to black hands. Cleage experienced and observed all these developments. From his theological perspective, the black nation was actually forming. And the black church needed to be more theologically self-conscious about leading that formation.

Cleage, ordained in the United Church of Christ, stands squarely within the black political theology trend. The issue of political power relations dominates his theological viewpoint. In *The Black Messiah* Cleage introduces his position:

> Our basic struggle, then, is to get some kind of power. We must not be ashamed of power. We must mobilize the entire black community to secure political and economic power. Without power we are helpless and psychologically sick.[1]

Within the black political theology group, I define Cleage's interest as a Black Christian Nationalist Theology of Revolution. His only concern is *black* people. For him Jesus was a black-skinned person; as a result, one can only speak as a black *Christian*. The substance of Cleage's *theology* indicates a black God aggressively involved in the business of black people. Thus Jesus came as a *nationalist* to set the black nation free. And this road toward freedom follows black *revolution*.[2]

Because the intricacies of Cleage's theology unfold around his highlighting the life of Jesus, Cleage spends less time on God, per se. In fact, his theology equals his veneration of the life of Jesus. Therefore, a look at Cleage's centerpiece of Christology sheds clarity on his black political theology.[3]

Christology

For Cleage, Jesus was a black, revolutionary Zealot, leading the fight against a white Rome in order to realize a revolution for the black nation of Israel. When Cleage writes "black Jesus" he does not mean ontologically, symbolically or psycho-culturally. Cleage means a black-skinned Jesus.

> When I say that Jesus was black, that Jesus was the black Messiah . . . I'm not saying, "Wouldn't it be nice if Jesus was black? or "Let's pretend that Jesus was black" or "It's necessary psychologically for us to believe that Jesus was black." I'm saying that Jesus WAS black. There never was a white Jesus.[4]

With the death of John the Baptist, in Cleage's opinion, Jesus assumed the political leadership of the revolutionary Zealots. This black movement waged war against the white oppressor, Rome, in order to reconstitute the black nation. The black scribes and Pharisees collaborated with white Rome to preserve their privileges. Consequently Jesus came as a revolutionary and an organizer of the black revolution. He had to be crucified for political reasons because "this is the kind of life that Jesus lived." He died due to his sole purpose—making black revolution to reconstitute the black nation.[5]

It is something of a misnomer to classify Cleage's interpretation of Jesus as Christology in the classical conception of the doctrine of Christ. Cleage hardly displays any interest in the resurrected Christ. For him the messiahship belongs to Jesus not because of Good Friday and Easter, but strictly as a result of Jesus' life and earthly activity in attempting to reconstitute the black nation. Thus Cleage apparently avoids a dichotomy between the Jesus of history and the Christ of faith. With Cleage's black Messiah, the Jesus of history is an identical twin with the Jesus of faith in the fight against racism and for black liberation.[6]

Liberation

Cleage attacks the black church for incorrectly nurturing a gospel of salvation instead of a gospel of liberation. He maintains that the salvation gospel caters to an individualistic, other-worldly, pie-in-the-sky quandary. Confusion in its gospel has become the black church's basic theological problem. Belief in salvation by faith, and not by work, and in the sacrifice of Jesus on Calvary will not justify the black church's engagement in the black revolution to make a heaven on earth.

In contrast Cleage offers the gospel of liberation, which aims to achieve a black earthly heaven here and now. For Cleage, the gospel of liberation fosters the black church's collective participation in reconstituting the collective black nation; the constructing of a nation "as if it had a capital, a Congress and a president." Though rebuilding the nation does not immediately require a contiguous geography, in the liberated black nation black people would still seek to control their own communities. This "Promised Land on earth" would operate in a communal way with black people sharing love for one another.[7]

In sum, the thrust of Cleage's liberation comprises an immediate, earthly kingdom in the form of a black nation within the over-all American white nation. He glues together the historical ultimate goal during Jesus' time, the contemporary ultimate goal for black Americans, and the breaking in of the end time with the theme of reconstituting a black nation. But how will Cleage consummate his liberation, that is, the building of the black nation? Since he places so much weight on the black church as the center of the black nation process, a review of Cleage's ecclesiology is relevant.

Ecclesiology

Unlike other black theologians, Cleage functions primarily in the capacity of pastor of his Shrine of the Black Madonna. He faces the daily running of the black church and the immediate implications of that church for the black community. Thus practicality of ecclesiology figures high in his black theology.

For Cleage, the black church will initiate liberation, the building of the black nation.

Our basic task is bringing black people together and building a Nation. This church [referencing his Shrine of the Black Madonna] is the hub of the emerging Black Nation. From it we go out in all directions to educate, to set up action centers.

The reconstituted black church will serve as the foundation in the "task of building an institutional power base." As the hub and base—the beginning of the nation—the black church will then spin off all other relevant black survival institutions.[8]

Once people are in the church, Cleage seeks to cleanse them of the white, slave, salvation gospel. To this end he has redone both theological creed and liturgy. He produced "The Black Christian Nationalist Creed," which incorporates his Black Christian Nationalist Theology of Revolution. When initiates undergo baptism at the Shrine of the Black Madonna, they accept baptism into the "hub" of the black nation. Likewise, communion signifies each person's and the collective unit's willingness to shed its blood and sacrifice its body for the rebuilding of the nation. Cleage ridicules the classical doctrines of baptism and eucharist as mere ploys of the white, slave theology in an attempt to guarantee individuals a place in heaven. At the shrine, in contrast, members worship not the physical resurrection of Jesus' body, but the resurrection of the black nation started by Jesus two thousand years ago. Black people's labor to construct the black nation symbolizes Jesus' immortality.[9]

When Cleage speaks of the restructured black church's relation to the black community, he compares this to the connection between the Temple at Jerusalem and Israel. The black church does not limit its ministry to those inside its walls. All black people belong to the purview and congregation of the Shrine of the Black Madonna. If the black church serves as the seed of the nation, then the church ministers to the entire Pan-African black community. In fact, the Black Liberation Movement "is the Christian Church in the 20th Century and that Christian Church cannot truly be the church until it also becomes the Movement."[10] Ecclesiology holds up Cleage's entire black political theology. The Shrine of the Black Madonna is the black nation. And the Shrine of the Black Madonna becomes the entire black revolution.

Reconciliation

Cleage lauds voluntary, permanent separation between the races. Since the American government and white people have systematically segregated blacks outside the basic institutional structures and the centers of power, the black church should build on this segregation by developing a theology of separation. Reconciliation, therefore, indicates a separate black political power.

Here Malcolm X's black nationalist politics directly affect Cleage's reconciliation doctrine. Paralleling Malcolm's claim that the white man is the devil, Cleage views whites as the enemy. Indeed, from Cleage's vantage point, the black race undergoes a life-and-death ordeal for political nationhood and freedom from America, the modern-day "white Roman oppressor." In warfare against the enemy there exists a no-compromise power struggle. Cleage describes an inevitable "disaster course" of conflict and violence between black and white. Black people want their nation, but white people refuse to make changes to allow blacks to experience dignity and justice. So the Shrine of the Black Madonna rejects nonviolence both practically and philosophically. On the contrary, the black church may be forced to launch young blacks against the white enemy in a holy war for the black nation.

In order to understand Cleage's doctrine of reconciliation, one must appreciate the historical and brutal slaughter of blacks by European and American whites. Cleage urges black Americans to not lapse into historical amnesia. He reminds us that the "white man"

> took [blacks] from Africa packed on slave ships like animals. He killed more than one hundred million Black people just bringing us across. He raped a continent and destroyed a civilization. He made us work for nothing to build a country [America] for him and make him wealthy.[11]

Cleage's reconciliation viewpoint not only originates from a sober assessment of black history, it also follows his theological and scriptural exegesis wherein Jesus, the black Messiah, organized to reconstitute the black nation and separate it from the white oppressor, Rome. For Cleage, reconciliation takes place only among blacks. Toward racists he calls for conflict, not reconciliation; he seeks separation for the black nation, not integration into America's white supremacy.

JAMES H. CONE

Since the 1969 publication of *Black Theology and Black Power*, the first systematic treatment of black theology in North America, James H. Cone of the African Methodist Episcopal Church remains the father of contemporary black theology. Formerly Cone participated in the National Committee of Black Christians and the Congress of African Peoples. He is currently a member of the Ecumenical Association of Third World Theologians, the Black Theology Project (Theology of Americas) and the Society for the Study of Black Religion.

Black Christian Theology

Like Albert Cleage, James Cone's black theology developed in response to the Civil Rights and Black Power movements and northern urban rebellions. Cleage, however, dismissed the approach of systematic theology, utilized the homilectic form, and keyed in on the most militant wing of the black freedom struggle to such a degree that his black theology appeared to border on worshipping a religion of black power politics. Cone, on the other hand, began his black theology by interpreting the black liberation movement through the systematic doctrines of classical theology. In this comparative sense, Cone remained in the mainstream of classical theology and Cleage flanked him on the left within the black political theology trend.[12]

Among the political theologians Cleage contributed his notion of a black nation. Cone notes Cleage's unique emphasis and goes beyond him by introducing liberation of the poor, specifically the black poor, as the controlling norm of a political black theology. Cone wrote his first text during the upheaval of 1968. A white assassin's bullet had ended the life of Martin Luther King, Jr., in April of that year. With that bullet the movement for peace, nonviolence and racial fellowship ground to a halt. Within a week of King's murder, one hundred and thirty cities went up in flames. The national guard and army troops descended upon the black ghettoes. Forty-six civilians died; over three thousand were injured; and twenty-seven thousand were arrested. The white power structure had intensified its war on black America.

Prior to 1968, however, and throughout his graduate studies and early teaching career, Cone knew of the increased attacks on the black community. During 1967 while teaching at Adrian College in Adrian, Michigan, seventy miles from Detroit, he was deeply affected by that city's rebellion. Moreover, he read about the loss of black life at the hands of cold white power. Between 1965 and 1968, three hundred urban riots erupted with over eight thousand casualties and fifty thousand arrested. Furthermore, Cone sensed the racist, white backlash epitomized by the 1968 presidential election of Richard M. Nixon. Nixon campaigned and won on a law-and-order platform. He pledged to reverse the civil rights gains of the 1960s. He decreased open housing, halted busing for school desegregation, reduced government funding for ghetto improvement, removed curbs on police departments and gutted affirmative action policies. During this same year Nixon and J. Edgar Hoover resumed counterintelligence programs to disrupt black protest organizations and assassinate black militants. While blacks died, white theologians toyed with Barth-Brunner debates and the "death of God" fad. When the white church and theologians did speak, they hypocritically condemned the counterviolence in the ghettoes. But they remained silent on the initiating, structural violence of white racism.

For Cone in 1968, therefore, the survival of his community and his own black identity were at stake. He had to write on black theology and black power. If Christianity had any meaning for powerless black America, Cone wrote, it placed black liberation of the poor at the core of the gospel.

Thus, Cone formulated his black theology in direct relation to the Black Power Movement and urban rebellions in the 1960s.[13] He perceived Black Power and black theology as co-laborers in the field of black liberation:

Black Power and Black theology work on two separate but similar fronts. Both believe Blackness is the primary datum of human experience which must be reckoned with, for it is the reason for our oppression and the only tool for our liberation.[14]

Cone subscribed to a black theology that sought power for oppressed black people, a rearrangement of power to eliminate racist oppression and to enhance black freedom. Similar to Malcolm X's faith claim, Cone professed a religion whose primary theological cornerstone undergirded the political eradication of racial discrimination. Reviewing the birth of his black theology eighteen years later, he says: "I think when I first began [writing black theology], I saw the political as the most crucial. I still, in many ways, do." However, he wishes to "balance" the political-cultural dynamic "a lot more." Now he more tightly interweaves his understanding of these two strands:

> I see the political and the cultural now with the political really dependent upon the cultural. I don't see how you can sustain a political analysis and movement without cultural resources.[15]

Here too, one recognizes his penchant toward the black political trend. Though hindsight has informed his theological integration of the political with the cultural, Cone remains committed to a black theology that employs cultural resources *for* the political movement, the political liberation of black people.

I characterize the theological bent of Cone, the major representative of the black political theology trend, as a Black Christian Theology of Liberation. It is *black* because he equates the black experience with the primary datum of black theology. It is *Christian* because the foundational inquiry for his theology remains: "What does the Christian gospel have to say to powerless black [people] whose existence is threatened daily by the insidious tentacles of white power?" It is *theology* because Cone reflects on the very presence of God "actively involved in the present-day affairs of [black people]." And it is about *liberation* because he surmises liberation as the "central idea for articulating the gospel of Jesus."[16] The Christian gospel of liberation and the liberation of the poor form the heart of Cone's systematic theology.

Liberation

What does the gospel of liberation mean in Cone's theological system? Similar to Cleage, the target of liberation for Cone centers on the destruction of the structure of American white racism. This demonic system has crushed the black person into a non-person. "The white structure of this American society," Cone elaborates, "personified in every racist, must be at least part of what the New Testament meant by the demonic forces."[17] Though he later broadens the target to include women's oppression, cap-

italism and imperialism, his entry point in the development of his black
theology hinges on black people's struggle against racism.

For Cone, the human procession toward black liberation against this
demonic structure originates in divine freedom. The freedom of God "is
the source and content of human freedom." Grounded in divine freedom
(meaning God's own free choice to create humans in freedom and to be
with them in the realization of freedom and liberation in history), black
liberation or black freedom denotes the divine will to execute human emancipation. The *imago dei* (God who is freedom in being, will and function)
mandates humanity's created state and telos. At the same time, one cannot
have divine freedom — and human freedom — without divine justice. Freedom or liberation accompanies justice. And divine justice makes black liberation more than a human effort and goal; it makes liberation a divine
intent. God's righteousness changes God's freedom into a practical realization of human liberation in history.[18]

In addition to anchoring the concepts of divine freedom and divine jus-
tice/righteousness, liberation also links up with salvation and with "God's
Kingdom" in Cone's theology. Salvation is no longer a supposedly inward
calmness or elusive balm in the afterworld; thus it no longer creates opiates
in support of racism. On the contrary, God, through Christ, saves humanity
by entering the depths of oppression and liberating humanity from all human evils, including racism. Finally, Cone sounds a universal note of liberation in his doctrine of the kingdom. The kingdom stands for all the
world's poor because they have nothing to expect from this world. Ce-
mented in historical liberation, the kingdom embodies the poor's hope and
empowers them toward organizing for practical liberation in history.[19]

Christology

God's liberation of black people through Christ's cross and resurrection
marks the centrality of Cone's Christology. For Cone, the New Testament
witness reveals Jesus' person as the Oppressed One. Because black people
suffocate under extreme afflictions, the locus of Jesus' work is a black Christ
identified with liberation from black suffering. The Bible tells the story of
Jesus' oppression; the contemporary story tells of black people's oppression.
In a word, the Oppressed One in black suffering expresses divine being
and divine activity. Christ is black because of how Christ was revealed and
because of where Christ seeks to Be. Having intersected the liberation of
the oppressed with the person and work of Christ and having situated that
liberation in the black community, Cone boldly asserts in his first published
book, "Christianity is not alien to Black Power; it is Black Power."[20]

Within the political theology trend Cone dismisses both J. Deotis Roberts' belief that blacks need a black Christ because of a psychocultural
crisis[21] and Albert Cleage's statement about Christ's literal black skin
color.[22] Cone then cites a distinction between the literal and symbolic nature

of Christological blackness. In explicating the contrast, Cone offers a proviso for the possible interim nature of a black Christology. "I realize," he confesses, "that 'blackness' as a christological title may not be appropriate in the distant future or even in every human context in our present." But today the literalness of Christ's blackness arises from Christ literally entering and converging with black oppression and black struggle. Furthermore, Cone continues, Christ's symbolic status of blackness resides in Christ's "transcendent affirmation" that God has never left the universal oppressed alone.[23]

Cone's political doctrine of Jesus adds a new dimension to that of Cleage's. In order to fight white theology Cone brings together both the Jesus of history with the Christ of faith to complement the liberation theme; we cannot have one without the other. Similar to Cleage, Cone does argue that we know what and where Jesus is today based on what Jesus did while on earth. But moving beyond Cleage, Cone creates new political meaning in the crucifixion and resurrection around the thread of his liberation axis. Calvary and the empty tomb prove key in Cone's Christology. Jesus' "death and resurrection" reveal "that God is present in all dimensions of human liberation."[24] In contrast, Cleage recognizes black liberation against white supremacy because Jesus executed liberation on earth before death.

Finally, Cone's black Christology privileges the poor. Christ died on the cross and rose from the dead in partiality to the liberation of the poor and the oppressed and in direct opposition to the satanic on earth. The being and work of Christ express the divine intent to liberate the oppressed. Christ rescues the downtrodden from the material bondage of "principalities and powers." In this liberation process the oppressors also realize their freedom because the object of their oppression—the now freed poor—no longer occupies an oppressed status.[25] The dialectical effect of Jesus Christ rendering deliverance for both the oppressed and the oppressor raises the question of the importance of reconciliation in Cone's black theology.

Reconciliation

Even though his first book expresses the thundering challenge of a manifesto against white people and their racism, Cone, however, never excludes the possibility of reconciliation.

> I do not rule out the possibility of creative changes, even in the lives of oppressors. It is illegitimate to sit in judgment on another man, deciding how he will or must respond. That is another form of oppression.[26]

The white oppressor might change and become reconciled with the black oppressed in the latter's liberation movement. Here too, within the black political theology trend, Cone differentiates his doctrine of reconciliation from both Cleage's and Roberts'. Cleage's position excludes reconciliation with the "white enemy." If one could construe reconciliation between black and white in Cleage's doctrine, the substance would be black people's voluntary, permanent separation from whites! At the other end of the spectrum, Roberts argues a scriptural basis for reconciliation with white people as the essence of the Good News.[27] All three political theologians seek reconciliation, but they differ on its achievement.

Yet, like Cleage and unlike Roberts, Cone develops his doctrine of reconciliation primarily and consistently with concern for the liberation of oppressed blacks. Therefore, in order to yield meaningful and productive reconciliation, only the black community can set the conditions for reconciliation. On the other hand, the "white oppressor" suffers from an enslavement to racism and forfeits any capability to offer suitable reconciliation terms. Instead, the oppressed lay down "the rules of the game." The rule established by oppressed blacks aims at the heart of white racist power. In fact, Cone writes, "there will be no more talk about reconciliation until a redistribution of power has taken place. And until then, it would be advisable for whites to leave blacks alone."[28]

Cone describes two types of reconciliation — objective and subjective. Because Jesus Christ died on the cross and rose from the dead, the devil and satanic forces experienced defeat. The cross-resurrection triumph manifests the objective reconciliation. Now that God has objectively liberated the oppressed from the finality of demonic clutches such as white racism, oppressed humanity (black people) must assume its responsibility to subjectively fight with God in Christ against injustice. Divine victory at Calvary and the tomb objectively shattered the walls of hostility between white and black. Now the oppressed must act as if they are truly emancipated subjectively; that means fighting with total effort against white racism and for freedom. This is subjective liberation. Therefore Cone maintains the consistency of his liberation theme in both objective and subjective reconciliation.

Furthermore, Cone assigns the task of fighting white oppression as the example of what reconciliation implies for blacks. For whites reconciliation can only mean one thing — coming to God through black people.[29]

J. DEOTIS ROBERTS

Black Theology of Balance

Black Power and the late 1960s freedom struggle by black America gave rise to Cone and Cleage. But J. Deotis Roberts (an ordained Baptist) predated this period. Roberts studied Christian Platonism during the 1950s at Edinburgh and Cambridge Universities. He gravitated to epistemological questions of faith, disclosed in his first two titles (*Faith and Reason*, 1962, and *From Puritanism to Platonism in Seventeenth Century England*, 1968).

Roberts' interlocutor was classical European-American philosophical theology. However, with urban rebellions inundating Dr. Martin Luther King's movement, Roberts began to theologically respond to the radical alteration in black people's political scenery.

To understand Roberts' black theology, one has to see him as the product of two larger political trends — civil rights and black power. He and Dr. King finished their doctoral degrees around the same time in the 1950s. Both came out of a Southern Baptist environment, which suggested that blacks could improve their social status through hard work, impeccable educational credentials and a reliance on Christian nonviolence. Concomitantly, a successful black achieved the reward of integration with white people. Hence Roberts matured in the King-civil rights ethos. But while a professor at Howard University, the political turmoil and violence of Black Power also directly affected him. In fact, he taught there while Stokely Carmichael was enrolled. Consequently, Roberts tried to stay within the Black Power Movement, yet bring his insights from the King-civil rights era.[30]

Roberts is a member of the Black Theology Project (Theology in the Americas) and the Society for the Study of Black Religion. Currently a professor at the Eastern Baptist Theological Seminary, he set out to develop a black political theology. He was the third member of the black political theology group to publish a book (*Liberation and Reconciliation*, 1971). Further situating himself with the political theologians, he explicitly named his second black theology book *A Black Political Theology*. But even in his controversial first work one finds his explication of black political theology:

> The reason why Black Theology is "political" is that the one-to-one approach is inadequate and unattractive to any black man who is aware of the serious and insidious character of racism.[31]

Within this theology, Roberts establishes a clear intent which guides his entire theological system. "What I am seeking," writes Roberts, "is a Christian theological approach to race relations that will lead us beyond a hypocritical tokenism to liberation as a genuine reconciliation between equals."[32] He intends to combine liberation and reconciliation. As a member of the political trend, Roberts hopes to build on and go beyond both Cleage's black nation thesis and Cone's liberation-of-the-poor contribution.

I depict Roberts' thinking as a Black Christian Theology of Balance. He explains his *black* theology as "inner city" theology reflecting upon black awareness and black power. It is *Christian* because he makes it synonymous with a "constructive restatement of the Christian faith" and sees the "raw material" for black theology embedded in the black church. As *theology*, Roberts describes his activity as "reasoning about God." And he adheres to a theological methodology of *balance*. Referring to his theological outlook, Roberts summarizes:

I tried to bridge the two generations of Dr. King and the one of the new black power and black consciousness movement. . . . My whole methodology and whole outlook would mean that I would almost have an equal balance. . . . I'm on both sides of the fence.

The most noted issue around which controversy brews deals with Roberts' "balanced" handling of the Christian liberation-reconciliation doctrine. Within the political trend, Roberts stakes out his fundamental claim here. "Thus I have spoken of . . . liberation and reconciliation. A worthy Black Theology has to be balanced in this way."[33]

Liberation and Reconciliation

Within the black political theology trend Cleage restricts reconciliation to blacks, and Cone will come to it after a redistribution of white political power. Roberts, however, stands for black liberation against white racism and, simultaneously, for genuine reconciliation with white people. Because of Roberts' theology of balance, I treat liberation and reconciliation together. He targets both liberation and reconciliation as the "twin goals" and "two main poles"[34] of black theology. Liberation implies black people's freedom from the bondage of white racism. And reconciliation suggests that black freedom does not deny white humanity but meets whites on equal ground. Roberts seeks to develop both aims, the bedrock of his black theology, in a balanced way, that is, in terms of (a) always explaining one in relation to the other, and (b) utilizing them as the core around which he weaves his systematic theology. Yet as one carefully examines Roberts' books and articles, an apparent unresolved tension over the twin goals surfaces.

Referring to white "tired liberals" and "angry black separatists" Roberts argues in *Liberation and Reconciliation*: "Both need to consider the meaning of liberation in the context of reconciliation." Situated "in the context of" reconciliation, liberation here leans slightly toward a status *subordinate* to reconciliation. "Beyond liberation we chart the guidelines for a true Christian reconciliation." Here reconciliation seems to have more value than liberation in the sense that liberation of black people acts as a *stepping stone* to get beyond itself to reconciliation with white people. An authentic reconciliation waits on the other side of liberation. Then one finds, "*The* priority consideration at present is liberation for the black man. . . . Liberation is *the* theme of Black Theology" (my emphasis). The lack of reconciliation as one of the priorities or themes in black theology stands out glaringly in its omission. Further on, he writes, "Liberation is a proper precondition for reconciliation in the area of race relations." Again, liberation of blacks serves as an intermediate measure or *means* toward the *end* of reconciliation.

Moreover, in his essay "Black Theology in the Making" Roberts describes how "liberation from oppression is the heart and center of my program." No longer the "precondition," liberation is now the "heart and center," suggesting that all other doctrines—including reconciliation—revolve around and subordinate themselves to it. On the next page he appears to challenge his own "heart and center" contentions with these statements: "Reconciliation is the more excellent way. . . . Reconciliation . . . is beyond liberation, beyond confrontation. . . . Blacks as well as Whites need to seek reconciliation as an ultimate goal." Here "the ultimate goal" of reconciliation (with no mention of the "twin goal" of liberation) is more excellent and beyond the "heart and center" of liberation (with no mention of the "twin goal" of reconciliation). Yet Roberts maintains his goal is "human liberation from racism." But a nagging question mark presses to the fore with his comment that "reconciliation is the very essence of the good news" and his concern that if reconciliation between the black oppressed and white oppressor "is the final goal, then all matters must be placed in Christian theological perspective."

Finally, Roberts admits that "reconciliation is the goal of black theology. But reconciliation is built on liberation."[35] Still, it appears as if Roberts has incompletely synthesized a movement for political liberation from white racism with a movement toward reconciliation with whites.

Christology

Roberts seeks to place Cleage's and Cone's Christology in proper perspective. Cleage argues for a literal black Christ. Cone believes Christ was never literally white and the divinity assumes blackness by his presence among the oppressed black community. In *Liberation and Reconciliation* Roberts also adheres to a black Messiah, though not in the literal historical sense. For him the black Messiah speaks to a psychocultural crisis engendered by white American religion's demand that only the white Christ is worthy of adoration. In Roberts' opinion one must not limit Christianity merely to the white Christ's worthiness. The black experience has to also be a major source for contemporary Christology. A need materializes to make Christ and the gospel address the black person directly. As a black image Christ becomes one among black people, and the black person retrieves his or her own dignity and pride.

Furthermore, Roberts does not wish to challenge white Americans to worship a black Christ. Thus Roberts does not demand a vengeful repentance from them for worshipping a white Christ. This type of "revenge" would dehumanize whites as they have done to blacks. Besides, affirmation of a black Christ, for Roberts, includes room for a white Christ. But, applying his balanced methodology, if whites could overcome their superior-inferior state of mind and color-consciousness and could worship a black Messiah, then reconciliation would be nearer. Still, Roberts claims, real reconciliation through black and white equality would allow American blacks and whites to transcend the skin color of Christ and reach out to a "universal Christ" without color. At this point Roberts clarifies the black Messiah-colorless Messiah relation in his liberation-reconciliation paradigm. The black Messiah functions in a symbolic and mythic capacity. In the black experience the black Messiah liberates blacks. At the same time the universal Christ reconciles black and white Americans. Jesus Christ the Liberator offers liberation from white oppression and forgiveness from sin and exploitation within the black community. Jesus Christ the Reconciler brings black people together and black and white people together in "multiracial fellowship."

Roberts' *A Black Political Theology* further elaborates his Christology. In this text (a) Christ operates above culture and in culture while liberating the whole person and speaking to the need for peoplehood. Christ is the focus of a theology of social change and political action. And Jesus is the liberator who casts his lot with the oppressed. (b) Along with "mainstream Protestantism" Roberts agrees that the *essence* or *substance* of Christology lies in the universal Word—the lordship of Christ over each people. Black Christology takes for granted this universal definition and particularizes it in the *form* of the black experience. (c) The existential and personal Christ liberates and the universal Christ reconciles all Americans, black and white.[36]

WILLIAM R. JONES

Black Theology of Humanism

William R. Jones is a philosopher of religion. At present he teaches in the department of religion and serves as director of the Afro-American Studies Program at Florida State University; he is also a member of the Society for the Study of Black Religion. Having pursued doctoral work on Sartre, he cultivated an interest in existential, philosophical and humanistic issues. Indeed, his primary speciality is a sobering, philosophical critique of black liberation theology's common belief, in the face of black existential suffering, that God's being and work are good and omnipotent. Attempting to remove the presuppositions of every shade of black liberation theology, Jones poses this challenge: Given the ceaseless black American suffering, is God a white racist?

As a Unitarian-Universalist minister and professor, one can also understand how he would go for the jugular vein—God's incarnation of Jesus Christ Liberator—in black theology. All political theologians agree Jesus is black. But only Jones dissents on the Messiah's liberation work. The fourth and final member of the black political theology trend, Jones challenges Cleage's black nation tenets, Cone's liberation gospel claim and Roberts' liberation-reconciliation approach. To combat white theology and white oppression, Jones believes he surpasses his colleagues with his contribution of black humanism. To the other political theologians Jones adds this unique question: How should the black community best survive white political, economic and social oppression; by relying on a racist supernatural being or ultimately relying on the human efforts of the black community?

I label Jones' theology a Black Theology of Humanism. As a black religious philosopher he hopes to make the humanistic wing of black religion the norm of all black theology. Obviously his Unitarian-Universalist faith strongly determines his specific input into the political theology group. Likewise he believes he is in line with a historical humanist movement within the black community. From his perspective, poet Countee Cullen, Rev. Nathaniel Paul, Bishop Daniel A. Payne, James Baldwin and Carter G. Woodson all put black suffering and white evil on their agendas. Jones also aligns himself with the political theologians because he (a) chooses the political theological proponents for dialogical partners, and, more important, (b) believes that "the issue is first to get some consensus and clarity about how economic, social, and political oppression operate."[37]

Most of Jones' documented efforts are critiques of other black theologians' positive programs. To date he has not presented his comprehensive viewpoint on a black theology of humanism. Moreover, Jones eschews other theological, doctrinal propositions for his singular concentration on theodicy. Therefore it would not be fitting to attempt a review of his position by subsuming his thinking under the headings used thus far—black theology, liberation, Christology and reconciliation. Instead of squeezing out what may not yet exist, we will travel the road of Jones' own argument.

Theodicy

Jones proclaims that theodicy acts as the necessary ground for Christian soteriology, for it logically precedes liberation. When other political theologians talk of God's liberation of the oppressed blacks, Jones asserts, they presuppose the essential goodness of God. Yet they assert divine benevolence without acknowledging the pre-existent evil that necessitates divine goodness in the first place. In brief, for other political theologians there can be no black liberation theology unless they *a priori* conclude God's benevolence toward humanity. But the *logic* of other black theologians, that is, their theology of liberation from black suffering, can only reply in the affirmative to Jones' "threshold question," Is God a white racist? Therefore, theodicy, the *a priori* of the *a priori*, should be the controlling category in black theology. Why this conclusion?

For Jones, the evidence of black suffering seems to point away from a divine liberation activity in human affairs and toward a white racist God. First, blacks experience a *maldistribution* of suffering relative to the rest of the United States population. Second, if one can differentiate between negative and positive suffering, black suffering falls under *negative* suffering. It has no essential value for humanity's salvation-liberation. Third, blacks undergo the *enormity* of suffering. They suffer out of proportion to their over-all numbers. Finally, black suffering is *noncatastrophic*. It does not strike and leave following a short and devastating siege; it is transgenerational.

After detailing these four aspects, Jones connects this observation with the next piece in his philosophical construct of theodicy. He calls for the "multievidentiality" of black suffering. This means that for every assertion of suffering as divine favor, a demonic deity stands as a possible alternative cause of the suffering. Divine suffering can be either favorable (the suffering servant model) or unfavorable (deserved punishment from God's curse).

Next Jones advances the principle that God is the sum of God's acts. Given the four dimensions of black suffering, other black theologians must identify where in black history and life one discerns the actual events in which one views God's benevolent and liberating work. If God is the sum of God's acts, what does the demonstration or lack of demonstration of God's liberating activity prove about God's being and work?

Black theologians must then establish criteria to unravel positive from negative suffering. Positive or favorable suffering toward the end of salvation demands that blacks must endure. On the other hand, there must be criteria for negative suffering, which would then allow for human rebellion. Jones extends the following proposal. The criteria for negative suffering (one demanding human rebellion against the status quo of oppression) stipulate a radical shift in the status of black suffering—the elimination of suffering. Jones calls this shift the exaltation-liberation event. If other black theologians cannot justify a negative black suffering by designating an exaltation-liberation event, then black people should submit to favorable suffering and, consequently, endure quietism, that is, not engage in corrective activity against white racism.

Since all other black political theologians subscribe to a doctrine of God's active involvement in the liberation of black people in human history, what Jones labels "the politics of God," they must decide where, in fact, God effects God's purpose of liberation and join God in that struggle. Jones surmises: Given (a) the four aspects of black suffering; (b) the multievidentiality interpretation of black suffering; (c) that God is the sum of God's acts; and (d) the lack of an exaltation-liberation event, one can only conclude that God is a white racist. Therefore the black theologians bear the burden of refuting Jones' conclusion before they can employ the politics of God in their variegated black theologies. Furthermore, because black theologians cannot manifest an exaltation-liberation event in black history and life, black suffering shoulders the burden of positive suffering. Undergoing God-ordained, positive suffering to achieve salvation-liberation, black people should adhere to an ethic of quietism and not rebel against the white status quo.

To avoid the debilitating alternative of quietism brought about by the failure of other black theologians to refute the "threshold question," Jones develops his black theology of humanism. He seeks to remove the prop of quietism in the edifice of black liberation theology. Jones' criticism attempts to dismantle the basic premise of God's goodness, all-powerfulness and justice for the black poor. From the rubble of his deconstruction he puts forth the singular capacity of solitary humanity. He would have the black church replace God's sovereignty with secular humanism. In Jones' logic the "functional ultimacy of man" accompanies secular humanism. Even though one may argue that the ultimate source of human values issues from God, humanity (in the material reality of black history and life) acts as the supreme arbiter of its own values. In the final analysis, humanity not only decides values and ethics, but also whether or not God is the source of human values and actions. Thus, functionally speaking, humanity holds the ultimate reins on interpretation and practice.

Before proceeding with his project, Jones qualifies his proposal by distinguishing his endeavor of secular humanism from what he terms "humanocentric theism." In other words, he wishes to use a radically new theistic tool, humanocentric theism, which is not his actual position, in order to clear the soil for the seed of secular humanism, which is his root concern. Humanocentric theism becomes a handy spade to prepare the ground for secular humanism by virtue of both instruments harvesting the fruits of human functional ultimacy.

Though advocating the "functional ultimacy of man," Jones believes he leaves a role for divinity in the scenario of human activity. In this sense he explains secular humanism as akin to humanocentric theism. The latter assigns an exalted status to humanity, in particular to human freedom and control over human destiny. What makes Jones' secular humanism a form of theism? Secular humanism discovers its theistic ground from a belief that human functional ultimacy results from God's will and God's ultimate purpose and plan for humankind. Intrinsic to humanity's created ontology (human nature) is humanity's capacity of codetermination with divinity. In conclusion, humanocentric theism provides a consistent constitutive feature of a liberation theology; it grants human freedom. And it provides a "sturdy refutation" of divine racism; it removes God's overruling sovereignty from human history.[38]

CRITIQUE

No! to White Theology

The black political theology trend sets out a clear path for black theology. Black people cannot achieve their God-given humanity and dignity until white racist relations are transformed in society, the church and theology. Black theology of liberation cannot proceed without challenging and confronting white supremacy. The political theologians correctly unfold their project around the political, economic and social oppression in the black community. A genuine black theology of liberation is accountable both to a liberating God and black freedom.

In contrast to white theology, the political theologians justifiably begin their understanding of God in the oppressed community. White theological tradition evolves out of positions of privilege; black theology sees God in the faces of the disinherited. When white theology dabbles in esoteric and obscure academic issues, black political theology anchors itself in the concrete movement against racism. As the community fights for survival and liberation, black theology also has to be the critical arm of that fight. When white theology teaches that religion and theology are individualistic private affairs, black political theology urges the black church and community to struggle collectively. White theology supports the subjugation of black life by justifying the normalcy of "whiteness"; black theology unequivocally sides with the marginalized. While white theology deceptively argues about the objectivity of "God-talk," black political theologians claim that all theologies reflect either the oppressor or the oppressed; theology is not neutral.

Furthermore, white theology speaks of a spiritual salvation in the hereafter; black political theology talks about a material freedom here and now. White theology considers itself the legitimate scientific "classical" discipline; black theology fights for the right of the black poor to think critically about their faith. White and black theologies occupy two opposing social contexts. Thus they do theology in radically different ways. When white theology sings "God Bless America," black political theology pictures the white church's support of police departments, white ethnic enclaves and the white backlash. The black political theology trend, therefore, correctly rejects European-North American theology's pretentions of authenticity and normalcy.

Black Theology of "Liberation"

All four political theologians make contributions around the *liberation* theme. Albert Cleage's black liberation theology (the right of black self-determination, including the right of separation) is a sorely needed, straightforward condemnation of white theology and its antithetical relation to the gospel. His separation motif represents those particular periods in black history when only separation can save black life from the quasi-genocidal attacks of white America.

William R. Jones' attack on liberation presuppositions awoke all black theologians from the slumbering, preconscious assumptions about the politics of God. Such a critique warrants serious analysis simply because it scrutinizes primordial tenets of black liberation God-talk. When in-house discourse appears to *automatically* justify its claims of divine liberation activity by merely repeating the phrase "God favors the suffering blacks," it is time to clean the theological house. Jones' secular humanism plays the important role of a potential cleaning broom. His challenging critique of the liberation assumption weaves together a black experience context, a rigor of philosophical logic and a materialist methodology.

In constructing a black theology for the entire black community, Jones' non-Christian challenge is important. It is important because the norm for an inclusive black theology is all theological factors enhancing the liberation of the black poor. God manifests God's liberation purposes in diverse ways in the black community. Therefore there are diverse ways of faith witnessing to God's liberation.

Jones' resolution of his theodicy position, however, is not persuasive, particularly to the black church. For example, my own Christocentrism, as well as that of the black church, provides the lens for me to appreciate other examples of God's liberating activity for the poor. Stated differently, for me it is only through God's work in Christ that the possibility for God's power to arise in other areas of life and history achieves reality. Still, a cultural-political theology includes both non-Christian and non-"religious" segments who have and will continue to question the liberation thrust of the Christian sections of the over-all black community's theology. Malcolm X was a prime example of a non-Christian black theological voice who launched a devastating criticism. He insightfully charged that Christianity was the "white man's" religion. Similarly, the Black Panther Party, representing a faith in black liberation in the "streets," voiced the non-religious sentiment. Though a Christian cannot follow Jones' path, Jones does present a persisting query.

Of all the political theologians, James Cone has done the most to develop and institutionalize black theology as *liberation* theology. His groundbreaking work, *Black Theology and Black Power* (1969) and *A Black Theology of Liberation* (1970) were the first two texts to present black theology systematically. Moreover, he is the first American (black or white) to link comprehensively the theological concept of liberation of the poor with the gospel. Moreover, his liberation concern has influenced students throughout seminaries. In different parts of the United States, graduate students interested in black theology write their theses and dissertations on his liberation perspective. He produces the most doctoral students and has written the most articles and books on black theology and its relation to the black church. Furthermore, his black theology has had an impact on the developing liberation theologies in Africa, Asia and Latin America. For instance, South African black theology assigns its development directly to Cone's impact. With liberation of the oppressed, particularly black people, through Christ the Liberator, Cone's theological concept of liberation has reflected an over-all cogency and consistency since his first published writing in 1968. He remains the dominant force in black theology of liberation today.

In his black theology of balance, J. Deotis Roberts exhibits strength in his attempt to develop a holistic liberation theology. He carves out a program that theologizes on both the political and personal situations of black

Americans. An authentic theology should relate to the external structural constraints on blacks as well as the personal, spiritual and negative lifestyles within the black community. He raises the political liberation of the external critique against the systemic racism of American society. Roberts also calls for a forthright internal liberation of deleterious black-on-black practices. He associates the "social context of experience with existential concerns." He thus sketches a picture of black collectivity along with personal individuality. For him, social oppression produces personal crises. This holistic, internal-external aspect of his balance methodology is a positive contribution to the activity of the black church and community. Because his method seeks to be all-inclusive, he opens his black theology to cultural dimensions too.

On the negative side, one encounters an inconsistency in Roberts' liberation theme. An incongruity appears in the treatment of "balance" and in his sources for theological normalcy.

One receives the distinct impression from Roberts' declared intent that his black political theology of balance really lacks the evenness he sets out as twin goals in his project. His "balance" inconsistency confuses the liberation-reconciliation impact in his political theology. In *Black Theology Today* he develops a quasi "which way forward" for black theology under the heading "A Brief Constructive Statement." After criticizing Major Jones, William Jones and James Cone, he outlines the salient points of his own black theological endeavors. While mentioning liberation, nowhere does one detect a hint of the other goal—reconciliation. Similarly, in the same text but under the rubric "contextual theology," he deletes the reconciliation concern in a discussion on the importance of the incarnation. Today's implication from the incarnation, Roberts contends, directs us to a "theology of liberation," an interpretation of "a gospel of liberation." And in his latest work, *Black Theology in Dialogue*, he concludes that the future of black theology is a black theology that is "essentially a liberation theology." Except for William R. Jones, no political theologian would question the liberation impulse. But Roberts specifically stakes his claim on his dual aim of liberation *and* reconciliation.[39]

In a situation in which oppressed black people cry out for liberation (justice), and the oppressor white community, perpetuating the yoke of oppression on the necks of poor blacks, cries out for reconciliation (without justice), one has to take a stand. Roberts' "liberating experience of reconciliation for the white oppressor as well as for the black oppressed" dilutes the force of liberation and thus fails the test. South African Archbishop Desmond Tutu once observed: "If you are neutral in situations of injustice, you have chosen the side of the oppressor." By desiring to liberate blacks and reconcile them with their white oppressor, Roberts keeps the status quo. Either the poor have to support the rich in the persistent effort at black genocide or the rich have to join Christ in liberating the poor blacks. This latter scenario demands a destruction of everything that is "white" in the United States and making everything that is white black with Christ. One cannot bridge or balance two conflicting movements—the Civil Rights and the Black Power movements—without taking a stand. The civil rights era fought to integrate *Negroes* with white people by acknowledging white power and values as the norm. The black power era fought for the liberation—the power to implement self-determination politically, culturally and economically—of *black* people.

Roberts also hints at the *normalcy* status of white theology and intimates his real goal is reconciliation with white people's theology. For example, he insinuates the narrowness of black theology. He wishes "to admit the black theologian to the comprehensive field of theology."[40] This presumes that mainstream Protestant theology determines the comprehensive theological field. Elsewhere Roberts implies that the black religious experience equals the narrow way but the white "broad field of theology" equips blacks with the ingredients for a mature and constructive black theology. Likewise he describes black people's study of their faith-claim as "too often subjective to be sufficiently critical and evaluative." Therefore white theology can be supplementary to black theology "by being more objective by bringing careful analysis and critical judgement upon [black people's] affirmation of faith." For Roberts, white theology is more critical and objective, while black faith-claims may be subjective and lack the noetic.[41] But how can black theology fight for liberation by accepting the normalcy of that from which it seeks liberation? Stated differently, we have to build a black theology of liberation from black indigenous cultural resources.

Blackness

Influenced by Malcolm X, Cleage worked to correct the abject self-negation of black Americans in the church and theology. By cursing everything white he struggled to give blacks a sense of their own power. We pinpoint Cleage's strengths in his practical application of his black theology. From his ecclesiological standpoint—the reconstituted black church as the black revolution's center—he attempted to organize his Christian community to march toward self-determination and black liberation. First, he wrote a new theology for his church so that the congregation would not only separate physically from whites but would also have a theology to justify separation. Second, his church developed a black studies school as an ongoing institutionalization and popularization of black life and culture. Third, he sent church members to the community as organizers. Finally, he guided all church activities toward the unification of the black community around a common philosophy and commitment to transform a servile black existence into a political power base.[42]

While appreciating his reaction to the brutalities of white America, Cleage's theology sometimes appears to subscribe to a genetic deterministic anthropology. Commenting on the metanoia possibilities for whites, he asserts:

> If white people could change (and we do not think that possible unless our analysis of human nature is incorrect) and begin to love black people, we would note the change.[43]

His one-sided use of human nature connotes an inherent evilness on the part of white people and, conversely, an inherent divineness in blacks. Cleage could have developed his position more comprehensively in the following way. Because Jesus dedicated himself to the least of these, that is, the black poor, and because the black poor in the United States are labeled satanic (as opposed to the "purity" of whiteness), and are the lowest of the low in American society, metanoia and liberation for whites — as well as middle class blacks — result from their recognizing a black Jesus and joining with him in the struggle of the black poor.

Moreover, part of Cleage's simplistic "white skin equals the devil and black skin equals the divine" springs from his absolute disdain for the use of class interests and Marxism as tools of social analysis in his account of "blackness." He proclaims that "Marxian philosophy and economics do not apply to America for the very simple reason that we have a physically distinguishable [black] group which is oppressed. . . . Marxism offers no solution to the Black man's problem." Cleage's weakness in Marxist political economy has implications for his goal of black community control. In the United States, black community control cannot succeed without moving toward the total dismantling of monopoly capitalist ownership. Instead of democratic, community control, Cleage's writings seem to leave monopoly capitalism intact; this would allow regressive black elected officials and like-minded black churches to replace or act in concert with the exploitative role of whites. However, in black theology Marxism can perform the important function of promoting the liberation of the black poor as the primary criteria.[44]

Regarding Cone's treatment of blackness, one observation on African lineage will suffice. The issue of Cone's slighting black people's African heritage emerged around his now-famous statement: "The black church was born in slavery. Its existence symbolizes a people who were completely stripped of their African heritage as they were enslaved by the 'Christian' white man."[45] Charles Long and Gayraud Wilmore have pioneered critiques of Cone's initial one-sidedness vis-à-vis African lineage to black America. Moreover, Josiah U. Young has most recently resumed the critique along similar lines.[46] However, to put the criticisms in perspective, Cone's statement was made in the context of correctly exposing the heinousness of white "Christian" slavery. And since the critique of his colleagues Wilmore and Long, he has corrected his gross overstatement.

Still, I wish to draw out possible theological implications of black Americans' Africanness from his earlier writings. First, Cone denied God's creation of black Americans' Africanness by citing white slavemasters' ability to totally *re-create* (for example, strip) what God had created. Because black Americans reflect the createdness of God, to have denied their Africanness was to deny the fact that they reflected the *imago dei*. Second, by stating that Africanness was completely stripped, Cone's view objectively denied the omnipotent creativeness and ability of God to *maintain* God's own creation. Last, Cone's position yielded to the demonic forces of "whiteness" by implying that the white Anti-Christ forces destroyed the gift of God's grace to black Americans — their Africanness.

Black Liberation Movement

All four black political theologians exhibit some weaknesses in their theological views on the black liberation movement. Both J. Deotis Roberts and James Cone believe that black theology is church theology. Therefore a critique of Cone also covers Roberts' views.

In *God of the Oppressed*, Cone claims:

> What then is the form and content of black religious thought, when viewed in the light of the social situation? Briefly, the form of black religious thought is expressed in the style of story and its content is liberation. Black theology, then, is the story of black people's struggle for liberation in an extreme situation of oppression.

One observes two contentions. First, black religious thought matches with black theology and both include liberation as the content. And second, black theology, here, concerns itself with the struggle of all segments in the black community. In this black struggle Cone perceives the working of God's will. He also states that black faith is not only in black churches but also *outside* of the institutions of black denominations. Cone then homes in on the black theological task: "It is not the task of black theology to remove the influence of the divine in the black community. Its task is to interpret the divine element in the forces and achievement of black liberation."[47] Cone links black theology and black religious thought in a broad way to speak to the struggle of every liberation effort in the black community. And in that Christian and non-Christian effort at liberation Cone sees the work of the divine. The presupposition for the divine's work, in this emphasis of Cone's, does not require the entire struggling black community to accept Christianity. In fact, he clearly asserts: "When I speak of black faith, I am referring only secondarily to organized religion and primarily to black people's collective acknowledgment of the spirit of liberation in their midst."[48]

Yet, tacking more toward a Barthian and Tillichian understanding of theology,[49] Cone also believes that "theology is the discipline arising within the Christian community" and "black theology is Christian theology." Continuing along the same vein he understands that "theology is a church discipline — that is, a discipline which functions within the Christian community."[50]

Cone moves between a bi-polar definition of black theology: Black theology covers the entire community versus black theology circumscribes the Christian community. However, the paradox could possibly be resolved as follows. For a black theology the essence resides in God's liberating activity in the total black experience. God presents God's self in the black church and outside of the black church, in the sacred and in the secular, as both intermix in the black reality. For the total black community, Jesus Christ does not delimit the norm. In a broader sense black faith, "the spirit of liberation in [the black community's] midst," judges the efficacy toward emancipation. Thus the black Christian theologian seeks to identify God's Christian and non-Christian activity in the entire black community. At the same time, from a Christian perspective, the theologian identifies the decisive revelation of Jesus Christ, the Liberator.

However, to say *Christian* theology is for the entire black community leads to at least three potential obstacles that could hinder the unity of all blacks. One, it could impose God's activity in Christ on God's activity in non-Christian movements in the black community. Second, and concomitantly, it could restrict God's liberating activity to a rational discourse concerning God in Christ alone. And third, it could undermine the implementation of a black political theology for the black community (church and non-church) by excluding the vast number of progressive black community non-Christians, those allies who are on God's (non-Christian) side. At issue is how a Christian develops a black theology as part of a larger black community. A black Christian critically reflects on her or his faith and believes that Christian theology is for all black people (in the sense that Christian theology supports black freedom). But that statement needs to be modified by simultaneously and consistently acknowledging God's unlimited revelation of liberation beyond black *Christian* theology. The total black community spawns black theology; it is the discussion of and witnessing to and with God's liberation of the poor, particularly the black poor. The norm for black theology is *all* factors enhancing black liberation; Jesus Christ is one factor, and, for the black Christian, the decisive factor.

Albert Cleage's understanding of the black liberation movement suffers like Roberts' and Cone's. Certainly Cleage is right when his black ecclesiology does not limit its liberation ministry to its parishioners. And he is possibly correct that the black church might initiate and build the black freedom struggle. But Cleage overstates an appropriate ecclesiology for black liberation by declaring that the movement is the Christian church and the Christian church is the movement. Such a statement might exhort the black church to shed its white theology and become involved. But it tends to one-sidedly subordinate the non-Christian radical elements in the black struggle. The black liberation movement is not "the Christian Church in the 20th Century," as Cleage states. A more appropriate ecclesiology for the entire black community would view the black Christian church as one part of the "hub" along with other radical representatives of God's black liberation movement.

Opposing Cleage, Roberts and Cone, William R. Jones approaches the black liberation movement from an entirely different angle. He questions the black church's liberation practice in the movement by questioning its faith claim in a liberating God. But his method of critical engagement does not deal with other black theologians on their own terms. All other black political theologians dialogue with the presupposition of belonging to and speaking for a particular faith community whose pre-belief is in what God has done for blacks even since Africa. Jones does not share this starting point. Hence there will never be an adequate reply to secular humanism's philosophical attack on the black church's *faith* in God's presence in the black liberation movement. Either the black church has to liquidate its faith, tradition and historical practice, or secularism will have to join the masses of black folk in their struggle alongside a liberating God. Otherwise both will forever pass each other like strangers in the dark. As long as Jones critiques the liberation-salvation power of God's work in Jesus Christ, he separates himself from other black theologians. However, since Jesus Christ does not delimit the norm for the entire black community, Jones' critique does not necessarily remove him from the black theological discourse. On the contrary, as long as he upholds liberation as the theological norm, he remains within a black theology of liberation.

Jones believes his *coup de grâce* is his question: Why has God not eliminated black suffering? Black church politics, however, do not begin here. The black church affirms its faith claim by praising and thanking the Lord for black survival and for the fact that "trouble does not last always." The black church and a large section of the non-church-going black community appreciate a God of liberation who empowered black resistance on slave ships, during slavery itself, from Montgomery to Memphis, through black power and urban rebellions, and in today's local community organizing efforts and Rainbow formations.[51] Faith in this God of liberation yields empowerment, hope and resistance in the practical movement; all the basics which the human functional ultimacy has not substantiated. For the black church the decisive exaltation-liberation event took place in Jesus Christ. Between Christ's first arrival and the parousia, the black church believes in and experiences various penultimate exaltation-liberation events — freedom from slavery, the abolition of legal segregation and the denial of the right to vote, and so on.

CONCLUSION

This chapter explored the political manifestations of black theology in the United States. We followed the path of theology and power relations and black power confronting white power. We observed that the black political theology trend was strong on the political dimension, the political struggle against racist power, of a black theology of liberation. However, as a group they lacked a consistent relationship between politics and culture. The following chapter brings the cultural theological motif to the forefront. We will pursue theological issues of God and black people's Africanness and blackness. We will appraise liberation from a cultural perspective. Here too we will find differentiation within a single paradigm.

CHAPTER THREE

No Black Culture, No Black Theology

Princes shall come out of Egypt;
Ethiopia shall soon stretch out her hands unto God.
Psalm 68:31 (KJV)

It is a peculiar sensation, this double-consciousness, this sense of always looking at one's self through the eyes of others, of measuring one's soul by the tape of a world that looks on in amused contempt and pity. One ever feels his twoness, — an American, a Negro; two souls, two thoughts, two unreconciled strivings; two warring ideals in one dark body, whose dogged strength alone keeps it from being torn asunder.

W.E.B. DuBois

Representatives of the North American black cultural theology trend present a clear contrast to their political colleagues of the previous chapter. From the perspective of the cultural trend, the black political theologians waste too much time and attention reacting to white racism and the white American aspect of DuBois' "double-consciousness." The cultural theologians distinguish themselves by indicting the white supremacist, cultural structure of religion and the discipline of white theology. They accuse the political theologians of waging an attack on European-American theology and religion while, at the same time, accepting a white intellectual framework. Cultural theologians demand a total shift in definition of religious structure, a refocus away from theology and an excavation of primordial black worldviews. They require unwavering allegiance to the African and black side in DuBois' "two warring ideals in one dark body."

We shall review the theological perspectives of Gayraud S. Wilmore, Charles H. Long, Cecil W. Cone and Vincent Harding as paradigmatic of the black cultural theological trend. The categories of (a) black theology, (b) sources, (c) Africanisms, and (d) liberation will assist our investigation.

63

The cultural theologians' black theology derives from the same Civil Rights and Black Power movements that shaped the black political theology trend. But the cultural theologians uncompromisingly see their line of demarcation at two points—the role of theology and the primacy of black cultural resources. Wilmore accepts black theology as a worthy discipline but argues that it is subsumed under the larger, non-Christian category of *black religious thought*. Long substitutes *religious language* in place of theology. He forcefully argues that theology *qua* theology has acted as an imperialistic morphology, and he denies any success at constructing a genuine black theology. Cecil W. Cone embraces black theology's validity but adamantly specifies its root in *African religion*. Finally, Harding holds theology at arm's length and desires not to use such a stifling, European-American term. He prefers to simply let unself-conscious *spirituality* arise from the black community.

GAYRAUD S. WILMORE

Black Religious Thought

Gayraud S. Wilmore has had a major impact on contemporary black theology in the United States. Wilmore, an ordained Presbyterian, participated in the very early meetings of the ad hoc National Committee of Negro Churchmen. He first chaired the committee's theological commission and crafted its pioneering black theological direction. Though trained in social ethics, Wilmore shifted emphasis to black history and black theology. His 1972 edition of *Black Religion and Black Radicalism* filled a major gap in the nascent black theological movement—the need for a fresh account of the myriad streams of resistance in black religious history. *Black Theology: A Documentary History, 1966-1979*, which he co-edited with James Cone, is still the classic textbook on black theology. He is a member of the Black Theology Project (Theology in the Americas) and the Society for the Study of Black Religion.

I refer to Wilmore's theology as Black Theology of Religious Thought. The phrase *religious thought* comes directly from his self-description. Wilmore wants to date any discussion of black theology long before the polemics against white theology of the 1960s. Furthermore, he evaluates theology within the generic "black religious thought":

If we are going to talk about black theology, we really need to go back to the beginning and not assume that black theology began with the publication of Dr. Cone's book in 1969. But when we do that, we have to agree that we are not using theology in the strictly academic and technical sense. What we really might use better is the term . . . black religious thought.[1]

Wilmore argues for this designation of black people's religious experience because he believes black *Christian* theology grows out of black religious thought. He wants to dig deeper, for he discovers something broader beneath academic theology, which, in his opinion, mainly reflects the confessions of the Christian church, the apostolic faith, the Old and New Testaments, and church disciplines. Given the priority of black religious thought, how does Wilmore define theology?

Black theology, Wilmore professes, is not the mere opposite of the dominant Christian theology, a black version of white classical theology. On the contrary, black theology gains its validity in plumbing the meaning of black freedom from specific black theological resources. Wilmore advances this query: In what ways do black Christian, *non-Christian* and *secular* groups comprehend, feel and practice liberation as their ultimate concern? Unpacking this ultimate concern is the theological work of black theology. Hence, continues Wilmore, black theology fulfills its proper task when it points the way toward the total black community's emancipation. Furthermore, the norm of black theology is freedom for black people and, in that process, freedom for all God's humanity.[2] Thus Wilmore works on a black theology leaning more toward the liberation strands in non-Christian black movements.

Even when one sanctions the validity of black theology, one still has to begin at the beginning, which is before the black church. In that sense Wilmore does not view theology as merely a church discipline.

> The seminal Black Theology of the African slaves on the plantations of the New World existed prior to the existence of the black church as such. Its first theologians were not theologically trained professors, but preacher-conjurers.[3]

Although theology goes back to the period before and during the historic black church's resistance against slavery and racism, the thought of the black religious experience embraced the attempts of all black secular and non-Christian groups to express the meaning and values of the black reality in the United States, Africa and the Caribbean. Even today theology extends beyond the black church as an ecclesiastical institution. It includes aspects of black life and culture, contends Wilmore, which white scholars would call secular, non-Christian and sometimes anti-Christian.

One could contrast Wilmore's church history, and attendant theology, with the religious social ethics of Dr. Peter Paris. Paris specifically chooses for examination two of the oldest examples of black Christianity in the United States, the African Methodist Episcopal Church and the National Baptist Convention, U.S.A., Inc.[4] Paris' text outlines a move beyond black liberation theology to the precept of "the black Christian tradition." He derives his theology from the official records of the institutional black church. Wilmore, on the other hand, does not mention theology or church in the title of *Black Religion and Black Radicalism*. Though acknowledging the import of black church theology, he travels the road to theology via black religion — ecclesiastical and non-ecclesiastical.

Wilmore writes in order to create a new set of interpretive tools, a new hermeneutic for the black community. How does the over-all black community bring forth its ultimate concerns and solutions in a situation of racist exploitation? For Wilmore the area of probing is neither European-American theology nor simply black church documents. He searches the black oral tradition and literature, sifting through mythology, ethical norms and folklore.[5] There he ascertains black religious thought.

Sources

Black religious thought becomes the precondition and preconscious ingredient for a black theology. Offering a panoramic view, black religious thought allows Wilmore to move from the confines of a systematic church theology to the unbounded religious experience nourished by the masses of black people. For the entire community, black religious thought operates on a basic norm: an indestructible belief in freedom, a freedom born in the African environment. This informal, uncategorized religious thought of black folk, therefore, opens up a whole new world of sources with which to sharpen a new black hermeneutic for liberation. As long as belief in freedom regulates the sources, following Wilmore's line of reasoning, the possibilities of black cultural, theological creativity seem endless.

In *Black Religion and Black Radicalism*[6] Wilmore uncovers four locations for theological sources. He does not directly include scripture and early church tradition in his three-sources division. The presuppositional status of the Bible and apostolic faith hints at their de-emphasis in the development of his black religious thought. Wilmore wishes to promote non-Christian resources. First, he highlights the lower-class black community's folk religion. In his judgment black faith as folk religion has powered all major revolutionary and nationalist mass-based movements of blacks and has maintained some semblance of Africa's cultural importance in black America. Sometimes folk religion overlaps the black Christian church. Other times it unfolds in movements like the Nation of Islam, Marcus Garvey's efforts, black Islam, black Judaism, the Azusa Street Revival and Daddy Grace.

The second source is the "writings, sermons, and addresses of the black preachers and public men and women of the past." Wilmore agrees that not all historic black heroines and heroes were members of the clergy. But he claims that almost all experienced religious conditioning from the black community. They reflected the unique spirituality of black life and culture erected on black faith. Both the black clergy and the black literati have drawn on the religious and theological themes of suffering, struggle, hope, justice, faith and survival and liberation of black people. Therefore one must also seek theological implications in the essays of Alice Walker, the poetry of Countee Cullen, the novels of Richard Wright and the tales of Langston Hughes. For Wilmore, one does not develop black theology primarily in white seminaries. Properly molded, black theology is found "in the streets, in taverns and pool halls, as well as in churches."

Traditional religions of Africa make up the third source of black theology. Wilmore points out the non-*ex nihilo* origin of black Americans; black people are an *African* people. Consequently the religious and theological connections to ancient and modern Africa bear heavily on contemporary black knowledge of God. The particular way God revealed God's self in pre-colonial Africa contributes to the survival and liberation of black people on both sides of the Atlantic. A modification of African traditional religious beliefs, values and practices could very well engineer a revitalization of Afro-American religion in North America. Here Wilmore also calls for a cooperative venture between black Americans and Africans to rediscover and uncover common "belief structures and worship practices" in black religious norms and conventions.

Wilmore contends that any future work on black theology has to go back to the period of African-American life in slavery. I include this as his fourth and his final source. In the slave epoch various theological and religious motifs come together to formulate the basis of black religious thought. The following typifies Wilmore's position on the black cultural elements in slavery-based black religion.

> In the formation of a new common language, in the telling of animal tales and proverbs, in the leisure time practice of remembered handicrafts, in the preparation of foods, homemade medicines, and magical potions and charms, in the standardization of rituals of birth, marriage, and death, in the creation of modes of play and parody, in the expression of favorite styles of singing, instrumental music, and the dance . . . the slaves wove for themselves the tapestry of a new African-American culture.[7]

These unified cultural aspects were integrated into a basic religious conception of life and reality. To understand the elementary religious cosmology of black Christians and the entire black community, one has to go back to the cultural elements just cited. In the unique way in which black culture formed itself one discovers the rudimentary theology of black religious thought cut from the African spiritual survivals in the slavery of the New World, for example, Africanisms.

Africanisms

Black cultural theological trend members unanimously assert that Africanisms occupy a prominant role in black religion and, therefore, the construction of an authentic black theology of liberation. They advocate upgrading the religious implications of the remains of African values and worldview. Wilmore points out several religious themes that he believes survive from Africa in today's black community:[8]

(a) In black life, there exists no sharp dichotomy between the secular and the sacred, religion and life.

(b) Religion is pragmatic. It relates directly to food, shelter, economic life, childrearing and recreation. Religion must work in everyday life.

(c) Like Africa, the over-all black community places a premium on family and solidarity in communalism as opposed to excessive individualism.

(d) Black folk worship God with the fullness of the body, mind and spirit. This links to liberation because the Spirit descends and unbinds both the soul and the body. "This same Spirit which calls us out of the rigidity of our psychosomatic entity, calls us out of the tyranny of our political bondage." For Wilmore, pneumatology includes the freeing of the body and the soul.

(e) When the black community speaks of the presence of God and the Spirit in its midst, this indicates the spirit of black ancestors' lives.

With these religious Africanisms Wilmore wishes to carry out a correction of "the whitenization of black religion." At the same time, and probably more important for his project, he lifts up these themes to generate "a constructive and positive development of a creative black religious thought, a creative black theology." Africanisms mean God, the Lord of all peoples and cultures, created the Africanness in "black Americans." As God-created, Africanisms inherently contain creative, positive theological value for black people and all humanity. In brief, they contain possibilities for liberation.

Liberation

To understand Wilmore's theological conception of liberation or freedom, one has to keep in mind his proclivity to African culture. Wilmore describes how the black masses' religious experience toward freedom represented an outgrowth of the ancestral African environment. In this primordial ethos freedom pointed to existential deliverance, liberation from all powers that inhibited the holistic release of mind, body and spirit. Any power that prohibited the full advancement of the individual in community would be defeated. At this juncture Wilmore emphasizes that liberation signals more than politics and economics. It means

freedom of the person as a child of God, the freedom to be himself and herself most fully, to realize the most creative potential of his or her psychophysiological nature . . . the freedom that black religion celebrates and black theology seeks to explicate is simply the freedom to be a child of God.[9]

For Wilmore, freedom, in the theological sense, is each individual of the community attaining the height of his or her God-given possibilities. One achieves divine initiated liberation once one exhausts the fullest potential of one's mind and body. Divine freedom results in full human creativity; therefore, blocking human wholeness attacks divine purpose.

Wilmore sees a necessity to talk in theological language about black people's ultimate concern for liberation because of the derivation of black folk's yearning for liberation. Liberation evolves from blacks' pristine consciousness of a transcendent reality. In that reality freedom intertwined inseparably with the essence of the definition of humanity created in *imago dei*.[10] Thus in addition to being a *child* of God and reaching full *wholeness*, a black person undergoes a liberated experience with the complete realization of God's *image* in her or him. In fact, attaining maximum human potential mirrors the *imago dei*. God created humanity to be human in the fullest sense of the word. To be human is to succeed in all that is humanly possible. For black Americans, then, there is an African religious and cultural sense that human creativity incarnates God's image.

Furthermore, liberation discloses divine imperative, a mandated theological ethic. The black Christian community, Wilmore writes, needs to regain "a sense of cultural vocation that relates to their experience of struggle in terms of both spiritual formation and social transformation."[11] Wilmore establishes the phrase *cultural vocation* and pinpoints at least two things. First, liberation does not come from a whimsical human decision about what to do in life. On the contrary, the divine calls and bestows upon humanity the vocation—a lifelong pursuit in response to God's word—to be free. Second, spiritual formation and social change coalesce in a vocation of culture. Culture acts as the umbrella for the holistic liberation of and interplay between the spirit and body. Wilmore's preference for culture as the context for politics becomes clear in this instance. For him, to see liberation primarily in political terms would narrow black people's religious ontology to political liberation in reaction to another (whites). Whereas culture, employed by Wilmore, expresses a total mind-body-spirit religious way of life. A cultural matrix seems to imply a proactive black religious mode of being.

Though he gives preference to culture, Wilmore does indeed recognize the inseparability of political and cultural liberation. Yet he shuns a one-sided goal of only political liberation because he believes that it yields a deformed achievement. In Wilmore's view, one cannot consummate the fullest measure of human liberation while remaining captive to the oppressor's culture. People have "to appreciate and value their own traditions in art and music and literature and family life and childrearing habits and recreation and all the multiflex aspects of human life."[12] The black community does not engage in these cultural activities as an idle pastime. Again, for Wilmore, in these very activities, that is, in culture, one identifies sources of religious and theological values held over from Africa. Until black folks appreciate the cultural way, and thus the religious way, political liberation is a Pyrrhic victory: Black people would win the political battle but lose the over-all cultural (religious and theological) war to their white oppressor. Thus only with success in the cultural sphere will black liberation illustrate a thoroughgoing victory over demonic principalities and powers on earth.

CHARLES H. LONG

Black Religious Language

Throughout the 1970s Charles H. Long waged a vehement struggle against attempts at creating a black theology and against neglecting the primacy of culture in black life and religion. Past president of the American Academy of Religion and member of the Society for the Study of Black Religion, Long does not credit himself as a black theologian. On the contrary, he obtained his formal studies in history of religions. Previously a professor at the University of North Carolina at Chapel Hill, he now teaches history of religions at Syracuse University in New York. Indeed, his discipline directly impinges upon his interpretation of black theology. Therefore a look at his definition of history and religion will aid this study.

> By "history" I mean the particular temporal-spatial cultural situation in which man responds to that which is sacred and by "religion" I mean the structure of the myth, symbol, or religious response through which man apprehends the sacred. The historian of religion is interested in understanding the enduring structure of these responses.[13]

History operates as cultural location for humanity's response to the sacred. Put differently, the plane of human activity and intercourse with the holy is cultural. Culture gives birth to religion. And religion denotes structures through which humanity apprehends the holy. Here Long hopes to elude any coloring of religious structure from a white to a darker hue — an error of blacks aping white religious structures.[14] Rather, he targets the very (white) religious structure itself and attempts its deconstruction and subsequent reconstruction from something religiously new.

Long agrees with Wilmore's accent away from strict Christian sources and broadening black religious thought to include non-Christian and secular elements. Long builds on Wilmore's work by using his unique definition of religious language. In fact, I label Long's perspective a Black Religious Language. He characterizes religion as the fountainhead out of which all other discourses, including theology, emanate. "For my purposes," Long writes, "religion will mean orientation — orientation in the ultimate sense, that is, how one comes to terms with the ultimate significance of one's place in the world."[15] Religion, then, deals with how a people negotiates its ultimate significance in a cultural time and space. Hence the *entire* black community is religious because it confronts the question of ultimate significance. As a result, for Long, all languages extend out of religion: language about God, salvation and creation.

Language has an exact meaning for Long. In a certain sense language does not mirror reality; language is all of reality. "All you have is language," comments Long.

> There is nothing behind, before, underneath, overarching or whatever. So whatever reality you want to talk about is in the language.... So that language has its own materiality. It is not so much that there is a reality there and I'm using these words just to say what I want to say about it. I am saying that in language is the reality that I am expressing.... I do not think language is just something that represents something else.[16]

Here one can better grasp the fundamental problem Long has with the meaning and origination of discourse. He does not view religious language as a mechanical epiphenomenon or a flimsy shadow of some other real religious substance. Religious language *is* religious substance. In his perspective, discourses express power when they authenticate the modes and structures of the people for whom discourses speak. Therefore genuine black religious language speaks the actuality and materiality of what proceeds among black culture and life.

With his definitions of religion and language Long submits both theology and Christianity to a deconstructive critique. He dismisses the notion of a black theology because he believes theology originated and presently acts as a "power discourse" used by the white oppressor in that oppressor's interests. Long attacks the very structure (as opposed to reinterpreting theological categories) of theology because theology as theology represents a discourse of those (white) people who have the power to define cultural categories. Black people and poor people, posits Long, have not had the privilege of establishing cultural categories. Thus why should black people enter the "imitative game" of saying they will attain their liberation by virtue of mimicking those who have oppressed them? Again, theology is white people's power discourse.

Relatedly, and similar to Wilmore, Long voices primary problems with black theology because, in his words, "it is church theology." Yet in Long's assessment, churches only incorporate that segment of black religion and culture that has self-consciously fractionized itself as Christian. In fact, the black community also fosters a great deal of other religious life that boasts Ultimate Concern. By naming themselves advocates of black theology black religious intellectuals miss the non-Christian mode of religion in black culture. Hence theology and black theology, in particular, narrow the categories of religious language in the black community.[17]

With a like-minded rationale, Long cautions against Christianity as an authentic religion for the liberation of black religious language. He states that Christianity is probably the only religion that accommodates a theology. Why? Because "Christianity is not a grassroots religion . . . that grows up out of the ground of the people."[18] Even when Christianity spread across Europe, one has to presuppose that some other mode of religious discourse preceded it. One has to presuppose, in Long's opinion, the vitality of a people's cultural and religious life wherever Christianity goes throughout the world. Briefly, both theology and Christianity operate as dominating power discourses. And so, one needs other sources for black religious language.

Sources

Long approaches sources in order to answer this question: What are the religious elements in the cultural experience of black folk? He contrasts his approach to that of two representatives of the black political theological trend, James H. Cone and Albert B. Cleage. Cone and Cleage function essentially as "apologetic theologians working implicitly and explicitly from the Christian theological tradition." They have accepted the theological structure of Christian religious discourse. Long then raises the theological methodological shortcomings in apologetic theology. "This limitation of methodological perspectives" on the part of Cone and Cleage, Long contends, has resulted in a truncated understanding and the exclusion of certain creative possibilities among black folk.[19]

Long turns his eye toward the more vitally important discourses forthcoming from the black community itself. There one begins with the raw data of black religious language. For example, Long "would spend as much time with Count Basie, Jimmy Lungford, and Cab Calloway, and black poets, and all these kind of folks as I would with ministers." He includes other such notables as Carter G. Woodson, W.E.B. Dubois, George Washington Carver and Jelly Roll Morton.[20] Both ministers and non-ministers struggle to give religious significance to black life and experience. The non-ministers occupy a position in black religious language just as creative and just as powerful as the ministers.

Long's religious and theological sources fall into four groups.[21] Agreeing with Wilmore, he first points out the involuntary presence of Africa's descendants in America. When the first Africans arrived in the New World, the process of creating black Americans commenced. Involuntary presence proved and continues to prove key to that creation. Slavery, and today's oppression of the black community, had to have affected in a unique way how bound Africans viewed their Ultimate Concern. Therefore involuntary presence and orientation communicate deep-seated religious meaning. The slave experienced negativity in bondage and, at the same time, created a different reality from a unique perception of Ultimate Concern. The confines of slavery, then, permitted transformative creativity on the level of religious consciousness.

Like Wilmore, Long also looks for the black community's engagement with the holy in tradition, a second source. The oral tradition of black folklore offers a gold mine of creative religious possibilities. What does a combing of slave narratives, black sermons, the words and music of the spirituals and the blues, the cycle of Br'er Rabbit, and High John the Conqueror stories yield? "These materials reveal," Long writes, "a range of religious meanings extending from trickster-transformer hero to High Gods."

In addition, slaves adopted and invested new meaning in the biblical imagery of the Bible, a third source. They interpreted God's deliverance of Israel from Egyptian bondage, Long professes, as a sign of hope. Furthermore, the slaves saw God as the omnipotent, moral deity, who had power to set things right. And the slaves never or hardly ever accused God in situations of theodicy. For example, to conserve their humanity in confrontation with the majority population's debilitating norm, slaves experienced the biblical God as a "transformer of their consciousness." In particular Long inspects the slaves' conversion experiences and discovers a combination of a practical "God acting in history" and a concern for "mystification of consciousness." Here in these narratives, the encounter of God overwhelms the slaves in the black religious experience and not in the trinitarian dogma. Accordingly, these theological structures — God acting in ordinary events and transformation of religious consciousness — combined in such a radical metanoia, can render clues about black religious consciousness for the entire black community. In other words, in the slaves' interpretation the transformer God of the Christian Bible is also found in the religious consciousness of non-Christian movements like "the Black Muslims and the Black Jews."

The slaves also distinguished God from Jesus Christ; consequently Long concedes that to the extent blacks have adhered to Christianity, trinitarian language has appeared, though more for an experiential rather than a dogmatic rationale. The slaves simply experienced Jesus as another form of God and not as the noetic second person of the Trinity. Particularly in biblical imagery they appropriated definite Christological attributes as dominant symbols. The appropriated biblical Christ evolved into a fellow sufferer, a little child, companion and person who understands. Long cites the essence of the Jesus' religious structure in Jesus' role of companion and creator, "a deity related more to the human condition than deities of the sky, and the subjection of this deity to death at the hands of men."

Also reflecting Wilmore's concern, the image and historical reality of Africa remain Long's final source. Admittedly white people's barbarity during slavery did splinter and thus adversely affect whatever cultural forms Africans brought with them from their home continent. Yet, Long purports, one cannot overlook the ebbing and flowing of the image and historical reality of Africa within the religious consciousness of black America since its creation. More specifically, the image and the reality have manifested themselves in black dance, music and political theory. Thus, part of black folk's Ultimate Concern is a manifest lack of homeness. On the one hand black ontology is an American ontology, suggests Long. But on the other hand, being black in the world (in America) casts a forlorn transience, a precognizant yearning for a connectedness to the Continent.

Africanisms

Long defines an Africanism as a mode of orientation toward and perception of reality. He claims this method of grasping and functioning in reality has probably persisted from Africa to black America. Africans did not touch the New World shores with a religious *tabula rasa*. Despite white cruelty in breaking up families and forbidding the speaking of African languages — all aimed at cultural domination — the structure of viewing the world, on which African languages thrived, endured. Since Long describes religion as orientation toward one's Ultimate Concern in life, black people's African cosmology intimates religious importance. For example, though West Africa evidences diverse social and linguistic formations, underneath empirical difference lies a structural unity revealed in religious and language forms. Because a great majority of American slaves originated in West Africa, the prevention of obvious language and cultural usages among slaves did not necessarily mean the abolition of the subterranean religious structural unity. Long mentions the examples of shout songs on the part of slaves, their secret meetings of "conjuring," and the continued presence of African rhythm and dance in American culture.

However, the major area of Africanism study, for Long, appears to be the religious implications of the image of Africa in the minds of slaves. Even if the slave could not directly remember Africa, the imprint of Africa's image stuck as a place of historical departure. Brutally removed from their homeland, Africans still maintained the remains of Africa which loomed like a beginning, like a form of creation. Theologically the Africa-image presents these queries for Long: Does the forced removal of black folk from their homeland indicate a peculiar divine teleological intent? This question somewhat images the Hebrew people's sojourn in the wilderness on the way to Canaan. Are black Americans on the way to a land of milk and honey? Are they to reconnect to their sisters and brothers on the Continent to help in their God-ordained freedom or perhaps, as a remnant of God's purpose on earth, bear the burden of leading in the realization of America into what God has created all humankind to become; that is, to overcome the tower of Babel cultural cacophony and establish the harmonious unity of diverse American cultures "speaking in tongues" about the same God? Long's exploration of the image and history of Africa opens up further religious avenues pregnant with theological possibilities.

Long's religious and historical image structure of Africa in black religious consciousness also touches on "eschatological hope" for black Americans. The religious value of the land (Africa) implies that it is unnecessary to actually return to beginnings, in the sense of massive pan-African migration. Yet a clear imprint of Africa in the religious consciousness could undergird the future potential of black freedom. The knowledge that God created a black lineage from a definite land could imply that the movement toward independence and wholeness in Africa has an inextricable link to black America. Just as God moves in mysterious ways in African liberation, cannot and will not God move in an appropriate kairotic manner for the same blood and flesh of Africans in America? Africa may portend Afro-American liberation.[22]

Liberation

Understanding what Long sees as the target of liberation facilitates an appreciation of his goal of liberation. Long charges European-Americans with executing a second creation in the case of black communities in America. "The oppressed must deal with . . . the fictive truth of their status as expressed by the oppressors, that is, their second creation."[23] The West forged black America out of the West's own history and language. Africa's descendants would not be in the United States, asserts Long, if Europeans had not brought them here. Since Africans' arrival, whites have continued the definition of what it means to be black in white America. The dominant America, then, employed its cultural language, mode of perception and religion to make blacks invisible. Referencing European conquest of African slaves (and Native Americans), Long asserts,

> The economic and military conquest was accomplished, but another conquest more subtle and with even longer-lasting effects had taken place. This was the linguistic conquest.[24]

Within the linguistic conquest theology marks a discourse that obfuscates attempts at black cultural meaning. More often than not theology functions like an imperialistic discourse. Linked to Christianity, it superimposes itself upon pre-existing religious structures.

The spurious, second creation by European cultural practices comes after the first creation, the work of God. Thus black people's struggle for liberation has been to reaffirm their truth and autonomy given in the first creation. In a sense, black liberation resides in black people renaming themselves in accord with the first creation. Admittedly they cannot literally return to the beginnings. Therefore liberation, eschatologically speaking, should bear salutary fruit in a third creation, God's new creation of a new humanity.[25]

Liberation will come with a new discourse, Long reasons, not merely in regard to its content and semantics, but in the essence of its structure, rhythm and texture. A liberative language helps humanity to become human in the world. For instance, the restrictions of slavery permitted Africans to perform transformative action mainly in the religious consciousness. Thus the locus of new language has to be situated in the religious consciousness, the orientation toward Ultimate Concern.

In addition to liberation in new discourse and the religious consciousness, blacks' fight for their God-created humanity takes the form of validating cultural identity. Long asserts:

> A great deal of the fight for human rights [by black Americans] is not only economic but a fight for the legitimation of Black cultural forms—those that have survived from Africa and those created in America.[26]

Long indicates a Christological role in this move toward legitimation. Denied cultural forms of identity, the black theologian has heard the voice of Christ speaking to the cultural and psychological identity issue. Thus Christ's identity with the black reality makes a way amidst cultural chaos.

Part of rectifying the cultural identity chaos entails a return to the black past, a requirement of intellectual and cultural deciphering. Long calls for a project to clarify the meanings of "those strange, profound, comical and sober deposits of [black folk's] past." This effort has momentous implications. Non-interpretation of those remains means perpetual slavery. Therefore, those deposits "must be vindicated or we shall never be free."[27]

Pursuing his liberation in cultural identity, Long has proposed that a study be undertaken of the interrelatedness of myriad religious traditions in the United States. In the dialogue each tradition would hold equal status with no one assuming "the normative structure of discourse." Culture would be the locus of investigation and the participants would use a "hermeneutic of deciphering." The result of such an equitable give-and-take might reveal a new, genuine structure of religious meaning for America.[28] Remembering Long's description of language possessing its own materiality, one can see how a normative discourse created from equality and liberation affects and effects a new religious relation among America's cultural distinctions.

CECIL W. CONE

Black African Religion

Trained in systematic theology and supportive of a black liberation theology, Cecil W. Cone nevertheless starts his black theology neither with white academic theological norms nor with the exigencies of Black Power. Cone, of the African Methodist Episcopal Church and formerly president of Edward Waters College in Florida, concludes that black religion is the only proper point of departure for black theology.[29]

A third member of the black cultural theology trend, Cone accepts Wilmore's and Long's broadening of black theology beyond academic theology and into culture, for example, black religious thought and religious language. But Cone extends his theology by linking all black American religious manifestations to a particular African perception of the divine. I term Cone's theology a Black Theology of African Religion because of the centrality of African religion in his view of black religion. The latter, in Cone's project, entails black Christian religion yet supercedes it. Black religion denotes the religion practiced by the people of African descent. And its determining characteristic is its roots in African religions.

Black theology, then, relates directly to the genesis of black religion in the United States. Indeed, black theology dates to the very moment that Africans arrived as slaves, and especially when they reacted to the slavemaster's Christianity. This introduction to Christianity, says Cone, afforded slaves the opportunity to "transpose" their African tradition and African religions into the context of this new religion. Thus an African understanding of God deeply penetrated the theological content of black Christian religion and black religion generally.

Black religion comes first and black theology interprets that religion from a theological perspective, guided by the Bible. But Cone does not confine black theology to a mere "theological discipline." In his opinion,

> Every time a black preacher mounts the pulpit . . . or a black Sunday school teacher begins to talk with her class . . . or on Wednesday night, a black layperson testifies . . . , they are actually making black theological statements.[30]

Thus black theology transcends the activities in seminaries.

Cone's black theology hinges on the conversion experience in black religion, the slave's radical confrontation with the (African) Almighty Sovereign God. Amidst the cauldron of slavery, the slave encountered not the God of white missionaries, but the God of his or her lost African heritage. The "omnipotent, omniscient and omnipresent" Almighty Sovereign God forced God's self on the slave in a terrifying experience. At that moment the slave realized how utterly sinful he or she was. The discovery of human unholiness and divine holiness revealed the radical distinction between the contingent and the absolute.

This recognition of human wretchedness prepared the slave for the actual conversion in the black religious experience. Conversion marked the entrance of the divine in the soul of the slave, the placement of humanity in God's hands, the literal removal of the slave from this world. As one slave actually testified to the experience of conversion, "God struck me dead!" Conversion brought on a new humanity. Now God had allowed the slave to contemplate new possiblities in the world because the slave, post-conversion, saw himself or herself only as a child of God and not of anyone else.[31] By correlating the African Almighty Sovereign God with the oppressed slave in the conversion experience, Cone hopes to set right "the identity crisis in black theology."

Sources

Cone posits the identity crisis in black theology at two sources. First, he chastises black theologians (in particular, J. Deotis Roberts) who, for Cone, obsequiously cater to European standardized, academic respectability. This path will lead to the destruction of black theology. In fact, black theologians need to distance themselves from European-American theological customs. How can black theology flirt with academic theology, which ignored black religion as a source? Black theologians need to prepare themselves to do theology that the white majority will not label "good" theology.

Second, Cone targets the politics of Black Power as a false theological base for black theology. He sees a fundamental contradiction in the eager acceptance of Black Power and the simultaneous attempts at maintaining connection to the black religious tradition. A theology of Black Power merely offers a rebel theology. God, not politics, is the starting point in black religion. Against the theology of James Cone, Cecil Cone asserts that the motifs of Black Power radicals do not shape the concerns of black religion and black theology. Neither black power slogans nor white seminaries determine black theology. Black theology identifies with the faith of the black church—the Almighty Sovereign God of Africa in the conversion experience of black religion. Cone's primary impetus is to place the institutional black church at the center of black liberation. To accomplish this he attacks the black political theology trend (James Cone and J. Deotis Roberts) for its foreign theological influence.

Cone avoids the morass of the identity crisis by scrutinizing the essential elements of black religion. He starts by suggesting these general source areas: sermons, prayers, testimonies and slave narratives.[32] Next he proceeds to give three specific source classifications. Like Wilmore, he includes African traditional religions, the first classification. Black theology emerges out of black religion, whose central element is the Almighty Sovereign God. And African traditional religion gives birth to this God. Cone claims:

> I would say that any theology that has its roots in the African tradition or the African way of viewing reality is black theology. And the African way of viewing theology is you begin with the Almighty Sovereign God. That's the starting place for African theology. And that's the real starting place for true Black Theology—the Almighty Sovereign God.[33]

Cone proffers the claim that Africans and black Americans are theological soulmates because they share the same religious fountainhead, the same divinity in worship found in African traditional religion.

Similar to Wilmore and Long, Cone accepts the environment of slavery as the second source classification. From the seventeenth to the nineteenth centuries, Europeans created a cultural custom of involuntary servitude for Africans brutally brought to North America. Europeans used baracoons (holding places for Africans to be loaded on slaveships bound for North America), the Middle Passage across the Atlantic, slave auction blocks, and severe torture and punishment to break Africans and transform them into black Americans. One cannot develop a realistic black theology, claims Cone, without sifting through the details of the black religion that arose from one of the most concentrated processes in human history, the forced birth of a people called black Americans. In this ethos African traditional religion converted into black religion.

Finally, agreeing with Long, black religion comes from the slaves' appropriation of the Christian Bible. Slaves reinterpreted the Bible, Cone submits, in light of their African religious background. They struggled to maintain their humanity and live out their conversion experience as children of the Almighty Sovereign God while white "Christians" sought to recategorize Africans in North America as property. In sum, the African Almighty Sovereign God provided the normative lens for the slaves' interpretation of scripture, Christianity and all reality. When today's black theology speaks of the source of scripture, it has to comprehend African religion as the building block of black Christian religion.

Africanisms

Cone's first and foremost Africanism in black religion is the Almighty Sovereign God. This divinity permeates Cone's black theology from beginning to end.

The all-encompassing Almighty Sovereign God causes black religion to value reality in a specific manner. Echoing Wilmore and Long, Cone distinguishes between the African way and the Greco-Roman way.

The African way of viewing reality is one that sees God as part of all reality and sees all life as sacred and views life as a totality that somehow or another has a religious dimension to it.

Contrasting the Greco-Roman cosmology, Cone continues:

In the Greco-Roman and the Westernized way of looking at life, life is chopped up into categories; [this grows] really out of that Greek tradition where man and his mind, in order to understand, he has to put things into categories. So you have your religious life here, your political life here, your economic life here.[34]

Such a holistic approach on Cone's part implies that the ingredients for a black theology can be found both inside and outside the black church. The traditional white church usually pits itself (the sacred sphere) against the world (the secular sphere), whereas black theology finds black religion incorporated in the secular world. Thus the secular-sacred complement in black religion signifies a larger African way of perceiving reality. This method of expressing, experiencing and orienting reality withstood slavery's destruction of the empirical forms of African religion and language.

Also like African societies, black American communities, Cone contends, dwell on the supernatural as a major focus of concern. For instance, religion in the slave era did not develop simply in reaction to the dehumanizing effects of bondage. Far from a mere coping device, black religion, in itself, dwells on and worships divinity regardless of situations of oppression or liberation.

Liberation

Cecil W. Cone wants to maintain the slave's conversion encounter with the Almighty Sovereign God at the center of liberation. At the same time, he does not deny that black religion definitely exhibited yearnings for emancipation.

While striving for freedom and equality is an element in black religion, it nonetheless is not identified with its essence. The essence of black religion is the encounter with the Almighty Sovereign God.[35]

Cecil Cone contrasts his view of liberation with that of James Cone. The black theology of the latter, in the opinion of the former, suffered from the ideological influence of Black Power.[36] In Cecil Cone's opinion, James Cone's discipleship to Black Power forced him to see liberation narrowly in political terms. Thus James Cone missed the broader dimension to liberation in the black religious tradition, displayed by the slave's response to his or her God-encounter. The conversion of the slave rendered him or her an entirely new creature, completely transformed and totally free. In this freedom the slave felt the experience of a new humanity. In Cecil Cone's liberation in black religion, the doctrine of pneumatology occupies a key aspect of the conversion experience. He writes: "The main ingredient of [black] religion is the encounter with the Almighty Sovereign God, which produces a new life of freedom in the Spirit."[37]

In fairness to Cecil Cone, one cannot say that he avoids the issue of political liberation. In his view the majority of the slaves did participate in some degree of liberation resistance against the white oppressor. Post-conversion life of freedom in the Spirit meant that nothing on earth, including the slave system, could hold back the slave's being free in the Spirit. But Cone concentrates on setting priorities. The question is what comes first—the Almighty Sovereign God or black liberation politics? For Cecil Cone political liberation follows as a by-product of first "getting right" with God. The slave recognized his or her wretched, sinful existence and acknowledged the holiness of the divine. Next, having experienced the forced presence of the divine, the slave underwent a metanoia that freed his or her being in the Spirit. After all of this the issue of politics came to the fore. To have "good religion," for Cecil Cone, one has to have one's house in order with the Almighty Sovereign God of Africa.[38]

VINCENT HARDING

Black Spirituality

Vincent Harding (a Mennonite and present professor of religion and social transformation at the Iliff School of Theology in Colorado) has had a profound effect on the development of contemporary black theology in the United States, particularly the young black theology of the 1960s and early 1970s. For example, Gayraud Wilmore lavishes the following notable accolade on Harding. Harding's work "more than any other," Wilmore confesses, "except W.E.B. DuBois, provoked me to turn from social ethics to history."[39] Harding was a major religious thinker and historian for Dr. Martin Luther King, Jr., during the Civil Rights Movement; he also helped to organize the Institute of the Black World in Atlanta.

Prior to the publication of James Cone's *Black Theology and Black Power* Harding penned three important articles. They conveyed serious theological questions for the religion and theology of the black church and the theological groping of the National Committee of Black Churchmen. His "Black Power and the American Christ" essay (January 4, 1967) linked Black Power favorably to divine sovereignty, divine immanence, religious dimensions in black power, Christology and ecclesiology. "The Religion of Black Power" (1968) continued with other doctrinal issues: love, theology, ecumenism, messianism, eschatalogy, resurrection and creation. In "Religion and Resistance Among Antebellum Negroes, 1800-1860" (1969) Harding unearthed and codified black religion in black slave resistance.[40]

Uniting with the other black cultural theology trend colleagues' expansion of theology's definition, Harding adds his unique contribution on black spirituality. I call his religious view a Black Theology of Spirituality because of his stress on a pneumatological centrality and his downplaying of the theological discipline. Harding appraises theology as a European-American way of handling religious experience. If permitted, he emphasizes, theology could become an oppressive "kind of operation." The categories and ideas of theology certainly don't grow out of [black] people's religious experience.

Furthermore, in his judgment, most non-Western religions possess no categories that could be called theology. Hence Harding handles theology "somewhat lightly."[41]

However, Harding perceives the tremendously important role of the "systematizers of black theology," especially in warring with white theologians in seminaries. Yet no one should overlook the black masses' theology, created out of their joy and pain. Harding values this latter "theology" because of its absolute unself-consciousness. Black folks do not feel they have to speak, comments Harding, "in Barthian terms." Harding refuses to lock black religious experience into intellectual categories of theology. For him, in "this time and age when lots of people are talking about liberation theology, I'm much more interested in liberation spirituality."

Sources

Harding espouses sources derived, not from the academies, but from an examination of what I view as the interaction of the "wildness" of the divine spirit in black history and today's black community. In his words:

> If theology has any kind of human purpose and task and rationale, it is a way of people, especially people in difficulties . . . , trying to come to terms with their understanding of the movements of God among them. It is their attempt to bring some order to the wildness of the divine.[42]

As one source he cites the Afro-American spirituals as profound examples of theological reflections in the black community.

With Wilmore, Long and Cecil Cone, he goes on to specify the nature of black religious life under slavery as another source. Having accepted Christian categories from white slavemasters, black chattel naturally ruminated over such theological questions as Jesus, Christianity, freedom, sisterhood and brotherhood. Slaves had to figure out theologically the difference between their religion and the slaveowners'. For Harding, the first written and "sung documents" on the Christian experience by enslaved black folks included liberation theology.

In addition to the source of slavery, Harding recognizes the importance of the 1950s and 1960s southern freedom movement. "I think the southern freedom movement," says Harding, "is one of the most magnificent and still unmined laboratories or resources for understanding liberation spirituality." He specifically focuses on the freedom movement's singing. Somehow, it seems, singing conjured up or communally solidified the spirit and yielded power and great strength. Harding thinks "that [singing] would be one of the most crucial parts of liberation spirituality."[43]

A final source encompasses the general category of the "noneducated" blacks, more exactly, the non-theologically educated blacks. The richness of this source, Harding believes, will be tapped once one has a sense of respect for non-literate black people. Then black religious intellectuals will begin to listen to the stories of the unlettered and also take seriously their available written materials for knowledge resources. The emphasis here is on reorienting theological epistemology.

Africanisms

In his sources for a black theology of spirituality Harding does not explicitly mention African religious remains. He nonetheless intimates the existence of Africanisms. Harding appraises the basic distinction between African and European spiritualities. Wilmore, Long and Cecil Cone particularize Africanisms on the cosmological and religious levels. Harding accepts similar African traits but deposits them on the pneumatological level. For Harding, the typology of European spirituality brings to light the individualism of the single person. In this mode one achieves a spiritual situation in "solitude and aloneness." Harding does not discount the necessity of spiritual nourishment for the individual. But African tradition kindles a spirituality in communal relationships. By this Harding denotes the need to keep faith with others as "part of the spirituality of keeping one going."[44] African spirituality glues the individual to the community and vice versa. In the same instance Harding discusses the individual and the community keeping faith with God. One's understanding of God in faith is inextricably woven with one's spiritual bonds to the community. Thus Harding cements theology and pneumatology. He observed such a spirituality (an example of Africanism) during his direct involvement in the southern freedom movement; he advocates it for today's black theology of liberation.

Liberation

Harding goes beyond an analysis of racism and capitalism in his dealings with oppression in America. He raises a third problematic for liberation, one which permeates more pervasively. Harding calls this target for liberation, "the ailment of the spirit." He has "long sensed that [racism and capitalism] were necessary but insufficient definitions of the malaise that has grasped the white mainstream of America." Beneath these twin evils he perceives a lack of attunement and a loss of awareness of self, all manifestations of the spirit requiring prescription. Harding asserts:

> There will be no hope for a truly just society on these shores until we address the issue of the human spirit and its role in our struggles for political transformation.[45]

Political liberation, for Harding, comes with a serious consideration and engagement with spiritual matters. Therefore he targets a healing of the American spirit.

The new spiritual society would accent human transformation and personal integrity as well as radicalized social structures. The struggle for black liberation, Harding surmises, has often appeared like a restricted political, economic and racial movement. But the core of black people's effort has always been attempts at realizing individual capacities within empowering communities. Furthermore, Harding appreciates the simultaneous linkage of human communal spirituality with human-God spirituality. And thus one deduces that his fully liberated, human spiritual society would also reflect a consummated eschatological spiritual reality.[46] In a word, pneumatology draws together individual and community needs with the Ultimate Spirituality.

Following the connection between liberation and spirituality further, Harding calls for an urgency in decoding those spiritual resources in black history that have not simply sustained black survival, "an absolutely inadequate kind of goal." Instead, pushing beyond a mere holding pattern, he searches for an exegesis providing spiritual resources on which black people have drawn in overcoming oppressive societal obstacles and transforming themselves. For "the struggle for freedom and justice was a fundamental element of the contextualization of [black] spirituality."[47] Thus political movements are part of and express the deeper spiritual presence, that is, black people's encountering the "wildness of the divine" spirit liberating in their midst.

CRITIQUE

The black cultural theology trend highlights the dimensions of black faith beyond "academic" theology and also refocuses on black folk culture.

Beyond "Academic" Theology

Gayraud Wilmore reconstructs the parameters of the theological sources for a black theology. This is extremely important in order to draw on apparent and cryptic resources for creating a black theology of liberation representing all (mainly the unrecognized non-Christian) faith traditions in the black community and to remain accountable to God's liberation movement in both black Christian and non-Christian projects. One has to pause at the theological excitement and challenge posed by Wilmore in his claim that the novels of Richard Wright and poems of Claude McKay propose theological sources just as valid as scripture and church dogma.

Similarly Wilmore expounds the liberative elements in black theology beyond Christianity. The black Christian church does not stand alone with its tradition of religious faith in liberation. In fact, the Spirit unbinds even on street corners and pool halls and performs a very definite, non-Christian unbinding for divine liberation of all black people.

However, Wilmore needs to sort out more clearly theologically the encounter between a black Christian theology of liberation and his heavily emphasized, non-Christian theology of liberation. He takes a step in this direction by granting non-Christian liberation sources a general revelation status. In his own words, "God has spoken in diverse ways"[48] in the black community. By citing this generality, he implies the particular significance of God's liberation revelation in Jesus Christ for Christians. Here by way of intimation, Wilmore correctly avoids the problem of portraying, and thereby imposing, black Christian theology of liberation as *the* theology of all black people. But this avoidance of imposition, coupled with Wilmore's heavy leaning on non-Christian sources, does not excuse a seeming unclarity on how a black Christian theology of liberation, committed to the black church, should relate to non-church and non-Christian theological sources.

This imprecision surfaces the issue of Christology. Wilmore's Christology requires further refinement. The joy in praising God's work outside the black church should not blind Christians to their essential identity, which comes from Jesus Christ. Where and how does Jesus Christ play a role in Wilmore's black religious thought? How comparable is Jesus Christ to the black faith expressed in a street corner crap game or the anger of a Bigger Thomas? Does Jesus Christ have a decisive revelation for black Christians?[49]

Charles Long, like Wilmore, does not take for granted preestablished theological language and categories. He understands the power of language; what one says and how one says it count. Not only does he instruct us not to imitate the oppressor's theological discipline and linguistics, but he also questions the structure and "rhythm" of God-talk. Finally, he forcefully introduces the vitalness of Africa, particularly in the Afro-American religious consciousness. He makes a point: how can African-Americans worship God in the United States and not be aware of some religious and theological relatedness to Africa?

Long, nonetheless, falls short when he depicts theology as inherently an unusable tool for black political and cultural liberation. All black religious intellectuals with advanced degrees have trained in disciplines of the white power structure. This includes history of religions. The question becomes one of appropriation for the black community, and for all of God's poor humanity in general. However, Long perceives a fundamental distinction between history of religions and theology. In his position the former discipline is an objective phenomenological comparison between existing religions. Theology, on the other hand, dabbles in subjective faith claims, thus leaving itself open to imperialistic manipulations by whites. But is this objective-subjective framework valid? I think not. Human beings engage in both disciplines: theology and history of religions. Since both portray themselves as human enterprises involved in God's activity, history of religions and theology are inevitably constrained by human limitations. God may be objective in God's liberation relation to humanity. But human fallibility denies history of religions' claiming an advantage over theology.

Long also weakens black ecclesiology with his deconstructions of theology and Christianity. Removing the Christian religious and theological aspects of black faith in order to salvage authentic, indigenous, black religious discourse is a false and harmful dichotomy. To strip the black church's historical relationship to Christianity and theology is also to tear away both positive and negative aspects in *black* Christianity and theology. Long fails to see how oppressed blacks resubstantiated the dominant discourse and faith for black liberation needs to combat *white* imperialistic Christianity and theology. A complete dispensing of black Christianity and theology, then, throws out the baby with the bath water, that is, the black church's liberating use of Christianity and theology, with white theology's religious presence in the black church. Such a one-sided approach to black faith negates the black *Christian* church's historical transforming role in black liberation. The black church has been the oldest and, despite bourgeois influences, most consistently progressive institution for organizing and hope in the black community.

Like Wilmore's and Long's theological critique, but from the angle of black church hegemony, Cecil Cone shows a tension in his ecclesiology. He claims that black religion exists wherever one finds blacks of African descent practicing religion in North America. From Cone's definition one would suspect that black theology arose wherever black religion thrived. In this manner black theology would reflect the total black community. Yet Cone writes:

> The theologian merely takes these statements [of black Christians] about God and organizes them into a coherent system to make sure that they are in harmony with God's revelation of himself in the Old and New Testaments. It is in this way that theology helps the Church understand her confession of faith and regulate her mission in the world.[50]

Pursuing Cone's interpretation of black theology's relation to black religion and the over-all black community, both Christian and non-Christian, his statement presents a half-truth. Black theology covers the entire black community's religious orientation. Certainly, the black church has been a preserver of black religious faith, but not the exclusive preserver. Therefore black theology interprets more than one segment of the black community's encounter with the Almighty Sovereign God.

Black Folk Culture and Religion

Charles Long contributes to black theology with his perceptive redefinition of black culture and religion. In the very cultural language of religion — its structure and texture — we encounter liberating elements. But Long borders on, if not advocates, the belief that religious language about liberation creates a religious reality of liberation. Granted, cultural language does have a material force on the black liberation movement. How black people rename and recreate themselves and their linguistic "rhythm" do influence their resistance to white power's control. Yet Long's one-sided emphasis downplays the dynamic between the political struggle of human bodies for liberation and its effects on religious-cultural and theological discourses, on the one hand, and religious-cultural language and its effect on political movements, on the other. Cultural discourse and political practice go together. For example, black slaves re-created themselves on the religious consciousness level and, at the same time, redefined their chattel status by political opposition. A new cultural-religious life helped them to resist politically. Similarly, political resistance also showed them a concrete liberation practice on which to transform the language of their abject religio-cultural oppression. Blacks have to fight for liberation on both levels. Language is a materiality, but it is not complete materiality. In a word, Long breaks the two-sidedness of the soteriological process.

In his treatment of folk religion and culture Wilmore correctly promotes communal culture as an important model of an Africanism, a religious and theological tracing from Africa. He poses communal economics over against the exploitative political economy of monopoly capitalism in the United States. Communalism provides an opening to observe the bond between politics and culture. In his characterization of communalism Wilmore correctly unearths the complementing and equal marriage of power-sharing in society (politics) to the lifestyle and worldview of human sharing (culture). But in his depiction of black religious thought Wilmore espouses the subsuming of politics within culture and the secondary status of the former to the latter. First, his argument that culture acts as the umbrella for politics does not sufficiently counter the reverse theological claim that God lords over politics as well. And consequently, politics adumbrates religious and theological implications too. Finally, contradicting Wilmore's culture-over-politics pattern, the Africanism of communalism, which he himself cites, substantiates a better position—religiously and theologically, culture and politics mutually subsume each other in an equivalent endeavor toward liberation.

Cecil Cone touches on two crucial areas in the foundation of black religion and black theology. Those areas, the impact of Africa's religion and culture and the slave folk religion and culture, remain barely mined sources for a genuine black theology. No other representative of the black cultural theological trend hammers home such a consistent focus on Africa and slavery in the doing of black theology. Cone rightly concludes that if one wants to forge a black theology, one has to delineate the Africanisms of the continent from which all black Americans descend. And if one realizes that the phenomenon of black Americans was created in the slave environment, then the slave's black religion has to have a place in contemporary black God-talk. Cone's trenchant theological commentary on black religion could be illustrated in the following questions about other American minority theologies: Can an authentic Mexican-American theology develop without dealing with Mexico? Can an Asian-American theology develop without taking Asia into account?

Yet a problem arises in Cone's description of the role of conversion to the Almighty Sovereign God. He essentially depicts conversion and the divine as non-political. This strongly and wrongly hints that God is neutral in God's being and God's work. First, black theologians dialogue about God in the context of the United States of America. In this context, since at least 1619, poor black people have endured white racism and economic exploitation. Where was God and what was God doing? On whose side did God stand, the oppressor or the oppressed? When a black person experiences conversion with the Almighty Sovereign God, has this God decided against white racism and economic exploitation, or does this God decide afterward? In this folk religion, is not the reason the slaves converted to the African Almighty Sovereign God because the African High God had brought them and their ancestors "a mighty long way" through all types of tribulations? Furthermore, why did this God, if a God of both political and cultural liberation, force God's self on the oppressed black slaves and not the oppressor white slavemasters?

Second, Cecil Cone includes the Bible in his basic sources. It is true slaves translated scripture through their own religious and cultural grid. The slave narratives substantiate this point. But again, does the God of the Bible stand out as a neutral God? Even Cone admits that the slaves appropriated the justice parables of Yahweh in the Old Testament. Likewise in the New Testament slaves appropriated the picture of Jesus Christ as the everpresent Comforter in times of hardship, "able to lift them out of the slave-condition and grant them freedom."[51]

Of all the black cultural theologians Harding presses most determinedly on the one theme of a black theology of spirituality. He tunes in to the spontaneous and uncontrolled spirituality of black folk religion. One of his chief concerns is to ensure a correct theological approach to the human spirit—the humanizing of society in relation to God's presence—after all the combatants have completed their political fighting. After all the charges and counter-charges of white against black and black against black, what does it all mean for the sanctity and survival of our God-given spirituality?

From my perspective spirituality has to be linked tightly to both political and cultural liberation of black people. God endowed humanity with a spirituality. But, far from a life in and of itself, that spirituality expresses itself in cultural and political dimensions. Harding rightly perceives a malaise, a certain sickness in America's spiritual state, particularly in "white mainstream America." However, in discerning the face of spirituality, one discovers its reflection in political and cultural realms. For instance, the black spirituals and the freedom movement's songs resulted from a people engaged in acts to claim their *imago dei*. Black spirituality springs out of the community's striving toward a state of "somebodiness" and self-worth (a cultural thrust) and an acquisition of sustenance (a political aim) to facilitate God's grace of human wholeness. A humanized society would indeed display a salutary spirituality, which would reflect a healthy culture and politics. Yet a healed culture and politics would, in turn, reflect a sturdy spirituality. They all reinforce and interact with one another.

Two Trends in Black Theology

The cultural theologians' insistence on redefining theology greatly helps the movement for black freedom. Seeking a more inclusive theology than that of the political trend's church theology, the cultural group includes the religious impulses from the entire black community. If any black person hopes and fights for freedom, then such an ultimate concern is a black theology of liberation. The cultural theologians review black history and correctly perceive diverse radical strands, both ecclesial and non-ecclesial.

In addition the cultural trend advocates reliance on black cultural foundations. This trend justifiably contends that a liberating black theology has to adhere strictly to the God-given resources in the black community. The question becomes: How is a liberating black faith shown in black culture, history and a total black way of life? One has to concur with the cultural theologians. God has revealed God's self in sources unique to black America.

God also pervades black reality by not allowing a complete break in African lineage. Black people have a rich African heritage in the African side of their black American existence. The cultural trend insightfully and persuasively links the contemporary 1960s black theology movement to Africa's religious concepts. They know very well that today's black faith blossoms from an African root. Thus a person attains self-awareness through encountering his or her primordial experiences.

God likewise has provided a different black religious and cultural structure for dealing with life and black folk's divine interaction. Unlike the political theologians, the cultural theologians explore the rhythm and texture of black faith's linguistic structure. They raise important issues: What impact does black religious language have on black life? Does the syntax and cadence of black talk about God affect black folk's faith perception of God in their daily activities? Is singing an important part of black liberation theology? In summation, the cultural trend differs from the political trend by examining non-church theology, Africa's influence, cultural resources and black language.

The two trends contrast and complement each other. They both begin with black freedom from white oppression and white theology, and God's involvement in black liberation. From these issues of black and divine freedom, political theologians move to confront white power relations in systems. From the same issues their cultural colleagues move toward a deeper concern over blackness. Both trends include politics and culture. The political theme unites with the cultural but asks how a singular cultural emphasis assists God's movement against the white power structure. The cultural thrust, in turn, agrees with political struggle but questions how this facilitates God's movement in and validation of blackness. Each fills in what the other lacks. However, a unified black political-cultural theology of liberation needs a more integrated synthesis.

CONCLUSION

For the black cultural theologians' cautiousness with the use of "systematic theology," a paraphrase from Wilmore suffices: "Theology: Don't Get Hung Up on a Word!."[52] Theology takes whatever shape the black masses intend. Theology systematizes their reflections and practice of faith in God (and Jesus Christ for black Christians). From black religion one can decipher doctrinal questions and, in turn, provide the black community with more clarity of faith in the holistic struggle for cultural and political liberation. A war is going on regarding faithful witness to God and Jesus Christ. Should we black theologians leave the black theological battlefield to the white power structure or should we fight to comprehend our black parents' thought and practice in faith?

On the other hand, the black political theologians recognize the vitalness of the theological discipline in the eschatological earthly goal of political and cultural liberation. However, their explicit wading into theological waters heightens the tension of DuBois' "two warring souls in one dark body." Their danger lies in the seduction of white theology's seemingly rational cogency, overwhelming quantity and gratifying respectability. Black political theologians must strive to keep their heads and hearts with the faith of the black poor or else their theology will become, in the final analysis, a pathetic white theology colored black.

Chapters 2 and 3 have provided South African black theologians with the political and cultural mix of black theology in the United States. By hearing the American voices the South Africans will have a better idea of what the issues are and what is at stake. Clarity in dialogical concerns will aid the quality of the cross-Atlantic dialogue itself. We now turn to Chapters 4 and 5 to familiarize black North American theologians with South African black political and cultural trends.

Part III

BLACK THEOLOGY SOUTH AFRICA

CHAPTER FOUR

Non-Racialism as God's Gift

That South Africa belongs to all who live in it, black and white, and that no government can justly claim authority unless it is based on the will of the people.... And therefore, we the people of South Africa, black and white, together equals, countrymen and brothers, adopt this Freedom Charter.

The Freedom Charter of 1955

THE BLACK THEOLOGICAL SITUATION

Black theology in South Africa aims its attack against the apartheid regime. The system of white supremacy, openly backed by the white Dutch Reformed Church, proclaims itself God-ordained. Consequently, the black political and cultural trends unite to fight the main enemy—structural white racism and its theological justification. Though both trends have particular nuances, they comprise a single black liberation movement. They concur that the heart of black theology is a liberating gospel in contrast to legalized discrimination under apartheid.

In addition to their unified struggle against the prime target, South African black theological, political and cultural accents are drawn together for another reason. The apartheid government maintains absolute and rigid regulation over black life and thought and seeks to capitalize on distinctions in the black populace, including the black theological community. Therefore state repression has forced all black theologians of liberation into a close working relationship.

In contrast to the persistent use of brutal force by white South Africa, the white power structure in the United States employs a bourgeois democracy and provides a bourgeois theological atmosphere. On the surface both expressions of this bourgeois rule solicit "freedom" for blacks and the poor to theologize equally with the dominant classical theology in the God-talk arena. Thus North American black theologians enjoy the privilege of calling on academic freedom and constitutional freedom in the pursuit of a theology of cultural and political liberation. Black American theologians are not as sensitive as South Africans must be to their government's interest in their work. Hence a wide variety of public critiques and counter-critiques have taken place between the North American political and cultural trends.

In South Africa strict control over the expression of black thought has caused theologians to function with a tighter working relationship in the development of one cultural-political black liberation theology. In fact, apartheid equates any type of black theology of liberation with treason against the state and subversion of the gospel of Christ.[1] Because apartheid exerts such a ruthless hold on the totality of black life, black theologians, in turn, are more inclined to maintain a holistic (political and cultural) theological response.

Despite the iron grip of apartheid laws and the close unity between political and cultural theological liberation displayed by black theologians, one can discern shades of difference. For example, Frank Chikane believes that today's South African black theology operates within a different political context from that of the early 1970s. At that time Black Consciousness served as the sole rallying cry for most blacks. Today, however, divergence within black theological discourse springs from divergence among secular anti-apartheid groups. Chikane claims:

> Although the division on the surface seemed to be between the Black Consciousness Movement and the progressive democrats [the non-racial, Freedom Charter adherents] based on a play between the class and race models or the combination of these models in trying to understand the South African society, it seems that the real decisive matter was the attitudes of these groupings to the historical liberation movements African National Congress (ANC) and the Pan Africanist Congress (PAC).[2]

I would add that not only do theological disputes reflect the secular splits, but the latter also mirror the former. Essentially there exist two general theological approaches to black theology in South Africa.

BLACK CONSCIOUSNESS AND SOWETO

Black theology in South Africa, both political and cultural, emerged in the Black Consciousness Era and the radical events around the Soweto Rebellion of 16 June 1976. A look at these two foundational periods helps to contextualize the writings of South African black theology.

Black Consciousness and Black theology began during the harsh years at the end of the 1960s and start of the 1970s. The white government had "endorsed out" women, the sick, children and the elderly from "white" urban areas to their black "ethnic homelands." This breaking up of families and dumping people into arid bantustans was one of the most hated policies. With its pass books regulating the flow of black male workers into white industry, the influx control law also symbolized the non-human status of blacks in their own country. On the average police arrested 1,730 blacks a day for passbook offenses. The black prison population increased fifteen percent a year. Unemployment reached over twenty percent. In the bantustans (the "separate development" areas or "ethnic homelands"), one out of every two children born alive died by the age of five. Throughout South Africa white children received free education. Blacks paid for a "bantu" education characterized by overcrowding, insufficient equipment and poor staffing.

In the 1970s the legal and penal system intensified repression. The government instituted the Riotous Assemblies Act (1974), which increased powers to ban gatherings, increased penalties for attending meetings, and gave police wider latitude in dispersing groups. Torture in the forms of solitary confinement, denial of sleep, electric shocks to the genitals and, among other things, systematic assault increased.[3]

The Black Consciousness Movement, which began in 1968-69, proved to be a revolution in thinking and self-help, a black renaissance and reawakening of black self-confidence and black pride. Students led nationwide campus protests for better and more relevant education. In the early seventies, workers went on strikes. The Black Community Programmes (1972), a prominent black consciousness organization, worked with existing black organizations and established workshops, training sessions, cultural and political publications, literary classes, black theater and poetry events, and youth seminars.

Another major black consciousness group, the Black People's Convention (1971), functioned as an umbrella organization for students, social and cultural groups, a few politicians, the Interdenominational African Ministers' Association and the African Independent Churches' Association. The South African Students' Organization (SASO) spread its influence on college campuses while the South African Students' Movement (SASM) did the same in high schools. Black caucuses grew in predominantly white churches and black theologians had to strike a balance between black self-assertion and continued contact with whites. In a word, the first half of the 1970s showed two tendencies: growing repression, and the rapid spread of black consciousness and black theology.[4]

Soweto

On 16 June 1976 black students in Soweto gathered to march to Orlando stadium. The key demand was rescinding Afrikaans as the medium of instruction for black students. However the Afrikaans issue stood for an overwhelming black anti-apartheid sentiment, particularly expressed in the black consciousness ethos of the 1970s. Put differently, the Soweto students were the angry children of the Black Consciousness Movement. Before the students reached the stadium, police opened fire. The children scattered and countered gunshot with rocks. From 16 June to 18 June the police killed over *five hundred* blacks, mostly children, and wounded *thousands*.

For the next seventeen months, throughout South Africa, blacks rose up in response to the Soweto Massacre. Indians and "Coloureds" rebelled in solidarity with Soweto. Students throughout the country battled army fire with rocks. Government buildings went up in flames. Parents supported their children. Black workers engaged in periodic strikes. Even in rural areas and some "independent" homelands, students burned down government buildings and Bantu schools. Incidents of sabotage against the state occurred. Students conducted school boycotts and more demonstrations. Mass funerals turned into protest areas, with people vowing to continue the struggle. Often police attacked and killed mourners. Students marched, stoned and burned. Police launched tear gas, tortured and killed. South Africa was in a state of civil war.

With the police assassination of Steve Biko in September 1977, rebellions further intensified throughout South Africa. Consequently, during the following month the apartheid government banned seventeen black consciousness organizations. With loss of leadership the resistance movement went into a temporary lull. Still, the events of 16 June 1976 to October 1977 left an indelible imprint on the black community. It became clearer than ever that the politics of apartheid would attempt black genocide unless a new democratic government led the country. Between the Soweto Rebellion and the October bannings, over one thousand blacks were killed, thousands wounded, thousands detained and tortured, and roughly four thousand fled the country, with a great many joining the ANC and PAC military camps.

The Soweto Rebellion became a national and historic rebellious movement. It marked a watershed in black opposition to apartheid. It stood for a highly politicized generation of youth, who wanted freedom and were willing to use militant tactics to get it. Soweto was not simply 16 June. Soweto was a seventeen-month national rebellion against the white power structure. And the South African black political and cultural theology trends responded to this volatile and mercurial atmosphere of Black Consciousness and Soweto.[5]

The Black Political Theology Trend

Chapter 5 will look at the approach of the black cultural theologians in South Africa. In the present chapter we explore the representatives of the black political theological trend. The political theological advocates maintain both a protest against black exclusion from participation with whites and a desire to work with whites toward the elimination of the latter's fracturing of human fellowship between the races. Like the Freedom Charter[6] and the ANC, the political trend defines the "will of the people" not simply by the black racial majority population, but by all who currently live in South Africa, black and white. All races are made in God's image and all, black and white together, have been granted equal calling to have dominion over God's grace of creation. Furthermore, the black political theological proponents share an extreme sensitivity to the bastardization of the gospel by the South African government and its church. They understand that an attack on the white power structure is both political and theological; political because the separation of the races undergirds the *raison d'etre* of apartheid; theological because a heretical gospel confession and interpretation undergird white supremacy and the denial of racial fellowship. Therefore to disengage its political policy of apartheid, they must wage war on the theological justification. In brief, we discover a theology based on non-racialism (black and white together) versus a theology of apartheid.

Uniting with the *Kairos Document*,[7] the black political theologians would call the relation between the white Dutch Reformed Church and the apartheid government "state theology." State theology describes a situation in which both the oppressed and the oppressors pledge loyalty to the same church. For example, Christian policemen beat up and kill Christian children and torture Christian prisoners. State theology depicts the Afrikaner government justifying the state's endemic violence, racism and capitalism with Christian theology. Such a perverted theology supposedly gets its authority from scripture. It tells the oppressed in South Africa to automatically obey the apartheid government (Romans 13:1-7). It boasts biblical bases in Genesis 10 on human genealogy and Genesis 11:1-9, the tower of Babel. For the theology of apartheid God condones violence against the poor and sanctions "separate development" of ethnic groups.

The black political theologians would also agree with the *Kairos Document*'s characterization of "church theology." This theology reflects the superficial, unproductive criticisms by the white, liberal, English-speaking churches. Church theology opts for "reconciliation" ("let's hear both sides of the story") without justice or confrontation with apartheid's evils. It makes appeals to the apartheid government but fails to focus on and support the people's struggles "below." Finally, it calls for non-violence, thus equating the victims' practice of self-defense with the structural violence of apartheid.

Against state and church theologies the black political theologians advocate "prophetic theology": a biblically based, action-oriented theology of oppressed people that fights external (white) and internal (black) oppressions and also uses social analysis of "the oppressor and the oppressed."

To represent the political theology trend, this chapter examines the theology of Manas Buthelezi, Allan Boesak, Simon Maimela and Frank Chikane. We will use the theological categories of a) theology, b) liberation, c) Christology and d) reconciliation as the framework for theological comparison.

MANAS BUTHELEZI

Racial Fellowship

Manas Buthelezi was the leading proponent of black theology in the 1970s. In 1973 he became the regional director for the Christian Institute in Natal Province. Directed by Beyers Naude, the Institute was a white initiated group that sought to transfer leadership to black consciousness theologians. Buthelezi, a Lutheran, also led the fight to build black caucuses in predominantly white churches. His writings reflect a specific problem: How to uphold black dignity while pursuing some type of Christian relationship with white fellow church members in the midst of the Black Consciousness Movement. Furthermore, during the Soweto Rebellion, he chaired the Black Parents Association, the most prominent group mediating between the students and the authorities. Currently, he serves as a bishop in the Evangelical Lutheran Church of South Africa.

I interpret Buthelezi's thinking as a Black Theology of Racial Fellowship. Buthelezi grapples with the theology of apartheid. "Before us," he contends, "we have two theologies: the theology of Separate Development . . . and the theology of racial fellowship."[8] The white Dutch Reformed Church (the NGK) has opted against the "principle of fellowship." Therefore apartheid theology exemplifies a complete rejection of black people, thus truncating Christian fellowship. For Buthelezi the subversion of this fundamental principle results in the followers of Christ not gathering together for Sunday worship. Moreover, it prevents blacks and whites sharing together all of God's daily blessings offered to humankind. The theology of separate development attempts to obfuscate God's grace to God's creation.[9]

A theology that blocks black-white contact in society reflects not a mere skewed political policy, but a sacrilegious attack on *agape*, God's love. God's love provides the cornerstone for racial fellowship.

> What is it that is unique in the Christian Gospel? It is the love of God in Jesus Christ that transforms strange neighbors into loving brothers. It is very often said that points of racial contact are points of friction. What is unique about the Gospel is that it changes points of contact into points of fellowship.

Buthelezi is fighting for his interpretation of the unique and essential characteristic of the gospel. He resumes:

> Fellowship is by definition a situation of contact. It follows that there can never be Christian fellowship without human contact. Any delib-

erate elimination of points of human contact is a calculated sabotage
of the essence of Christian fellowship.[10]

The lack of black and white human contact confirms the lack of racial
fellowship. The absence of racial fellowship indicates the absence of divine
love. The denial of agape attacks the essence of Christianity. White South
Africans, then, cannot confess theological obedience to God while upholding the divisive "Christian" principle of separate development.

While exposing white theology Buthelezi's black theology of racial fellowship also suggests tasks for black South African Christians. If white
Christians will not pursue the essence of the gospel, then the effort falls to
blacks. First, black Christians must undertake a proselytizing posture toward racist white Christians. Though whites hinder Christian fellowship
and Christian love, blacks must, nonetheless, take the first steps toward
recovering this love. Their witnessing and confession as Christians are at
stake. There is no other option. According to Buthelezi, "It is now time
for the black man to evangelize and humanise the white man." To remain
a Christian in South Africa, black people have an obligation to pursue the
zeal of a missionary calling. The oppressed must initiate the quest for
Christian love with their oppressors. "For the black man's side," continues
Buthelezi, "this will mean the retrieval of Christian love from the limitations
of the white man's economic and political institutions."[11]

Because blacks have to take Christian love from the limitations of the
white power structure's political-economic institutions, the second task of
the theology of racial fellowship points in a similar direction. In other
words, black theology challenges black Christians to answer political questions. Black South Africans experience white power dominance over black
existential reality and ontological make-up. Accordingly, blacks do not
share any meaningful power; thus, their predicament has theological implications. Buthelezi concludes: Blacks are "therefore waiting for a theology
that wrestles with the question of the restoration and distribution of
power."[12] Blacks need both the material and spiritual resources to be human. To achieve humanity requires the power of liberation.[13]

Liberation

The gospel of liberation will free black and white simultaneously, but
each in distinct ways. "South Africa urgently needs the Gospel of liberation," Buthelezi contends, "a Gospel that will liberate the whites from the
bondage inherent in the South African way of life — a way of life that chokes
brotherhood and fellowship between black and white."[14]

The gospel will save black people from the effects of white rejection,
Buthelezi asserts, and thus empower them with their own sense of God-
given worth and potential. Freed from this rejection, blackness becomes
God's grace instead of the "biological scourge" concocted by the white

power structure and internalized by blacks. And whites will enjoy freedom from the urge to reject; the gospel will render white rejection irrelevant and inconsequential. Concomitantly, white people will remove their chains of unrealized love and injustice between the races. Blacks will appreciate that they are not less than human; whites will accept that they are no more than human.

Total liberation will occur with the active promotion of love between black and white. Normal fraternization among people should call forth instances of praise. Instead, recounts Buthelezi, such Christian advocacy brings down the steel arm of the South African Security Branch. Lack of love in racial fellowship is a refusal of God's love. Here lies the profound demonic consequences of the theology of apartheid. Such a theology wallows in the mire of sin to the degree that it separates human togetherness from divine love. It not only separates *agape* from any forms of human expressions of love, but it attempts to frustrate and kill divine love. The nexus between human love and divine love acts as a Christian sacrament. Again, Buthelezi identifies the locus of the degradation of human-divine love in the white power structure—the political and social governmental institutions.[15] By implication the ethical demands to achieve the uniqueness of the gospel (love in racial fellowship) come through an alteration of the white power configuration.

While prophesying liberation against the apartheid government, Buthelezi does not leave the evils of the church unattended. His call for liberation also impinges on the ecclesiology of separate development. One cannot struggle for a liberated society without a liberated church. Yet "over the past decades, the [white South African] church has been turned into a living monument of a race and colour-oriented society." However, the church should foreshadow the racial fellowship to come with the kingdom. Certainly a present witness of black-white worship would indicate the fullness of the gospel's uniqueness apparent in the eschaton. In fact, Buthelezi claims, "a racially mixed [church] service [would assail] the majesty of the god of racism and colour."[16] In a word, an ecclesial fellowship would undermine apartheid theology's reverence for a tower of Babel ecclesiology. In reality, the apartheid church has mounted a frontal assault on the unity of the body of Christ.

Christology

Buthelezi sees his Christological claims centered in the Bible. The Bible depicts humanity as a body in Christ. Unity in Christ serves as the starting point for racial interaction and not for the apartness of apartheid Christology, which preaches an incarnation of division and dissension. "The Church derives the shape of its life not from the divisions of sin but from the unifying salvation in Christ."[17] God's revelation in Christ resolves the tower of Babel predicament in the Old Testament. In the body of Christ human identities and differences come together to complement one another and to enrich fellowship. Thus the appropriate Christology brings together differences in unity, not in discord.

Buthelezi's Christology of unified differences argues strongly for more than simply ecclesiological unity. Primarily, he fights for unity in Christ in order to live out the uniqueness of the gospel.

> In Christ mankind becomes a family, a brotherhood. This is the uniqueness of Christianity. . . . This is the uniqueness which, according to my diagnosis, the South African way of life has done its share to undermine and almost destroy.[18]

God expresses God's love for humanity through Christ's work of transforming human enmity into love, fearful neighbors into affectionate siblings. In Buthelezi's opinion Christianity's sacred ground and line of demarcation materialize in Christology—the incarnation of Christ's unifying activity among humankind.

For black Christians Christology suggests the sobriety of crossbearing. The essence of Jesus Christ's message, from Buthelezi's vantage point, revolves around Christ's pain in being one with another, even after the other has turned his or her back on him. Christ bore the burden of his accusers even as they mocked him and nailed him on the cross in his own blood. Therefore Christ's cross symbolizes his person and presence among humanity. To be one with those who cause pain is to follow the way of the cross toward racial fellowship. Buthelezi emphasizes:

> As far as the racist is concerned, I take this to mean that I should try to be one with him in love, even if it is unilateral, unreciprocated love and to continue to minister to him even while he carves for himself a racist church.

Buthelezi knows that to travel this path involves trepidation and tremendous risk. He resumes:

> This is a hard thing to do. I believe that it is for this reason that it is called the taking up of the cross and bearing one another's burden.[19]

Christology pushes black Christians into a pastoral role of ministering to racist Christians in a unilateral and unreciprocated fashion. Indeed, Christ demands that blacks initiate reconciliation.

Reconciliation

In line with his racial fellowship theology, Buthelezi targets the erosion of Christian love on the part of white South African Christians. The white populace, the minority people, has unilaterally and systematically rejected black fellowship in society as well as in the ecclesial community. In effect, whites have banned Christ's commandment to love their neighbor. This banishing of fellowship makes a mockery of reconciliation possibilities.

> Apartheid is the antithesis of what the gospel is about. Whereas the gospel creates a possibility and occasion for even enemies to be reconciled, apartheid has, in fact, torn apart potential friends.

Therefore, the effort toward reconciliation represents "giving witness to the heart of the gospel."[20]

The realization of reconciliation would create at least two situations in South Africa. It would liberate white people from divine judgment, the coming wrath of God. Here Buthelezi draws out the eschatological connection between reconciliation and the Ultimate Judgment. In liberating whites as prevention against ultimate divine disfavor, reconciliation would tell them that God also loves them and desires to inspire them with power to love blacks. With a liberated love white people would, in Buthelezi's words, "not find it nauseating to share a meal with [a black person] in a public restaurant."[21] Thus a white person, freed through reconciliation and spared God's final punishment, would experience intimate contact with a black on a daily basis.

In addition to emancipating whites, reconciliation would bring security to all of South Africa, black and white. Buthelezi acknowledges the state of affairs in South Africa as a tense volatility between "the threat and the threatened."[22] Such insecurity has generated acute disquiet and apprehension. In a belligerent atmosphere, Buthelezi believes, an intentional creation of a state of reconciliation offers the only alternative to white-black annihilation. No amount of armaments or draconian states of emergency on the part of the apartheid government will result in security. Only Christian reconciliation yields genuine security.

We noted that Buthelezi's Christology demands that black South Africans bear the burden and pain inflicted by the white breach of racial fellowship. Logically, then, reconciliation comes out of a black initiative to witness to God's love in Christ for the white racist. Black allegiance to Christ's work of reconciliation urges black Christians to undertake acts of creative love for their fellow South Africans.

Specifically, blacks must preach the gospel to all nations, that is, to white South Africa. Reconciliation signifies evangelization. Consequently black people need to tell whites that they, blacks, bear the *imago dei*. Such a testament will evangelize the whites into accepting blacks as children of God. Foregoing any expectation of white approval, blacks must witness out of love for whites. South Africa, in Buthelezi's opinion, desperately needs the establishment of a black Christian mission to the whites in South Africa. It would strive toward the fulfillment of a general aim:

to enable the white man to share the love of God as it has been uniquely revealed to the black man . . . to preach love to the white man so that he may have the courage to see with consequence that his security is not necessarily tied to his rejection of the black man . . . to work for the salvation of the white man who sorely needs it.[23]

Having defined reconciliation and the method for its achievement, Buthelezi directly links reconciliation to salvation. God saves humanity to help others; first, salvation reconciles us to God and, second, to our fellow humanity. Salvation permits us to see ourselves as we stand in relation to divinity. Through God we attain an identity that fosters harmonious living with God and our fellow humans. In contrast to the theology of separate development God sets us free to become reconciled in a racial fellowship of love.[24]

ALLAN A. BOESAK

Word of God

Allan A. Boesak belongs to the Dutch Reformed Mission Church in South Africa, which is condescendingly considered a daughter church by the white Dutch Reformed Church (NGK). He also holds the distinguished position of president of the World Alliance of Reformed Churches. In addition, Boesak gave one of the major presentations at the founding of the United Democratic Front of South Africa (UDF) in 1983. The UDF falls within the political and theological lineage of the Freedom Charter movement. Therefore Boesak is one of the premier theologial spokespersons for the UDF-Freedom Charter political opposition.

Like Buthelezi, Boesak concentrates on the evils of apartheid theology. Boesak, however, seems to have more at stake. He is motivated by his theological project to dethrone the theological support given by *his* Reformed tradition to the apartheid government. For instance, when the National Party came to power in 1948, the official white Dutch Reformed Church (NGK) newspaper, *Die Kerkbode* stated:

As a church we have always worked purposefully for the separation of the races. In this regard apartheid can rightfully be called a church policy.[25]

Boesak is driven to undermine his church's theological backing for the apartheid state because the Afrikaner government is literally a collection of white racist politicians who are all NGK leaders. He feels called and challenged to confront his church for its continued justification of and initial suggestion to the government to establish apartheid in the 1940s.

He is further influenced by the following existential and theological dilemma: How can one be black and Reformed when the Reformed tradition sustains the white supremacy of the (Reformed) apartheid government? Boesak chooses to focus his theological energies on fundamentally changing the internal politics of the Dutch Reformed Church. Hence he attempts to subvert the white NGK theology by rediscovering a radical wing in the Dutch Reformed tradition itself.

I picture Boesak's thought as a Black Theology of the Word of God. In my opinion Boesak has expressed his Word of God theology in diverse ways. In "Courage to Be Black" (*South African Outlook*, October 1975) and subsequent writings in the 1970s, he appears to lean toward the Black Consciousness Movement and black theology. By 1987, apparently broadening his framework from "black" to "oppressed," we discover him shifting toward a theology for justice.

> It is a question of not really shifting from Black and Reformed to Black and Christian, but from Black and Reformed to oppressed and Christian, because the oppression is suffered by Christians, and the oppression is sometimes perpetrated by Christians. And that is why Black and Reformed can no longer deal with what we have here today. So we talk about Theology for Justice.[26]

The manifestation of his theology may have shifted, but the supremacy of the Word of God—the norm regulating his God-talk—has remained constant throughout his theological career.

Boesak vehemently opposes apartheid because of its sham, pseudo-gospel facade. Wrapped in the theological mantle of scripture, apartheid originated in the white NGK; the NGK leadership proposed apartheid to the government as a cultural way of life and political policy. Boesak insightfully describes this insidious apartheid-gospel connection:

> Apartheid is more than an ideology, more than something that has been thought up to form the content of a particular political policy. Apartheid is also pseudo-gospel. It was born in the church. . . . The struggle against apartheid . . . is, therefore, more than merely a struggle against an evil ideology.

The battlefront extends beyond the dethronement of a satanic political system. "It is," resumes Boesak, "more than a struggle for the liberation and wholeness of people, white as well as black, in South Africa. It is also finally a struggle for the integrity of the Gospel of Jesus Christ"—the Word of God.[27] Thus the white power structure (in this instance, the Afrikaner government) props up separate development with the Bible.[28] The white "Christian" government and church indulge in idolatry by theologically justifying the deification of apartheid.

Boesak has dedicated his entire theology and ministry to the sovereignty of the Word of God. "The first thing I should mention, then," Boesak confesses, "is the principle of the supremacy of the word of God. In the Reformed tradition it is the word of God that gives life to our words." The "Word of God" or "scripture," he continues, is the foundation of the Reformed church's life and witness in the world.[29] However, the Word of God or the Bible does not kneel to uncritical accommodation to culture, neither to the apartheid pseudo-gospel nor even to the context that engenders black theology. No, the Word encounters and challenges black theology and the world. And out of that confrontation, under the supremacy of the Word, black theology becomes prophetic, critical, challenging and transformational of all situations. Here Boesak wants to assert emphatically, in his view, the decisive role of the Word. In the final analysis the liberation praxis of black theology submits not to the judgment of the situation of blackness, but to the liberating gospel of Jesus Christ. In the Reformed tradition, Boesak correctly claims, all of life falls under Jesus Christ's lordship. On this point he maintains consistency with his church tradition by accenting the supremacy of the Word. But he also breaks continuity by equating the Bible and Christ's lordship primarily with liberation. In fact, the content of the Word of God is the emancipation of all oppressed people. And so, what God has done for Israel and revealed through the incarnation of Jesus Christ is, strictly speaking, liberation.[30]

Liberation

Buthelezi stands for a liberation in which black and white share racial fellowship in Christ's love. While not denying divine love, Boesak understands liberation of the *poor* as essential to the gospel proclamation. Neither a secondary aspect nor a tangential intersection with the gospel, liberation constitutes the substance and form of black theology's Word of God. "Black Theology is a theology of liberation," in Boesak's words.

> By that we mean the following. Black Theology believes that liberation is not only "part of" the gospel, or "consistent with" the gospel; it is the content and framework of the gospel of Jesus Christ.[31]

Liberation ends alienation from God, neighbor and oneself. It brings freedom from economic exploitation, dehumanization and poverty. For Boesak, God liberates us to do God's will of justice. Liberation, then, frees one in human fulfillment for full service to God in order to emancipate the people of God. Thus God's people, the church, proclaim a total liberation from all manifestations of sin and for a holistic humanity.

Describing prophetic proclamation, Boesak directly connects ultimate and penultimate liberation. The latter acts in anticipation of the former. In the prophetic task of freedom, Boesak believes, the vision of the prophet in the fullness of the Kingdom (the Ultimate) is realized in the signs of the Kingdom—the cleansed lepers, the sight restored to the blind, and the justice rendered to the poor and downtrodden (the penultimate).[32] Today's partial freedom, then, mirrors apocalyptic signs of the kingdom coming.

Boesak's attention to the poor and the downtrodden also directs his aim of liberation against both the "external" and "internal" enemy. For instance, as God did with Israel of old, God demands justice from today's pharaoh, the external enemy (the white oppressor), as well as from the rich and powerful within contemporary Israel (black oppressors). As a result the truly free fight against any curtailment of freedom because God guarantees a thorough human liberation.

The Word of God, the Word of Liberation, consistently judges all human situations, regardless of color, with a singular divine yardstick. Accordingly, black emancipation should never, in Boesak's opinion, duplicate white, bourgeois individualism. In one expression bourgeois individualism cloaks itself in individual selfishness at the expense of group well-being. In another fashion it masquerades under the guise of an overly pious, otherworldly concern about heaven. In this last manner it paralyzes and channels black people's effort into the escape mechanism of "heaven."

In a deeper sense, moreover, Boesak's consistent utilization of the liberating Word of God against all expressions of white and black oppression allows him to link racial discrimination with class exploitation. Posing the question "Is racism indeed the only issue?" in order to ferret out interconnecting examples of oppression against the poor, Boesak replies:

> It seems to us that there is a far deeper malady in the American and South African societies that manifests itself in the form of racism. . . . Even in South Africa there are signs that should circumstances but allow, some whites would be quite willing to replace the insecurity of institutional racism with the false security of the "black bourgeoisie."[Thus the issue is] the relation between racism and capitalism.[33]

The deeper malady in the form of racism, white over black, is the structural exploitation of classism, black over black. And so Boesak desires a new South Africa, and by implication a new America, comprised of possibilities for true humanity. Teleologically, God's purpose is for a black-white common world. Hence, for an authentic liberation blacks seek to share with whites dreams of a penultimate society of genuine humanness as a sign of the eschatological fullness of what it means to bear the *imago dei*, black and white. More specifically, Boesak depicts this image of liberation: "We are all committed to the struggle for a non-racist, open, democratic South Africa, a unitary state, one nation in which all citizens will have the rights accorded them by ordinance of almighty God."[34] In a word, commitment to non-racialism — liberation beyond racism and classism — affects the common ground for reconciliation.

Reconciliation

Boesak establishes several conditions for black-white reconciliation. First, reconciliation does not mean "feeling good"; it implies suffering and death. Christ had to die. Likewise we too must prepare to sacrifice our lives for the sake of the other. "If white and black Christians fail to understand this," Boesak admonishes, "we will not be truly reconciled."[35] Second, in political terms reconciliation follows the attainment of righteousness and social justice. The South African system of privileges for the few must first give way to a democratic power-sharing and an equal participation in rights and responsibilities for all.

Third, reconciliation exhibits the presence of both divine love and divine righteousness. But the love of God points to Yahweh concretely taking the side of Yahweh's people against the oppressor pharaoh. Boesak places the role of God's love within the context of God's righteousness of liberation. Perhaps here we can discern some tension between Boesak's view of reconciliation and that of Manas Buthelezi. The latter appears to emphasize more the role of blacks in unilaterally loving racist whites. In contrast, Boesak claims that *agape* is a manifest activity of God doing justice. In reconciliation the Word of God activates liberation. God loves his people into freedom, and thus reconciliation, through a love of justice. While Buthelezi seems to base reconciliation on black-initiated love, Boesak points to justice as the condition for reconciliation.[36]

What does reconciliation signify for blacks and whites? For blacks, the "gateway" to true reconciliation, according to Boesak, opens when blacks say farewell to the non-white mentality. Blacks must affirm their blackness as part of the reconciliation process. They cannot reconcile with whites while hating their black selves, while negating their "infinite worth before God." Black people have to grasp their *imago dei* as the constitution of their humanity. Like Buthelezi, Boesak does mention the task of blacks loving whites. But again, love comes through justice.[37]

For whites, reconciliation entails their acceptance of black humanity. Even more, it summons whites to a commitment and faithfulness to the struggle of God's liberating Word of reconciling black-white relations through justice. In fact, Boesak recognizes whites who have already assumed the condition of blackness, that is, of already displaying commitment and faithfulness to the word of God in the midst of oppression. At this point he makes the definition of "blackness" concrete in such a way that whites can enter blackness. "We must remember that in situations like ours blackness (the state of oppression) is not only a colour, it is a condition." Therefore, he continues:

And it is within this perspective that the role of white Christians should be seen. . . . I speak of those white Christians who have understood their own white guilt in the oppression of black people as corporate responsibility, who have genuinely repented and have been genuinely converted.

These particular whites, in Boesak's assessment, have clearly committed themselves to the liberation struggle. They "have taken upon themselves the condition of blackness in South Africa" and are now part of the black church. They, therefore, have presumably met the conditions that lay the foundation for reconciliation.[38]

One has to emphasize that Boesak's reconciliation stands under the Word of God, a liberating Word. In reconciliation blacks and whites assume the condition of blackness based not on color but fundamentally on whoever witnesses to the Word in struggle. Yet neither blackness nor whiteness conditions the Word; "reconciliation and forgiveness find their meaning only when regarded against the background of God's liberating acts in Jesus Christ."[39]

Christology

In the previous sections we saw how genuine theology, liberation and reconciliation undergo the test of the Word of God in Boesak's approach to God-talk. However, in Christology, when he describes an emancipatory praxis under the Word of God, the liberating work and person of Jesus Christ pinpoint the substance of the Word. In the final analysis the gospel of Jesus Christ judges all reflection and all action; the Word is the gospel.

Christ judges in the person of the Poor One and the Oppressed One. In Boesak's Christology Christ's birth in a barn and his parents' financial inability to bear him at an inn reveal him as the Son of the Poor. And his lacking a place to "lay his head" (his homelessness) reveals a state of destitution. At the same time, Christ suffered oppression at the hands of the political state for preaching the Word of God. He even bore unearned punishment from the wicked of his own people. Yet, his person (divinity assuming Poverty and Oppression) lay the basis for his work on behalf of all poor and oppressed. He sounded good news for the marginalized. He sided with the dispossessed. He effected liberation. And he fulfilled Yahweh's promise of deliverance for the captives.[40]

To the lordship of this Person and Work Boesak pledges paramount allegiance. At all costs one clings to the confession of Christ as Lord. Consequently the laws of the state and of self-preservation do not undermine the authority of Christ's Person and Work. Neither do the intimidating demands of any people, status quo or ideology dictate to the followers of Christ. Here, drawing on progressive strands within his Reformed tradition,

Boesak theologically justifies disobedience to apartheid and commitment to the Word in the liberation movement.

Divine lordship thrusts the faithful completely into the political arena. One has to trek the political path because even the "slightest fraction of life" falls under the lordship of Christ. Boesak employs a theological rationale for his lordship Christological claim. God created life and God is indivisible. Hence life is indivisible. Since the substance of the Word of God is the liberating lordship of Christ, Christ reigns over all life. Buthelezi's Christology situates its uniqueness in drawing black and white into a loving family. Boesak sees this Christological function, but within the context of apartheid theology submitting to Christ's absolute lordship.

In this lordship Boesak also perceives faith and hope for the church. The certitude of Christ's past resurrection confirms his current reign. If Christ rose, he lives and rules over us today. Therefore having risen from the dead, Christ guarantees us a future life in the eschaton. The ecclesia, then, witnesses as a church of the resurrection. Moreover, the resurrected lordship cosmologically altered the balance of forces over sin's dominion. So the kingdom of sin likewise submits to the kingdom of Christ. This knowledge provides faith and hope for the church in the struggle between aggressive disloyalty to sin and unswerving allegiance to the kingdom.

In summary, Christ's lordship of liberation defeated the devil in political places. Christ rose from the clutches of evil persons and forever placed the faithful in God's kingdom of liberation.[41]

SIMON S. MAIMELA

Black Anthropology

A member of the Evangelical Lutheran Church of South Africa, Simon S. Maimela teaches theology at the University of South Africa in Pretoria. He is one of the first, if not the first, black theologians to be appointed to a teaching position at a prestigious white university. Like Buthelezi and Boesak, Maimela develops his black theology in a white church and a white educational institution. He, too, faces the theological dilemma of affirming black humanity while fighting white power and, simultaneously, upholding a rapprochement with his white colleagues and churchpersons. Also, he is chairperson of the Black Theology Project in Johannesburg and a member of the Institute for Contextual Theology. Maimela, in my estimate, develops a Black Theology of Anthropology.[42]

Maimela establishes the context for his theology by confronting the treacherousness of Afrikaner and English anthropology. He charges white anthropology with the sin of falsely portraying the created reality of humankind. Humanity, in white anthropology, has fallen prey to self-centeredness, a drive to accumulate absolute power and wealth for a particular individual, group or class. This negative anthropology attributes a utilitarianism to human contact. In particular, the neighbor becomes a mere tool for the personal gratification of the individualist. Different peoples, then, pose an immediate danger to one another and can never experience creative interrelation. "It is against the background of this extremely negative, cynical, and pessimistic anthropological presuppostion of the human self," writes Maimela, "that we should try to understand White praxis in South Africa."[43] Maimela, therefore, claims that such a deep, socialized, indoctrinated anthropology causes whites to automatically discourage contacts between diverse black ethnic groups, thus the policy of bantustans, and between whites and blacks, hence the policy of separate development; that is, Maimela accuses white anthropology of creating apartheid. Among the black political theologians, Buthelezi targets the breach in Christ's love in racial fellowship, and Boesak unveils the incorrect use of his Reformed tradition to support apartheid. For Maimela, the heart of the matter is a heretical theological anthropology.

White anthropology's most severe weakness denies divine intent to fully immerse human creation, black and white, in a transformative process of the rest of creation. Maimela ventures:

Perhaps the most serious problem about this theology—this is true for English and Afrikaans churches—is that it is devoid of the conception of a dynamic God who actively involves humans now in the present in order to transform the natural and social environment.[44]

On the contrary, asserts Maimela, the will of God in creation places humanity, black and white, squarely into political action: the dismantling of apartheid. God's will produces God's grace: a) the grace of God's gift of creation to humanity; b) the grace of God's gift of human authority over creation; and c) the grace of God's gift of human ability to work naturally with other humans toward the new creation. As a result, a Christian theological anthropology critically reflects on what it means to be politically involved by God in God's creative and redemptive movement toward full humanity. Indeed, God involves us as fellow workers and co-creators, "footsoldiers and missionaries," in the completion of God's creation. Theology, then, asks: How does God relate to human beings; how does God call human creation to transform the world into God's kingdom? And so God's purpose is humanity struggling in the process to realize the kingdom—the epitome of created humanity in liberation.[45]

Liberation

Maimela argues for liberation from the sin of broken fellowship. Similar to Buthelezi's racial fellowship, Maimela's Black Theology of Anthropology depicts sin as a collective concept, a refusal by one group to have interpersonal relations with another group. Christian relations, on the other hand, denote love and being present for the other's well-being. But the denial of neighborly interaction exhibits a fundamental state of alienation. Such an estranged situation among humanity immediately has an impact on human connection with the Creator. In fact, it severs all fellowship with God. Since God created humanity to work one with another, black and white, to have dominion over creation and to co-labor actively with God in bringing forth the kingdom, a severance in contact between diverse peoples inherently disrupts God's intent. A breach in human fellowship, then, enacts a grave disobedience against God and against the created order.

After defining sin, Maimela recounts sin's products. The sin of discordance in human fellowship spawns a host of antagonisms among people. Maimela cites the bitter fruits of poverty, hatred, racism, denial of freedom, self-centeredness, isolation "and other forms of sociopolitical structures which put a person at odds with his fellows." Because sin functions in a collective manner, Maimela highlights the evils of its structural nature. Thus sin breeds systemic conflict and polarization between groups and peoples.

But most important, for Maimela, sin spawns the particular antagonisms of class and race. He explains the exactness of these political evils by contrasting the target of his black liberation theology with black South African theologians who espouse, in his words, "black consciousness."

> There are those [black] theologians who have been informed and are committed to black consciousness [and for whom] the question of race is the supreme question; [they would] like to do theology in light of that framework.

Maimela does not want to neglect the race issue. Nevertheless, he proposes a "broader" framework, which encompasses both race and class. Echoing Boesak, Maimela continues:

> And there are others who . . . think the question of race is an important one, but who have also come to realize that we blacks can become exploiters; that capitalism knows no color; and [they] have now incorporated Marxist analysis and have come to realize the problem of class and race oppression among blacks themselves is a serious one. So I would regard the latter [framework] as much broader. . . . I prefer to operate within that framework.[46]

Maimela advocates race and class because a concentration on blackness and culture, alone and in and of themselves, does not automatically solve the deleterious effects of apartheid; nor does such a concentration guarantee the prevention of black-on-black exploitation by a non-white elite. Moreover, for a theological anthropology a narrow race theology interferes with God's purpose of diverse humanity, black and white, co-creating to attain the fullness of God's gift of creation. We should also note that Maimela's theological anthropology of liberation draws on the tool of Marxist class analysis. Unlike most black theologians in the political theological trend, Maimela openly names the political economic approach in societal transformation.

Having labeled capitalist exploitation and racial oppression as sin's handiwork, Maimela defines his theological anthropology of liberation. A liberated humanity has faith in and witnesses to God's intended anthropology. God wills that people co-labor with divinity as one in the realization of the kingdom of justice and peace. The emergence of that kingdom, in the final analysis brought to fruition by God, is fully rooted in a continuing creative, historical process. Therefore today's partial victories in reaching racial fellowship and justice contribute to the growth of the kingdom, which awaits all humanity in the eschaton. True freedom situates different peoples in their joint dominion over creation and in God's movement to refine the created order.[47]

Reconciliation

We noted how liberation ensues from obedience to divine anthropological intent. Consequently, for Maimela, liberation necessarily requires reconciliation—blacks and whites jointly sharing responsibility for and acting as catalysts in creation; that is, black and white responding to divine telos. However, Maimela contends, an ungodly anthropology blocks a proper reconciliation in South Africa. For example, the white church teaches the impossibility of blacks and whites living and struggling together. Thus the white church avoids a Christian fellowship which would "eliminate points of friction" between the races. Such a warped anthropology restricts the meaning of reconciliation to the forced separation of antagonistic neighbors! The church, Christian oneness and fellowship, all elements of reconciliation, are confined to one's race, ethnic group or "volk." This deformed view of reconciliation, Maimela believes, fails to comprehend the common needs of real people who are, in fact, actual neighbors. Indeed, it destroys the image of fellow human beings with true personalities by construing a depersonalized artificial separation and reifying the rich, dynamic diversity in the South African anthropology. Thus white anthropological reconciliation justifies racial apartness with false and abstract concepts of "group" and "race."

Furthermore, white reconciliation cuts directly across the grain of biblical testimony. For instance, Maimela cites the mandate and optimism of scripture regarding reconciliation:

> By stressing the fact that we belong to one another and are related as those who are brothers and sisters [black and white], the Bible wants us to assume so trusting a posture that we regard all human

relationships—regardless of race or group affiliations—as potentially nourishing to all who meet as persons.

Hence the Bible instructs us that reconciliation offers the potential for mutual gain. Continuing, Maimela writes: "[Scripture] wants to teach us to assume that coming together in truly human fellowship is beneficial and enriching to both sides."[48]

Adhering to his biblical witness of reconciliation, Maimela draws the following lessons from the Cain and Abel account. In this particular narrative God charges Cain for the whereabouts of Abel. The presupposition behind the divine charge or calling illustrates that being human entails mutual caring and protection. Also it indicates human authority to freely choose different options in reconciliation. Contrasting white reconciliation, Maimela insists the Bible denies an inherent proclivity toward black and white suspicion. Instead of automatically destroying black and white life, racial groups can opt to work together and nourish life. The biblical teaching assumes our created nature does not predetermine our mutual annihilation.[49]

Besides the biblical instruction, Maimela claims that the generic, symbolic state of black oppression also provides a basis for reconciliation in South Africa. However, first he concedes that the particular, ontological definition of blackness limits parameters to the oppressed plight of dark-skinned South Africans. At the same time, Maimela concludes:

> But in its symbolic sense, [blackness] refers to every human situation of enslavement. . . . [It] may very well happen that people who have white skins may actually also suffer injustices. . . . For the issue in the struggle here is one of a situation of oppression rather than the colour of the skin, because as we have indicated already the problem of oppression as such and the colour of one's skin may or may not coincide.[50]

Based on the pains of injustice and the struggle of liberation for a new humanity in the kingdom, oppressed whites and blacks experience blackness. Thus, similar to Boesak, symbolic blackness also offers common ground for reconciliation in Maimela's view.

Christology

But the Christian message of reconciliation ultimately rests on what God has brought about in the incarnation of Jesus of Nazareth, the Christ. For Maimela, the man Jesus leaves us no alternative but to have faith in a positive anthropology. Yes, we take seriously the perversion of sin in the human reality, but not to negate God's redemption for all humanity in Jesus Christ. Christ brought redemption expressly to heal the most serious "diseases of the heart" and of human works such as lack of love and fellowship. In fact, the complete Christian message of "conversion and reconciliation" reveals an understanding and a faith "that humans have been and continue to be changed by God [through Christ] who continues to mould them into new creatures."

Why did Christ die on the cross? According to Maimela, Christ gave his life in order for us to undergo a healing and renewal from the perverted life of sin and the products of sin. Christ's death brought regenerated and reinvigorated life and love to distorted human relations. To say otherwise, in the manner of white anthropology, signifies a cynical attempt to a) take the heart out of the crucifixion and b) blasphemously mock God's power in the resurrected Christ to intervene in the affairs of God's created humanity.[51]

While affirming the power of the crucifixion, Maimela cautions against a spiritualized atonement. Such an incorrect view depicts "the problem of man largely in spiritualized terms." Even with the atonement, Maimela approaches from an anthropological persuasion. He begins with Christ's atoning work from the perspective of humanity entangled in the concrete web of sociopolitical oppression. Though Christ's death and resurrection did resolve the need for a general and spiritual forgiveness of sins and guilt, this confession alone ignores the more exact Christological picture of humanity's material reality. Hence Christ's basic work accomplished the physical transformation of humanity.

Here Maimela's introduction of the work of Christ with physical change shows us how his Christology bridges theological anthropology (Christ's transformation of material humanity) and reconciliation (Christ's atonement in socio-political oppression) with liberation. He includes liberation in such a construction by the correct juxtaposition of Christological activity to salvation and historical liberation. The former, salvation, Christ has achieved and promised to humanity. The latter, historical liberation, remains the joint project of both God (in Christ) and Christians. While ultimate salvation of the kingdom is a divine gift, co-creators — God in Christ and humankind — forge alienating social conditions into a more humane and just social relation. In short, salvation preconditions historical liberation, and Christ's work links both to anthropology and reconciliation.

Maimela succinctly states the intricacies of his entire theological perspective:

> Put differently, the fundamental message of liberation is that the life, death and resurrection of Jesus Christ [Christology] were aimed at the total liberation (salvation) of humanity [liberation] from all kinds of limitations both spiritual and physical, and that this liberation is a dynamic historical process in which man [theological anthropology] is given the promise, the possibility and power to overcome all the perverted human conditions [reconciliation] on this side of the grave.[52]

In Christ, it seems for Maimela, all things are possible: a healed theological anthropology, a just fellowship of reconciliation, and both a penultimate and ultimate liberation/salvation. Like Buthelezi's Christology, Maimela discovers racial fellowship but sees Christ's resurrection providing the condition for both races working together in radical social transformation-creation. And when Boesak advocates total submission to Christ's liberating lordship, Maimela links this to Christ's work of healing sinful anthropology between white and black.

FRANK CHIKANE

The Peoples' Theology

Frank Chikane is important within the black political theology trend for several reasons. First, theologically he represents a younger generation of black activists, which has been baptized in township and trade union resistance movements. Second, hailing from Soweto, one of the historic hotbeds of black rebellions, Chikane holds the general secretary office at the South African Council of Churches. This platform, as evidenced by the work of Desmond Tutu, offers broad influence over South African churches and, indeed, churches worldwide. Third, Chikane was the moving force in and first general secretary at the Institute for Contextual Theology (ICT). The ICT is one of the premier theological organizations in South Africa that intentionally works to develop and do liberation theology in opposition to apartheid. A minister of the Apostolic Faith Mission Church, Chikane has been detained, tortured and charged with treason by the South African government for his Christian activities. Finally, Chikane is the mover behind the world-acclaimed *Kairos Document.*

Among the black political theologians, Buthelezi looks to black-white racial fellowship, Boesak employs the word of God to judge both black and white theologies, and Maimela focuses on an authentic black-white theological anthropology. Chikane goes to the people (black and white) for his theology, concentrating on building a Contextual People's Theology over against the dominant theologies inherited in South Africa. He, therefore, adamantly opposes theologies developed "from above" on the part of priests and academics, who, according to Chikane, err in two respects. First, they fail to recognize the abstractness and irrelevancy of their God-talk. Expressing the musings of a minority situated on top of the majority — laypersons and other ordinary men and women — the priests and academics talk in the isolated world of the monastery and the academy. Similarly, a Contextual People's Theology contends, these theologians enjoy the privileges of Western culture and liberal capitalism. In essence, they pontificate and dominate from the heights of "middle class comfort and complacency."

Second, because these theologies represent the powerful minority contexts, they incorrectly enunciate their theological claims as universally valid and eternally true for the majority of people. They fail to acknowledge their own particularity and limited perspective on God. Indeed, their theology can only speak for those who reside in such narrow and dominating confines of privilege. Such an "incontrovertible" and arrogant theology can only mouth the insidiousness of the ruling minority sector of society.

Chikane seeks to speak theologically from the context of the people. In his judgment

> more and more Christians today are beginning to feel the need to be liberated from a theology or theologies that are determined and thought out by an academic and ecclesiastic elite.... Ordinary lay Christians today are discovering that theology ... can be done, and very effectively done, by the people themselves. This kind of contextual theology has many names. We can call it a people's theology.[53]

At this point, Chikane establishes his theological viewpoint in contrast to a contextual elitist theology. As just indicated, ordinary Christians ("the people themselves") do theology quite effectively. Any practicing Christian, then, can do theology. If one genuinely attempts to live a Christian life and theologize creatively about his or her faith, one does theology. At this point Chikane adds an important stress on "doing" in opposition to the "thinking" of liberal capitalism's elite. In fact, a Contextual People's Theology claims that one does not even have to be an educated Christian to do theology. In opposition to a people's theology, theology of the elite mesmerizes the people with a highly specialized enterprise reserved exclusively for academic experts.

Though rejecting ecclesial and academic elites, Chikane perceives a role in a Contextual People's Theology for progressive, academically trained theologians. These authentic theologians reflect on their concrete involvement with the people in the activity of God with God's people. Accordingly, for Chikane, any theologian not part of God's action stands suspect regarding his or her position vis-à-vis God's struggle for a just society. "Theology not grounded in liberating praxis is not liberating theology," writes Chikane. Theology "is demanding, because it means theologians must relinquish their position of privilege and choose rather to suffer with the people of God: from this experience, a people's theology can be born."[54]

In addition, a Contextual People's Theology has a similar word for black theology. For instance, by way of critique, Chikane warns black theologians about the dangers of a contextual elitist theology. In his judgment, today's black theology "sort of lost its liberating aspect." Pursuing his argument, he continues:

> To me, black theology should be a theology of the people who are in struggle.... I'm looking forward to a black theology that will emerge

from the context of struggle more than a black theology that emerges from the heads of people who enjoy reflecting on the situation.[55]

In summary, a Contextual People's Theology culminates from the activity of theologians experiencing the praxis of struggle and suffering in God's action toward liberation.

Liberation

The ultimate liberation, for Chikane, resides in the kingdom of God. This kingdom serves the masses of people by providing them with justice and peace, a resolution to their current suffering and pain. Indeed, the Bible witnesses to God's involvement in history with the Israelites as a revelation that all history unfolds toward liberation for the people. Therefore the kingdom of liberation for the people, Chikane contends, is the end product of God's providential care displayed by God's action in history.

Put another way, Chikane adheres to a salvation history in which God brought about creation for the purpose of attaining the kingdom of justice and peace. God realizes the divine will of justice through history. And God governs, determines and intervenes in history for the kingdom of justice for the people. In response to the question, What is the theological norm regulating his theology, Chikane replies:

> I've moved into the concept of the kingdom of God. . . . It is looking for justice, searching for justice. I'm measuring life in terms of justice. . . . I would look for that which produces justice, which in a sense is liberating. It makes people free. . . . If something is not liberating, I get rid of it and I have to fight.[56]

Because the kingdom accomplishes the most humane and just society for people, its nature determines what Christians should do today. Christian witness, then, is motivated by the quest to approximate on earth the kingdom of God. To this end Christians gear their "doing theology" for a full humanity wherever the people endure death by hunger and disease—in squatter camps, the bantustans' arid lands, and the ghettoes. In sum, Chikane groups together Christian witness (a radical social change), theodicy (the context of the people's suffering) and liberation (justice for the people in the kingdom).

Finally, and in agreement with all members of the political theological trend, Chikane envisions a liberation beyond blackness. Like Boesak and Maimela, he wrestles with the interconnectedness of race oppression and class exploitation in South Africa. Chikane claims: "I'm struggling with the balance between race and class. I'm starting from the point that race is a product of social relations." Again complementing Maimela, Chikane appears to propose a broader framework that encompasses racial liberation within class liberation. Resuming his comment, he states: "And therefore the social relations become more important to me and become the starting point." Thus the future kingdom of justice for the people and today's victories which adumbrate that kingdom, both reach beyond race. Concluding, Chikane believes:

> Purely from my faith perspective [and] not from being informed by Marx, justice for me has nothing to do with the color of a person. It means I don't want a black person to come and oppress us.[57]

Reconciliation and Christology

Chikane ties reconciliation and Christology closely together. Since the theological norm guiding Chikane's liberation perspective is justice for the people from white and black oppression, he suggests possibilities of black and white cooperation in Christian witness today. But, at the same time, this potential does not entreat a cheap reconciliation. Just as Boesak weds reconciliation and liberation, Chikane asserts that an oppressed-oppressor relationship will not permit reconciliation until the exploiter repents and ceases oppression. In fact, the incarnation of Jesus Christ instructs us to do away with the inherited and dominant theologies that teach a reconciliation of neutrality in the midst of injustice against the people.[58]

The incarnation of the historical Jesus, Chikane explains, epitomizes the archetype reconciliation. Jesus Christ came in identification with human weakness, suffering and pain. Therefore, divine incarnation tells us to make "a preferential option for the victims against the victimizers." Jesus came for the people and lived with the people. Accordingly, our act of reconciliation issues from doing justice for the people.

Chikane presumes that the incarnation reveals the distinction that differentiates Jesus and the Christ. In the eyes of the disciples it was the criterion of praxis that made the human Jesus the divine Christ. Consequently no true Christological knowledge validates itself in the mere concept of Christology. Only Jesus' action in the process of transforming human suffering into people's liberation guaranteed the disciples and guarantees us today that the Person of Nazareth was the Messiah of God. Thus, Chikane claims, the "logos of praxis" becomes our starting point in Christology and, concomitantly, reconciliation.

Finally, Chikane attributes the incarnation with resolving all antagonisms and debilitating incongruences in the world and, thereby, mediating reconciliation.

> The incarnation is a way of saying the "human" is the "divine" because in Jesus the "divine" became "human.". . . Thus there is no longer a dichotomy between humanity and divinity in our lives.

... The only differentiation possible is between good and evil, right-eousness and unrighteousness, justice and injustice, love and hate, and between Shalom (peace) and war or conflict.[59]

In summary, the Logos entered the world of human evil—a situation of oppression and exploitation of the people by the elites, black and white. Amidst these worldly principalities and powers the human Jesus opted preferentially for the people (the poor) and thereby became the divine Christ proffering reconciliation. Thus through Jesus humanity partakes of the "divine nature"—justice in liberation. And so a full and authentic life for the people becomes a liberated existence: a simultaneous "humaniza-tion and divinization" in justice.

CONCLUSION

In this chapter we have reviewed the black political theology trend in South Africa. We discovered diverse emphases. Buthelezi proposed a the-ology of racial fellowship. Boesak would agree with such a theology to the degree that it submits to the liberating Word of God. Maimela would not contradict a Word of God accent as long as it achieves a theological an-thropology of social transformation. And Chikane would embrace all po-litical theological nuances from the perspective of a radical theology from below, from the context of the people.

All four theologians represent, in my estimate, a political theological trend. They uncompromisingly oppose the politics of apartheid's racial di-mension. They correctly note white theology's heretical justification of white supremacy. They attack white theology from within the (white) ecclesial tradition and build on the radical theological streams in church history. At the same time they confess as Christians a belief that South Africa belongs to all, black and white, who inhabit it. In the opinion of the political the-ologians God intends black and white to work together in racial fellowship toward a post-apartheid society and to enjoy this new creation jointly, black and white. Furthermore, from their understanding of race and class, the political theologians show a sensitivity to both white and black oppression. Racism originates from capitalist systemic relations. And so they warn against the new South Africa falling in the hands of an oppressive black elite. For them the objective measuring rod in theology is justice for the oppressed, regardless of color. They do not wish to imply that their political theology will do to the white minority what white theology does to the black majority. Finally, while acknowledging the important link between Black Consciousness and black theology, they nonetheless classify black theology as one part of the larger, more inclusive liberation theology. They empha-size a "broader" theological framework. In a word, only a political theology of non-racialism will guarantee the future of free South Africa.

Despite its valuable contributions, the black political theology trend needs to consider additional aspects of a holistic South African black theology. When the political theologians "broaden" beyond blackness and detect a "far deeper malady" in class beyond race, they seem to falsely present an important theological question. Sin manifests itself in both class (politics) and race (culture). Terms like "broadens" and "far deeper" imply that class one-sidedly gives rise to race and culture. Such an interpretation of the relation between class-politics and race-culture is too mechanical and simplistic. This could deter the black political trend from exploring the positive, creative, transformative dimensions of culture. God's love of, image in, and liberation purpose for poor blacks sanctify their love of themselves. To love and reconcile among themselves means poor blacks have the political right to and strength for self-determination as an oppressed people. In brief, they can determine both their political future and their cultural reality.

Accordingly, a black theology of liberation cannot reach its full potential without serious attention to a liberating black culture. One does not sense the importance of black music, dance, language, folklore, art, literature, theater, poetry, African traditional religions and African Christianity in the black political theology trend. Do the African Independent Churches lend any strength to a black political theology? What does the pre-colonial indigenous religious history contribute to the political theologians' theology? Does a black political theology allow for today's South African whites (of the right and of the left "progressives") to give restitution or reparations for stolen land back to poor blacks? Is there not something sacred in the land for the original owners—black South Africans? The black political theology trend, it seems, has not comprehensively explored the liberating nature of the unique "Africanness" and "blackness" in their political theology.

The following chapter examines black theologians of the black cultural theological trend in South Africa. Admittedly, it would grossly misrepresent these theologians to even insinuate a lack of interest in politics on their part. Yes, they attend to politics. In fact, all black theologians agree to the need to politically dismantle and destroy apartheid's political system. But they grapple with black existence under apartheid with a slant toward exposing white colonial theology and valorizing indigenous African cultural resources.

CHAPTER FIVE

Black Theology: God's Unique Gift for Black Liberation

By National freedom we mean freedom from White domination.
... This implies the rejection of the conception of segregation, apartheid, trusteeship, or White leadership which are all in one way or
another motivated by the idea of White domination or domination of
the White over the Blacks. Like all other people the African people
claim the right of self-determination.

Programme of Action, 1949

The present chapter reviews the members of the black cultural theology
trend in South Africa in contrast with the black political theology trend of
the previous chapter. Again we are reminded that general trends shun strict
compartmentalization of description. By definition, a trend denotes a
broader direction. Therefore this theological study recognizes the political
and cultural theological overlap.[1] Still, we can observe two theological nuances in South African black theology. A brief schema of each trend follows.

The political theological trend incorporates the following features: a) it
emphasizes an argument against a theology of apartheid; b) it seeks liberation through a non-racial theology; c) it sees racial fellowship determining the future of South Africa; d) it promotes liberation theology, which it
claims includes but also extends beyond black theology to all the oppressed;
and e) it maintains that South Africa belongs to all who live in it, black
and white.

The cultural theological trend displays the following attributes: a) it
emphasizes a fight against a theology of white settler colonialism; b) it
promotes liberation through the use of African indigenous theological
sources; c) it claims that God's gift of blackness (or Africanness) suggests
blacks have the right to self-determination, in some sense like the Programme of Action[2]; d) it stresses that the particularity of the black South

African situation mandates a *black* theology of liberation and its necessary link to black consciousness; and e) it struggles for the reclamation of the land from the white settler colonialists and places high regard on the sacredness of the land for black people.

With this delineation between the two trends, we can begin an examination of the black cultural theology trend. Like their political colleagues in the previous chapter, the cultural theologians develop their theology in the historical context of the 1970s' Black Consciousness Movement, the Soweto Rebellion and the 1980s' states of emergency. The same repressive realities prompt both political and cultural trends. The present chapter reviews the theological thought of Bonganjalo C. Goba, Itumeleng J. Mosala, Takatso A. Mofokeng and Desmond M. Tutu. The theological categories of theology, sources and liberation will aid our review.

BONGANJALO C. GOBA

Goba served as the past president of the Albert Luthuli College of the Federal Theological Seminary in South Africa and as a former theological professor at the University of South Africa with Simon S. Maimela; he currently works for the United Church Board of World Ministries (New York City) and is a member of the Johannesburg Black Theology Project. Goba worked with Steve Biko and the Black Consciousness Movement in the 1960s and 1970s. He is also a minister of the United Congregational Church in South Africa.

African Christian Theology

Goba develops an African Christian theology of liberation. He indicates the centrality of African traditional religions but connects this indigenous religious worldview to Christianity. He then establishes linkages between indigenous religions, Christianity and the contemporary plight of black South Africans in their liberation struggle.

> The presence and the growth of Christianity in South Africa since the later part of the nineteenth century poses a challenge to those of us African Christians who participate in that reality to develop an African Christian Theology.

While noting the reality of African traditional religion out of which black South Africans come, nonetheless Goba describes his theology differently:

> I prefer to call it African Christian theology because of the significance of the Christian mythos which has become part of our worldview as opposed to African theology, which to my understanding suggests

a theology which deals strictly with African traditional religious experience without relating that experience to the Christian faith.[3]

However, the impact of the "Christian mythos" does not in any way negate the decisive influence of the African worldview. In fact, for Goba this worldview proves normative in maintaining the African "cultural ethos," while the Western worldview acts in a functional capacity to ensure Africans' ability to cope with the Western technological society of South Africa. Thus he situates the Christian witness of faith "within the African cultural religious milieu." As Christians, Africans appropriate Christianity out of African culture. Goba emphasizes "that theological reflection does not take place in a cultural vacuum but always in a cultural context."[4]

Indeed, Goba's African Christian theology operates simultaneously in three contexts. The wisdom of the African traditional religious heritage (the *cultural* context) regulates the Christian religious orientation. Then, in a dialectical process, the African Christian theologian "owns the Christian mythos" for himself or herself and brings the gospel of Jesus Christ (the *Christian* context) from this mythos to its fullness as a challenge to liberate the African community. And an African Christian theology takes seriously the contemporary political structures, the existential brokenness engendered by the politics of apartheid (the *current* context). Thus Goba weaves a tapestry out of the African cultural foundation, the Christian gospel and the political battle against racist apartheid.[5]

Goba builds his theology with this three-strand mix because he opposes the theology of the "white missionary mentality."

Taking into account that theology in South Africa has been dominated by the white missionary mentality and ecclesiastical paternalism, black theologians will have to develop and articulate a theology which reflects their cultural and political experience of oppression.[6]

In his opinion the first challenge confronting any black theologian in South Africa is to discredit all deleterious aspects of Western Christian tradition.

In addition to this necessary negation of "white missionary mentality" theology, Goba forges his African Christian theology primarily out of the positive application of the African "mode of theological thought." A major plank in this indigenous African thought is the "holistic approach" to life and religious orientation. Such a comprehensive approach integrates theological reflection on the context of the Christian faith with African culture ("at the aesthetic level") and with today's black experience of oppression ("at the political level"). Here too, from the positive angle, Goba's theology anchors the Christian context and the contemporary context in the African cultural religious context.[7]

Finally, we perceive a basic presupposition to Goba's African Christian theology. In his view today's black theology is linked to two historical precedents: the pan-Africanist movement and the Black Consciousness Movement. Regarding the pan-African lineage Goba cites the 1940s Africanist movement of the Programme of Action as the philosophical roots of black theology. And Goba sees black consciousness as the "essence of the political vision that continues to inform my view of the black struggle" in South Africa. The black theologian must continue to be informed by black consciousness because it correctly understands racism affecting the total and essential nature of the South African social order. He exhorts those theologians who incorrectly place class analysis above race:

> Those who view the black problem as part of the general problem of class oppression make a big mistake because this tragically underestimates the uniqueness of the black situation and black experience as a whole. Black Consciousness poses a challenge to Black Theology because of its commitment to the uniqueness of the black experience.[8]

Goba's strong reliance on the particularity and uniqueness of the black experience brings us to his indigenous sources for the development of an African Christian theology of liberation.

Sources

Goba utilizes at least four basic sources in his theology: the Bible, African tradition, black experience and critical theory. In his first source, the Bible, Goba pursues the liberation motifs in order to ground scripturally his African Christian theology of liberation.[9]

African tradition, the second source, comprises what Goba calls the "inner religious tradition," which informs African Christian theology. This specific tradition bares the unique structure of African religious experience, which sees God in a totally different perspective from the structure of western missionary theology.

The African inner religious tradition has a different rhythm of nature. For the individual, life progresses through birth, puberty, initiation, marriage, procreation, entry into fellowship of the departed, and concludes with communion with the spirits. Similarly, indigenous thought discerns life as a whole without mechanical separation of spheres of spiritual and material reality. It also evolves from what Goba calls "one of the strongest forces in traditional African life" — kinship. Further, it holds in high esteem the concept of "corporate personality." Whatever happens to the individual happens to the entire community and vice versa.[10]

In Goba's judgment the African tradition of corporate personality has practical implications for black solidarity and a dynamic black community today. He zeroes in on corporate personality as one of the centerpieces to black liberation in South Africa. In his mind black thinking and practice have fallen prey to individualism and capitalism. An African Christian theology of liberation, then, must seek an alternative source to the debilitating consequences of individualism. For example, the African Independent Churches[11] (and Goba also cites "the Black storefront churches in the U.S.A.") exemplify a principal location for encountering the African inner religious tradition of corporate personality. Rooted in scripture, these ecclesial gatherings evince a deep communal dimension, unity and solidarity in the unique African cultural milieu. While acknowledging the contribution of the indigenous churches to the development of "corporate personality," Goba also confesses these churches' limitations. Though his African Christian theology of liberation incorporates the inner religious tradition of corporateness, it critiques the Independent Churches for not politically engaging apartheid.[12]

In my opinion Goba divides black experience, the third source, into two aspects: (a) black people's everyday culture; and (b) their political struggle. The aspect of daily cultural expressions of blacks takes many forms. Goba contends:

Now if you look for sources of theology — their experience, their songs, what they say, their poetry, all that becomes sources of theology; the statements that they make about their life as they struggle, all that is the sources for theology . . . what is happening in their lives becomes really the source for doing theology. And that comes in many forms.[13]

At stake is Goba's insistence on the myriad and creative cultural possibilities in black theology's epistemology from the common folk perspective.

Regarding the second aspect, the political struggle, Goba's African Christian theology advocates liberation from the apartheid society and thereby defines political struggle as another part of black experience. This resistance to political oppression gives rise to an entirely new theological language. Determined by a radical faith in the presence of Jesus Christ the liberator, such language pronounces a continual commitment to oppose apartheid. To sum up, the liberating language in the political movement coupled with the daily cultural existence constitute the source of black experience.[14]

The fourth and final source for an African Christian theology of liberation entails tools for social analysis: critical theory. In such a theoretical framework Goba prefers his "revisionist Marxist" project over the "vulgar Marxist approach." The latter tendency incorrectly elevates class analysis over the racial variable in its cultural assessment. The vulgar Marxist employs a reductionist method, which does not give full play to the "strong racial character" in the South African context. Goba constructively disagrees with this narrow class analysis for not fully embodying the language of praxis for the ordinary black person.

Instead, critical theory, for Goba, satisfies the demands of the current black liberation movement.

> There are those of us who use what we call critical theory. . . . Critical theory uses a revisionist Marxist paradigm. . . . In other words, critical theory says, when you reflect as a theologian, you already have a bias and you don't hide it. You bring the emancipatory interests of your group.

Goba's revisionist Marxist paradigm notes the significance of class insights, but not at the expense of the racial "bias" toward the "emancipatory interests" of the entire black group. Continuing his explanation Goba elaborates another aspect of his critical theory model:

> Critical theory really involves praxis. . . . The theory-praxis issue is clearly well-defined in critical theory in that those two things are always not separated, a dialectic.[15]

Here critical theory accounts for the interplay between the development of a theological language from the black experience and the praxis of everyday cultural and political struggle for liberation.

Liberation

Goba's African Christian theology targets racism as a key evil in South Africa. He states:

> The struggle against white domination is also at the center of our concern in theological reflection. As we struggle to reassert our God-given dignity we shall continue to fight the monster of racism.[16]

In addition to its centrality and key locus in South Africa, racism, in Goba's assessment, is the *fundamental* problem that haunts the lives of all black people.[17]

Racism assumes two distinct forms. First, it is manifest in colonial, white missionary theology. From its inception this theology worked hand in hand with colonial administration. Today, Goba contends, it continues to support and defend the demonic ideology of apartheid. Unfortunately the black church has mimicked the "white image" and "theological formulations" that support the status quo. Therefore, for the black church and its African Christian theology of liberation to be servants of the black community's liberation process, theology and church must debunk these false theological myths and religious beliefs of racism.

The second form of racism discloses the white liberal element in South Africa. In this instance Goba identifies the culpability of the multiracial church. The white liberal Christians in this church display an incrustation of hypocrisy and paternalism. They call for black and white together in their multiracial ecclesial gatherings. But, Goba believes, whites merely want to assuage their own consciences.[18]

Having characterized these two forms of racism, Goba does not neglect racism's theological implications. Racism exhibits sin, a profound breakdown between God and humanity and among humanity itself. Racism denies that God's creatures embody the *imago dei* and, thus, participate in the divine purpose for liberation. By forcing people to turn away from God and God's purpose, white racism, Goba states, insults God. Accordingly, the only way to witness in faith to God and realize a liberated common humanity between black and white in South Africa is to destroy the demon of white racism.[19]

Beyond the target of racism, Goba envisions a liberated South Africa providing justice, peace and full humanity for the oppressed black community. In particular, he singles out the land issue. The white colonial and missionary settlers stole the indigenous population's land. Today black people inhabit only thirteen percent of the worst areas in their own country. For Goba, one cannot talk about liberation from socio-economic problems without addressing the land conflict. Besides, and more important from a theological viewpoint, land represents the sacred to the black community. Goba asserts:

We are also becoming aware as an oppressed people that [land] must be given very high priority in our theology especially because land to us black Africans has a sacred character. It is closely associated with deep religious ties that we have with our ancestors.[20]

Hence the struggle for the new humanity and the liberated South Africa centers on the reclamation of stolen and holy land for black people.

To attain liberation, Goba propounds the black community's right to self-determination. He articulates the necessity "for the black Christian community to set up its own agenda and priorities" apart from white Christians. He dismisses the charge of advocating racial polarization and grounds self-determination in the distinctions between the oppressed (the victims) and the oppressor (the victimizers). Specifically, he calls on the black community (the victim) to formulate a black united front for liberation. Goba justifies the front with features from the African inner religious tradition. For instance, kinship and corporate personality dictate that blacks come together as one body to fight for their freedom against racism and for land and a new black humanity. Moreover, to uphold the principle of self-determination, reflected in corporate personality, makes real the black community's God-endowed black dignity in the eyes of God.[21]

Finally, Goba situates his entire liberation project on a theological foundation. Liberation then becomes a divine imperative resulting from God's calling to black South Africa to forge an emancipating corporate personality out of the church's ministry to the world. Goba writes: "Black ministry is that response to God's call to participate in this liberating activity in the world."[22] Thus black liberation for the ministry of the church and the success of an African Christian theology of liberation hinges on divine vocation.

ITUMELENG J. MOSALA

Historical Materialism

Mosala, an ordained Methodist, teaches biblical studies and black theology at the University of Cape Town. He is also a major leader of the Black Theology Project in Johannesburg. I cite his theology as a Historical Materialist Black Theology of Liberation.

> Aware of the limitations of the Western, liberal sociological tradition, a historical-materialist sociological approach has become the basis for a black theology of liberation.[23]

A historical materialist black theology of liberation examines all societies from the internal development of class formations and class relations. Classes arise, Mosala avows, in response to the manifestations of specific economic systems in specific stages of human history. Moreover, all religions and theologies are inextricably tied to historical periods of class society. Consequently all theologies connect themselves to the material reality of certain periods in history; thus a historical materialist theology.

Similar to Goba, Mosala critiques white missionary and liberal theologies, but from another angle. Mosala fights adamantly for a historical materialist theology because he perceives the danger of idealism inherent in white missionary and white liberal discourses. He believes

> Christianity has been saddled with an idealist methodology. Simply put, idealism is that intellectual framework which separates ideas, beliefs, ideologies from the concrete historical society. It fails to see causal connections between consciousness and material reality.[24]

Idealism mistakenly advocates the rule of ideas and universal principles over material reality. Because of this false primacy of thought forms, the idealist method deduces social and material relations from the Idea. Accordingly, theological notions of God, salvation and history hang statically suspended from society and supposedly affect the nature of society. Hence in Mosala's view, idealism negates the particularity of society, history, "cultural bias" and class interests and, therefore, subverts the dynamic impact of material reality on theology and religion in distinct historical epochs.

In addition to the idealism of white missionary and white liberal theologies, Mosala devises his black theology against "contextual theology" — an instrument "of ideological manipulation." He lambastes contextual theology on three accounts. First, contextual theology implies that theology by definition is harmless and even liberating. Under such false premises the theologian merely has to grasp a non-political contextual theology and apply it to a situation, thus rendering theology political. However, the theologian fails to realize that Western Christian theology's context acts as a religious version of "capitalist ruling class ideology." Second, Mosala rejects contextual theology because of its social class origins. It appeals to white and privileged theologians and not to black, oppressed people. The white and privileged prefer the general and not the particular nomenclature of black theology. Third and finally, Mosala charges contextual theology with theoretical bankruptcy. To do theology out of a context is nothing new. All theologies grow out of social contexts. Again, Mosala attacks contextual theology for sanitizing the white oppressors' theology by not specifying a black theology of liberation located on the particular side of the oppressed.[25]

White theology, both missionary and liberal, and those black and white "progressive" theologians advocating contextual theology shy away from specifying the particular necessity for a black theology. They prefer to remain on the plane of universalities. White theology speaks of theology abstractly. And black idealists and white "progressives" obscure black theology by hailing a general "contextual" theology. Mosala blames an idealist methodology for this shift away from a black theology. His entire theological effort is motivated by a quest to reassert the centrality and specificity of a materialist *black* theology for the black poor.

Eschewing all forms of idealism, Mosala systematizes the hermeneutic to his historical materialist theology. First he surveys the particular classes in present-day South Africa in order to discover the revolutionary class forces. Here he identifies the black working class and poor peasant masses. Then he calls forth a new "exegetical starting point."

> Black Theology needs a new exegetical starting point if it is to become a material force capable of gripping the black working class and peasant masses. . . . The social, cultural, political and economic world of the black working class and peasantry constitutes the only valid hermeneutical starting point for a Black Theology of liberation.[26]

Mosala's emphasis on the class content of theology marks a development within those South African black theologians who still *link* black theology to Black Consciousness. Agreeing with Goba, Mosala maintains that "Black Theology is actually the theological version of black consciousness" and these two cannot be separated.[27] But a historical materialist black theology of liberation propels black theology further (a) to specify the political economy of apartheid, and (b) to name the poor in the black liberation movement so that they will not remain faceless and nameless and, thereby, lose out to other privileged class forces.

Sources

Mosala constructs his historical materialist black theology from four sources. First, African traditional religions teach today's black theology the importance of functioning communally in the struggle. In particular, communalism mandates a collective lifestyle among members of the black community and not an individualistic way of life. Also, African traditional religions worship a God who is "terrifyingly present" in the human struggle for survival. Put differently, indigenous religions teach the decisive need for black people to fight for liberation as a unit alongside a God of liberation.

Further, Mosala defines African traditional religions as part of culture. However he does not speak of a general culture of indigenous religions. Following his historical materialist hermeneutic, he dissects the material basis of indigenous religions into two historical periods: primitive African communal society, and African feudal socio-economic relations. To grasp the significance of African traditional religions today, one has to ponder the role of culture in these two "pre-capitalist social formations." Thus the revolutionary theological worldview for contemporary black struggle emerges out of the specific oppressed classes, as opposed to the reactionary classes, in these two historical cultural epochs. From its lessons in culture "African traditional religions can make a lasting contribution."[28]

Since culture includes more than African traditional religions, it too serves as a theological source. Indeed, Mosala employs a cultural category derived from the everyday black experience.

> There are things to find in the culture. But culture can be progressively appropriated in the interest of the struggle, in the interest of building a black theological weapon of struggle. . . . Because for me [black culture] is the mechanism that people develop as an on-going self-defense mechanism . . . on a day to day basis to produce and reproduce their life.[29]

More exactly, when Mosala "progressively" engages a culture of "people," he pinpoints the culture of the black working class and peasant people. At this juncture "Black Theology . . . will have to rediscover black working class and poor peasant culture in order to find for itself a materialist hermeneutical starting point" in the fight against the apartheid state. Similar to African traditional religions, Mosala's historical materialist theological analysis of social formations compels him to designate the culture of the most oppressed classes even within the black liberation movement.[30] Drawing one's hermeneutic from the poor's culture, Mosala attests, prevents the black theologian's entrapment in "ruling class" ideology and theology.

African Independent Churches, the third source, furnish Mosala with the location of black working-class and peasant culture. Paralleling the black American and South African ecclesial situations, Mosala asserts that an important area

> which black theology needs to address seriously and concerning which lessons from both sides of the Atlantic must be drawn is that of the black working class culture. The black churches in the U.S.A. and especially the African Independent Churches in South Africa provide a wealth of resources in this regard.[31]

Mosala, however, criticizes current studies of African Independent Churches for employing a liberal anthropological approach that underscores the static category of "Africanness." In his judgment black theology of liberation should avoid "Africanness" or "African culture" in order to adhere to a historical, materialist, "socio-cultural" interpretation of both (a) the pre-cultural history of the black working class, and (b) the contemporary conditions in the townships and rural areas. Such a study would contribute a dynamic basis for theological reflection on the emancipatory elements in African Independent Churches.

From their own distinct experience in the African Independent Churches, black migrant workers exegete the Bible, the fourth source. In this process the workers contradict the "metaphysical," (idealistic) biblical God of white missionary theology. Again in line with historical materialist theology, Mosala distinguishes class struggle within the Bible itself, clarifying the biblical roots of black theology.

> By the biblical roots of Black Theology it is not implied that the entire Jewish-Christian Bible is on the side of the struggle of the black oppressed people of South Africa. On the contrary . . . there are significant parts of the Bible that militate against the struggle for liberation and are usable as ideological support for maintaining the interests of the ruling class.[32]

To ascertain and appropriate the specific biblical God, then, requires a double mediation, that is, a dialectical interplay between the historical experience of the oppressed classes in the Bible and the historical experience of the black working class and peasants in South Africa. The God found in both historical experiences will be the biblical God of liberation. In the black cultural theology trend Mosala builds on Goba's sources of African traditional religions, particularly the African Independent Churches, everyday black experience and the Bible. But Mosala frames his sources *within* the historical materialist class perspective. For him, this hermeneutical angle is the way toward black liberation.

Liberation

The existence of class struggle between the reactionary ruling class gods (Mosala cites the oppressive regimes of the Davidic-Solomonic monarchies and the conquest narratives) and the liberation God of the oppressed classes necessitates a *liberation of the Bible* itself. Thus a historical materialist black theology of liberation has to discover the whereabouts of the liberation God in the Bible. Unfortunately, claims Mosala, South African black theology has swallowed white missionary and "liberal Western male biblical exegesis" in full. Such a lethal biblical hermeneutic has "to be exposed with all the might that can be mustered."

Mosala takes exception to Allan Boesak's Word of God theology for failing to identify which scriptural texts belong to the oppressive classes and which sub-texts exhibit the emancipatory interests of the oppressed classes.

> What then is meant by the Bible as the "Word of God"? If the Bible is the "Word of God," therefore, the implication is that even the "law and order" God of David and Solomon cannot be the object of criticism in the light of the black experience.[33]

Which God do the black workers and poor peasants worship, "Baal, or El, or Yahweh; the white God or the black God?" According to his historical materialist black theology of liberation, Mosala opts for the "black God."

In addition to the Bible Mosala calls for a *liberation of black theology*. In Mosala's view the initial definition of black theology only allowed black people to do theology. However, as black theology sought accommodation in the white "discursive terrain," black theologians allowed those white liberals and "progressives" who supposedly "thought black" to enter the black theological circle. As a result whites have virtually silenced South African black theology in favor of Latin American liberation theology. For instance, Mosala wants to know the difference between "contextual theology" of liberation and "progressiveness" theology, on the one hand, and the uniqueness of black theology on the other. Hence Mosala sees the need to guard against white racism from both the theological right and theological left.[34]

Mosala's theology also points toward liberation from the *oppressive apartheid economic system*. A historical materialist black theology of liberation, then, specifies the connection between apartheid and the "strategies of capitalist domination." The exploitative South African economy comprises an increased accumulation of wealth for the benefit of the white few in equal proportion to the increased poverty of the majority black population. Accordingly, the black poor suffer from dispossession of their land and the continued capitalist generation of a "reserve army of labor." Mosala insists that any black theology not founded on such a materialist economic analysis will prove "heretical and false prophesy."[35]

Finally, what will shape the contours of the liberated South Africa for Mosala? He supplies insight to this question with his theological position on liberation-reconciliation. Mosala defines reconciliation-liberation in light of reversing black alienation, which is not primarily from white people, but foremost from black people's land, other instruments and means of production, black history, culture, religious traditions and institutions. Therefore liberation from alienation accrues land, and so forth, for black reconciliation, first, and second, for black reconciliation with whites. Such a restitution to that from which blacks have been alienated will lay the groundwork for post-apartheid values of freedom and democracy. In a word, new South Africa unveils social relations based on a biblical understanding of reconciliation-liberation—restitution in the Jubilee year in response to divine imperative.[36]

TAKATSO A. MOFOKENG

Christological Black Theology

Ordained in the black Dutch Reformed Church, Mofokeng teaches theology at the University of South Africa (Pretoria). He is a leader in the Johannesburg Black Theology Project and editor of its journal, *Journal of Black Theology in South Africa*. Mofokeng accepts Goba's focus against "white missionary mentality" and multiracial liberal theology. He also agrees with Mosala's historical materialist approach. Yet Mofokeng discovers a deeper acceptance by blacks of their own suffering. He, therefore, builds his black theology around correcting black people's negative conception of themselves. The weight of suffering, in a sense, has forced blacks to acquiesce to suffering. Mofokeng's direct experience with black suffering in and around his township inspired him to do black theology. He writes about a farm worker who labored all year but "got almost nothing to show to his wife and four kids." Mofokeng saw black children "with tattered clothes playing soccer with a punctured plastic ball." Even as he left his home he looked at "the huge refuse-dumping hill that symbolized [blacks'] status as dumped people right in the middle of the township."[37]

Due to the pressing nature of black suffering, he formulates a Christological Black Theology of Liberation. Among the cultural theologians he sees the key to liberation with a black Christology. In *The Crucified Among the Crossbearers: Towards a Black Christology*, the foundational inquiry guiding his entire theological project seeks to answer one question: "How can faith in Jesus Christ empower black people who are involved in the struggle for liberation?"[38]

Why does black Christology become the plumb line in Mofokeng's theology? For Mofokeng, the black South African people suffer profound alienation from themselves as a result of a stultifying debasement of their black humanity. Prolonged dehumanization has effected a disintegration of black personality and community. Consequently, blacks experience alienation from their culture, history and land; all of which maintain their community intact. The institutionalized suffering from this alienation has forced blacks into a warped comprehension of Jesus Christ's suffering in relation to black suffering. Accordingly, blacks accept constant torture and death normatively, because, in their mistaken opinion, their prototype Jesus Christ likewise tolerated torture and death. Somewhat rephrased, blacks witness to the crucified among the crossbearers by accepting their own oppression. This incorrect perception of the cross forces blacks to conclude their Christian faith "in paralysis on the cross at Golgotha." Thus the resurrection disappears from blacks' theological encounter and faith.

Having pictured the ceaseless alienation from black culture, history and land, and the attendant self-deprecating Christology, Mofokeng underscores the issue at stake.

> The concrete issue is the creation and growth of the black human person who can be the acting subject of his own history of liberation that is in progress.

Yet how does Mofokeng envision the realization of the new black subject for liberation? Continuing, he describes how black South African experiences

> present a negative picture of the situation, a negative situation that can be changed only when the black man accepts the negativity of his situation, faces it and transforms it into a positive instrument of liberation. This means accepting the cross and the history of the cross, bearing it and moving toward the future that is made different from the present by engagement.[39]

A negative Christological anthropology of tolerated suffering converts into an instrument of liberation by way of accepting the particularity of black Christological negativity, bearing this oppressive cross, but moving toward an eschatological reality out of blacks' struggling in the present. In Mofokeng's assessment Jesus' historical incarnation—both crucifixion and resurrection—serves as the paradigm for transforming and mediating the negative cross into the positive cross of liberation. In other words, Jesus' liberating incarnation vivifies and, thereby, coincides with the actualization of God's creation of a liberated black subject in the subject's own liberated history.

Here Mofokeng presents a dialectic between creation and liberation of the black subject. As the alienated black subject hangs on its cross, Jesus suffers on the cross with this subject. However, the grace of the resurrection renders faith that the black cross will not last always. In fact, the resurrection comforts the suffering of the black crucifixion, provides hope in the future, and more important, drives the oppressed community forward in the praxis of liberation. Hence God in Jesus' incarnation empowers blacks to fight the negativity of their alienation and, through this fight, creates a new black subject of history. The created black subject, furthermore, undertakes this journey toward liberation as a "self-creating and self-liberating subject."[40] In brief, the alienated black subject undergoes Christologically created liberation.

For Mofokeng, a Christological black theology of this created, alienated and liberated black subject evolves strictly within the theological parameters of black consciousness. He discounts any general or neutral theologies in South Africa. Following black consciousness thought and paralleling Goba and Mosala, he contends that either one does black theology of the oppressed or white theology of the oppressor. In fact, Mofokeng perceives a "peculiar relationship between Black Consciousness and Black Theology. Black consciousness is a philosophy and praxis of Black Liberation inseparably united with Black Theology."[41] Thus black consciousness, in Mofokeng's lens, acts as black theology's dialogical partner, epistemological informant, philosophical framework and programmatic praxis.

Sources

Because Mofokeng articulates such an intrinsic link between black consciousness and black theology, the former is the first source of his theology, which is defined by his Christology. Not only does he integrate black consciousness and black theology dialogically, epistemologically, philosophically and programmatically, but Mofokeng also discovers Christological import in black consciousness.

> Black Consciousness as the birth of the new black subject has a character of negation as its first manifestation. The present situation and the value system of the whites are rejected. . . . In doing this [rejection, blacks] become subjects that do not react but respond to the situation that surrounds them.[42]

Paralleling the cross-resurrection incarnation of Jesus Christ, black consciousness, likewise, creates a black subject for liberation. Black consciousness empowers alienated blacks to negate their negativity, to become acting subjects of their own history. Through negation comes a pro-active black humanity, which self-creates and self-liberates à la Jesus' incarnation. In a sense, for Mofokeng, Christology is black consciousness and black consciousness is Christology.

In addition, black consciousness acts upon black history, the second source. Black consciousness targets black history because whites have alienated black people from their indigenous history by causing suffering, defeat and humiliation. At the same time white theology has "demonized" black history; white God-talk disdainfully depicted the "justified" defeat of a black heathen people at the hands of a liberating (white) Christianity. "Dynamiting" this alienated condition, black consciousness offers a new outlet through which black people can become one with their past. Therefore black consciousness radically alters negative history into a positive historical praxis of liberation. At this point Mofokeng clarifies the subject of black history. He prefers not to limit the makers of black history to certain "African personalities." On the contrary, black consciousness unearths black history to reveal the real bearers of liberated history: the poor masses at the bottom. Like Mosala, Mofokeng specifies black workers and peasants.

Similar to the experience of black history, black consciousness energizes black culture, the third source. Black consciousness confronts an imperiled black culture and, in a healing and reconciling Christological function, transfigures negative culture into its liberating components of "black solidarity" and "corporate understanding" of black cultural humanity. Black consciousness, then, yields revolutionary elements for the black liberation movement. Here too, as with black history, Mofokeng wishes to underline the particular culture of the black poor.

Mofokeng criticizes both Manas Buthelezi and Allan Boesak for ignoring the importance of culture in doing black theology. Buthelezi, Mofokeng states, "explicitly and emphatically" asserted the total destruction of black culture. Over against these two members of the black political theology trend, Mofokeng sides with Steve Biko, who, in Mofokeng's view, recognized the existence of a damaged but thriving black culture.[43]

With the fourth source, the Bible, Mofokeng distances himself from Allan Boesak's scriptural interpretation. Mofokeng writes:

> Allan Boesak, taking an orthodox Calvinist stand, would like to dispute the legitimacy of the reciprocal meaningfulness between scripture and praxis. To us the praxis of liberation is not totally devoid of effective light because of the presence of Jesus Christ in the struggle of his "little ones."[44]

What is at stake for Mofokeng? He does not wish to remove Jesus from the everyday struggle of the black poor and thereby obviate the poor's privileged relation with scripture based on their intimate Christological interaction. And so, Mofokeng thinks (like Itumeleng Mosala) that a word of God theology tends to blur reciprocity between text and context. In brief, the light shines both ways: from the Bible to the black poor's praxis (accompanied by Jesus' liberating praxis) and from the poor's praxiological encounter with the Liberator back to the Bible.

Black people also endured alienation from their land, the fifth and final source. Loss of land at the hands of white missionaries and settlers, for Mofokeng, intimates theological importance. Black South Africans communed with their land, the basis of their God-given self-respect and creativity. They regarded land as the mother of all people and creation. Here he suggests a maternal theological attribute; land "carries, cares and feeds all people."[45] Therefore, the development of a Christological black theology to reconstitute the black subject requires an engagement with the feminist and fecund religious elements of land. Mofokeng echoes the black cultural trend's concern with the land's sacredness. Yet he adds the feminine aspect to the discussion.

Liberation

Mofokeng desires both a theological and psychological liberation for the black subject. Theologically white theologians have been fighting on a "battle-ground" to achieve a fatal "theological dehumanization of blacks." In particular they propagate the erroneous notion that black people lack worth in God's creation. White theologians, Mofokeng surmises, represent their white oppressor class and black theologians, newly arrived in combat, espouse the theological humanization of the oppressed black class. Psychologically the conditions of material oppression have lodged a perception of black inferiority in the minds of blacks and whites. For example, white missionary and colonial devastation of black culture, history and religion has reached such a degree that it has created a black non-subject with "a hollow mind," capable of accepting white authority and white values. Hence liberation strives toward black humanization on both theological and psychological planes.

In addition, in the new society Mofokeng advocates liberation of the land from white control to achieve black people's humanity. A struggle to recover the land pervades the entire history of black alienation. In fact, so intimate is the relation between blacks and their land that land connotes black self-love, life and ontology. Mofokeng writes:

> In South Africa black people's expression of love for themselves ... includes a struggle to recover their land. This is the theme that recurs incessantly in different forms right through the entire history of black South Africans. . . . Why is land included in the realization of the black people's humanity?. . . It is the vital and essential part of the being of black people. . . . There is, in other words, an identity of life and of the means of life.[46]

Furthermore, the refusal to restore blacks' land indicates a blasphemy against God; a sin against both God's creation (the new black subject) and God's gift (the land) to God's creation. For God intended a new society of a reclaimed land wherein black people, particularly the poor, would communally share ownership and equally distribute the fruits of the land.

Precisely in this communal community Mofokeng discovers black people offering joyful praises to God in Jesus Christ for the gift of freedom to be human. Thus communal liberation on the land facilitates a correct doxological connectedness with the divine. And in this communal way of life and worship the "old man," the negativeness of blackness, dies and the new black humanity is born on the land.[47] Moreover, through dependence on and dedication to Jesus Christ's living incarnation, that is, death and resurrection, the negativity of blackness becomes a re-creation — a liberated black birth, life and praxis out of the black subject's own death and resurrection. Only in communal activity can Jesus Christ facilitate achieving and maintaining a liberated land.

Finally, in the movement toward the new society who constitutes the appropriate agency for liberation in Mofokeng's Christological black theology? In a strong identification with black consciousness philosophy Mofokeng assigns human agency only to black people. For him, all white people belong to the oppressor class and blacks belong to the oppressed class. Thus, exercising their right to self-determination in national liberation, black people "are the only people who can create a new society" not based on race or color.

In addition to positing the vanguard role of blacks in national liberation, Mofokeng acknowledges a shift in the definition within the black human agency. Instead of a general category of "all" black people, he considers the black working class to embody the new subject of a non-alienated liberated history. Dispossessed of their sacred land, black people have been forced into the primary class of dispossessed workers.[48] The new black subject, then, bears the imprint of the black working class leading the entire national liberation movement toward God's gift — the holy land.

DESMOND M. TUTU

Tutu, the last representative of the black cultural theology trend, served as the former and first black general secretary of the South African Council of Churches and received the 1984 Nobel Peace Prize. Currently he acts in the capacity of the first black Anglican Archbishop of Cape Town and president of the All Africa Conference of Churches. He is the only black South African churchperson to have a book of essays published in his honor.

Relational Black Theology

Resonating with others in the cultural theological trend, Tutu attacks the assault on African indigenous values. For him, black Africans underwent a Europeanization process in which Western values projected themselves *ipso facto* as superior and with global validity. The elevation of missionary and colonial values simultaneously brought a denigration of "things African, and by definition, therefore of things black." Tutu credits this western disparaging of African-black values with fueling the growth of a necessary black consciousness movement.

Moreover, the equation of Western, missionary values with universal truth also impacted the theological enterprise. In missionary theology, Tutu continues,

> black was the colour of the devil, white the colour of angels, of Jesus Christ, and perhaps even of God. The black races were devoid of light, wallowing in the gloomy darkness of ignorance and superstition. If you started from this premise, then your missionary policy was logically mapped out for you.[49]

White missionaries, therefore, denied any religious truths or values in Africa prior to the Christian era. For Tutu, this disavowal of primordial indigenous African theological beliefs desecrates biblical proclamation, which states that nowhere does God not have a witness.

Tutu's dismissal of white missionary theological claims of European universality allows him, then, to focus on the particularity of an African or black theology. In his view theology, of necessity, reflects on the experience of a specific Christian community in relation to God's work through Jesus Christ in that community. Questioning black theology's methodological intent, Tutu asks:

> Does black theology now appear to lay claim to a universality which it has been so quick to condemn in others? No, it joyously celebrates its particularity.[50]

Again adhering to biblical proclamation, Tutu bases his particularistic black theology on a scriptural paradigm. The Exodus story, he asserts, reveals that a liberating God is always heeding the anguished cries of particular oppressed communities. On this point he unites with other cultural theologians' demand for a specific black theology.

Given Tutu's theological concerns, how would one characterize his overall theological approach? In my judgment, Tutu devises a Relational Black Theology. Instead of an either-or hermeneutic, he opts for a both-and interpretation, which shows complementarity and relationality. Specifically he attempts to avoid pitting black theology against African theology, and the former two against liberation theology. For him all three work together synonymously. For example, although he uses black theology's prophetic inclination to criticize African theology's one-sided interest in a "static" African culture, nonetheless, Tutu establishes a complementary relation between the two theologies. As a South African, Tutu states, he represents black theology; as a son of the Continent, he signifies African theology. For him black theology is "an aspect of African theology." He handles the mutual relation between black and liberation theologies in a similar way. Liberation theology struggles to answer the theodicy question: Why do the poor agonize in organized oppression and exploitation? Within the particular South African context, Tutu argues, black theology, "which is a theology of liberation in Africa," measures the depths of the tormented black poor's existence.[51]

Liberation

Tutu's relational black theology follows a relational hermeneutic both in its *method* toward liberation and in its *goal* for a liberated South Africa. Methodologically Tutu condones (a) the black consciousness' right of self-determination precept, that is, the right of oppressed blacks to disengage from whites. At the same time, he advocates (b) reconciliation between the races in South Africa. How does Tutu negotiate a seemingly contradictory position? For him, the right of self-determination complements reconciliation. Black consciousness' separation policy must succeed, claims Tutu, because it actualizes the worth of a black person as a "child of God" who can live without white tutelage. Having gained the right to determine its own destiny, the black community can, then, reconcile with the whites on an equal basis in the movement toward liberation.

In addition to establishing the methodological relation between the right of self-determination and reconciliation, Tutu's theology contains a black-white relational dimension in the goal of liberation. He understands (a) black liberation as the relational complement for (b) white liberation. Tutu believes that God sides with and liberates the oppressed blacks. Yet blacks involve themselves in the liberation movement because they "are also deeply concerned for white liberation." In other words, no one in South Africa will achieve the goal of liberation *until* blacks attain emancipation by exercising "their God-given personhood and humanity." At the same time, while calling blacks to freedom,

> the Gospel of Jesus Christ also calls to limitless forgiveness . . . as participation in the divine economy of salvation.[52]

Briefly put, the goals of black and white liberation complement one another. Though Tutu believes in white liberation through the forgiveness generated by black liberation's "participation in the divine economy of salvation," he never sanctions a cheap forgiveness. On the contrary, in its pardon of white oppression black liberation does not rule out militant confrontation and demands repentance in order for white liberation to materialize; for Jesus Christ, in his own pardon to both liberate and unite humanity, died on the cross.[53]

Further pursuing his relational hermeneutic in the goal of a liberated South Africa, Tutu affirms the following: The new society will (a) halt the stealing of black people's land and allow them to enjoy political and human rights on the land. Still, a liberated South Africa, Tutu submits, will also be (b) "a non-racial South Africa for all of us black and white together."[54] He discovers a scriptural basis for the complementary goal of black ownership of land and a non-racial society. On the one hand black freedom results from the biblical God's grace in creation and not from the whims of whites; on the other hand the same God of black liberation proclaims unity and one humanity as the "heart of the Christian message." On the one hand the *imago dei* expresses the inalienable right of black freedom; on the other hand God created all humanity for fellowship with God and fellow humanity.[55] Thus Tutu, adhering to his relational interpretation, structures a complementary approach in both the method toward and the goal of liberation.

Sources

Tutu's relational black theology grounds itself completely in the Bible, the first source. "Whatever black theology delivers," writes Tutu,

> should be consistent with scripture, with what we discern of God in the face of Jesus Christ. But it must communicate this meaningfully to those whom it is primarily addressing—the blacks.[56]

A relational black theology assumes its rationale precisely in scripture. For instance, in my judgment, the reason Tutu can allege he represents black theology, African theology and liberation theology is because he assumes the Bible reveals a biased God on the side of the poor. Therefore, because all three theologies in some manner dwell on the status of the oppressed, marginalized and outcast, Tutu accepts them as portrayals of the "theme of setting free," which "runs through the Bible as a golden thread."[57] As long as these three theologies touch on the plight of poor blacks and thereby maintain the principal biblical work of God in Jesus Christ, liberation, they delimit Tutu's theological enterprise.

Tutu also molds his relational black theology out of the "African soil," the second source, to heal the damage inflicted by white theology. As a travesty to the biblical witness and at the expense of negating indigenous sources, white missionary theology forced black Christians into a state of "religious schizophrenia." The white man's "cerebral religion," Tutu professes, barely touched the African soul, redeemed Africans from sins that they had not committed, and posed questions that they had not asked. To rectify white missionary theological errors, Africans

> are now looking to our own spiritual and cultural resources, to our own value systems. There must be a radical decolonisation in cultural

and spiritual matters as there has been in the political. . . .
[Theological education] must become authentically African.[58]

Therefore Tutu relies on the "African soil" and African ways of communion with God to shape his theology. Following the cultural trend,
and particularly Goba, Tutu sees the African "Weltanschauung" in complete compatibility with the Old and New Testaments. Specifically, the
African worldview resonates with the Old Testament's belief in the corporateness of community, including, Tutu asserts, linkages back to the
ancestors and forward to the generations not yet born. The community
envelopes the individual; that is, communal participation designates individual religious ontology. Hence, the "summum bonum" is not independence, Tutu explicates, but sharing and interdependence. Capitalism,
unfortunately, facilitates a negation of this African thought form. Tutu
states:

> I lay great stress on humanness and being truly human. In our African
> understanding, part of Ubantu—being human—is the rare gift of
> sharing. . . . Blacks are beginning to lose this wonderful attribute, be-
> cause we are being inveigled by the excessive individualism of the
> West. I loathe Capitalism because it gives far too great play to our
> inherent selfishness.[59]

Furthermore, Tutu believes that the African theological worldview may
be too "dramatic for verbalization" and, consequently, pertinent only as
communicated in African dance and song. From such a theological representation one can detect African corporateness in opposition to Western
individualism, wholeness in opposition to Hellenistic dichotomies of soul
and body, the reality of the spiritual in opposition to the poverty of the
material, and the awesomeness of the transcendent in opposition to diffidence about the almighty King.[60]

Finally Tutu looks toward black American achievements, a third source.
More specifically, he hails black North American progress in sports, films
and black magazines for conveying to black South Africans a sense of God-
given somebodiness. Though oppressed, black Americans succeeded in certain areas; this success inspires black South Africans to acknowledge the
inherent divine gift in their ontology. Tutu describes how black American
achievement made

> a theological statement. It was saying that these whom you see de-
> picted there have the imago dei. That these too are created in the
> image of God and if they are created in the image of God they too
> are God's representatives and if they are God's representatives then
> we [black South Africans] in spite of all that was happening and still

happens to us, we too are children of God . . . partners in helping God to establish his kingdom.[61]

In brief, the complementary relation between black American and black South African struggles and accomplishments provides Tutu with resources for doing a relational black theology in South Africa. With these resources black South Africans can rightfully affirm their intended co-partner status with divinity on the way toward creating the kingdom.

Assessment

The black cultural theology trend notes the importance of black culture and sacred land. It sees the profound, harmful implications of "white missionary" theology. It understands how white South African society has a negative impact on black psychology. Therefore the cultural theologians build on indigenous resources to establish a positive black mind-set and link this to black liberation. They draw on the liberating elements in African traditional religions and the African Independent Churches. To develop a total liberating black theology all religious traditions have to be pulled together. Furthermore, they struggle for a proper relation between the total black community's racial oppression and the effects of poor blacks' class exploitation. These theologians are right in introducing the dialectical interplay between God's liberation in the Bible and God's liberation among the black poor. Christ's liberation in the Bible and Christ's liberation among oppressed blacks is a back-and-forth critique and complement. Here Mosala's hermeneutic leads the way. The cultural advocates also speak to the theological necessity for black self-determination. Finally, and justifiably so, they lift up the importance of keeping the designation "black theology." As long as a white minority has privileges and as long as God continues to bless blacks with the *imago dei*, the cultural theologians perceive a specifically *black* theology.

At the same time the black cultural theology trend shows several weaknesses. First, this trend is clear on black reconciliation among blacks. But it needs to describe more exactly the dynamic between liberation-reconciliation and white people. How should blacks relate to whites under apartheid? On what conditions and how does one implement black-white reconciliation? If black reconciliation comes first, what roles do whites play in the reconciliation process? Do whites actively involve themselves in the liberation movement while blacks are first reconciling themselves? It seems to me that theologically the oppressed black community has the right to attain its God-given humanity as a victimized people. Poor blacks, as the site where Jesus Christ operates, determine the conditions for white people's participation. As long as whites adhere to the theological principle of the right of black self-determination and the poor determining the means of their liberation, then the beginning of a black-white reconciliation process is possible prior to complete overthrow of the sinful apartheid system.

Finally, though the cultural theologians point out the theological significance of black culture, they have not consistently done black theology from their own indigenous resources. For example, they generally lack theological ingredients such as black songs, poetry, folklore, sermons, language or literature. From these black primary sources, an authentic black liberation theology will emerge. One has to dig deeper into the black reality to break with the white missionary way of theologizing. What are the specific contours of black culture and life in the townships and rural and urban areas? And how do these contours inform the liberation essence of black theology?

CONCLUSION

We have examined both South African political and cultural theological trends and black North American political and cultural theological persuasions. Thus we have accomplished our intent: to view the internal dialogical contrasts between the political and cultural theological trends inside black theology in the United States and black theology in South Africa. American theologians have some feel for the political-cultural issues in South Africa; South Africans have a comparable exposure of American political-cultural theology. So far the interlocutors have engaged in intracontinental contrasts. In the next chapter the black theological interlocutors will come from each side of the Atlantic. We can engage the two countries in a comparative intercontinental theological dialogue.

Part IV

DIALOGUE AND THE FUTURE

CHAPTER SIX

Black Theology in the USA and South Africa: What Can They Say to Each Other?

We depend on you [black Americans]. We depend on you because our liberation is your liberation. As long as we are unfree — to that extent you are going to be unfree [in the USA]. And let me say to you, there is no doubt we are going to be free.

Archbishop Desmond Tutu, 1984

My trip to South Africa ... deepened my convictions about liberation being at the center of the gospel. ... For in Jesus' cross and resurrection the reality of death has been encountered and defeated. But since the full manifestation of that victory is still to come, we must bear witness now to God's coming liberation. ... This is the message of hope I heard preached and saw in the lives of South Africa's black Christians.

James H. Cone, 1986

The previous intracontinental comparisons of political and cultural theological trends allow us now to place black theology in the United States (BTUSA) and black theology in South Africa (BTSA) in dialogue. What has been the history of the dialogue; what theological issues have emerged from the discussion; and how do we critically assess these concerns?

This chapter analyzes one direct theological engagement, a conference called specifically for BTUSA and BTSA exchange, and several indirect encounters. Because the two theological discussants have only held one formal BTUSA-BTSA session, I create potential dialogue out of indirect discussions. By indirect, I mean situations in which North American and South African blacks present their theological positions at conferences or in books that are *not* called or written to explicitly and exclusively engage BTUSA and BTSA. For example, the presence of USA and/or South Af-

147

rican theologians at African theology conferences is considered indirect contact. Similarly books on black theology written only by one member of the USA-South African interlocutors are likewise classified as indirect.

More specifically, the first formal BTUSA-BTSA conference occurred December 1-3, 1986, at Union Theological Seminary in New York City.[1] However, previous *indirect* contact between both theologies took place in the context of meetings on black theology in the United States and African theology, that is, theology for the entire African continent, in the context of South African black theology seminars in 1971, and in Allan Boesak's first book. Therefore, to weigh critically the similarities and dissimilarities of the two theologies, we will review both indirect and direct dialogical encounters. Here our main interest is to evaluate not so much the discussions within each country (as exhibited in Chapters 2 through 5), but the points of contact and tension across the Atlantic.

INDIRECT DIALOGUE: 1971-77

Tanzania, 1971

The first occasion for indirect dialogue between BTUSA and BTSA transpired within the initial conference on black theology and African theology held in Dar Es Salaam, Tanzania, in August 1971. The Africa Commission of the National Committee of Black Churchmen and the Christian Council of Tanzania sponsored a week-long consultation with the theme "Black Identity and Solidarity—The Role of the Church as a Medium for Social Change."[2] The conference marked the first time in contemporary black church history that blacks and Africans had talked face-to-face without a white missionary go-between. Twenty-eight black Americans and sixteen Africans focused mainly on three issues: economic development, education and theology.[3]

James Cone's and Gayraud Wilmore's theological input in Tanzania directly touch our purpose. Cone and Wilmore, premier representatives of USA political and cultural theological trends respectively, collaborated on a joint presentation. Among other emphases we can deduce their establishment of two levels. First, they demarcated BTUSA from BTSA; and second, Wilmore and Cone outlined major points of unity with both political and cultural theological trends in BTSA.

Regarding the differences in the black experience in the United States and in Africa, including South Africa, Cone and Wilmore write:

> In the United States it has been a minority experience, separated, for the most part, from the ownership of land, from a discrete tribal language and culture, and from a living, historical memory.[4]

With their description of the whole of Africa, they also specifically point out the uniqueness of South Africa in contrast to the USA black reality. Resuming this contextual distinction, they continue:

> Even where Direct Rule was administrated . . . under brutally repressive regimes, such as . . . the Republic of South Africa, there was for the White man always the pervasive, overwhelming reality of the vast and alien land and the conspicuousness of an indigenous people who had latent power to resist foreign acculturation and swallow up the transplanted White civilization in the bowels of blackness.[5]

Despite white supremacist theology, black people in South Africa possess the capacity, as a majority population, to flex their sheer numbers and "swallow up" the non-indigenous white race in the "bowels of blackness." On the other hand, and because of white supremacist theology, black Americans suffer from the possibility of genocide in their minority status. It is these divergences in majority-minority societal stations, indigeneity-lack of indigeneity to the land, a continuity to a distinct African culture, ancestry and tribal language versus a black American ontological schizophrenia (tugged both by an Africanness and an Americanness) that condition the contrasts in the development of black theology in the United States and in South Africa.

At the same time, Wilmore and Cone elaborate major theological affinities between BTUSA and BTSA (within African theology overall). They enunciate similarities germane to both political and cultural theological trends. Theologically, they depict one's *knowledge of God* deriving from neither "mystical communion" nor "abstract rational thought." On the contrary, God renders knowledge of God's self through revelation in history in the liberation of the oppressed. Through faith, the poor recognize that their deliverance from stultifying bondage executes the Divine teleology, penultimately and ultimately. To know God, then, is to have faith in God's doing justice toward liberation.

Wilmore and Cone's *constructive definitional* task of black theology also parallels that of their black counterparts in South Africa. In the United States, they contend, black theology bursts forth in response to the existential predicament of black "folk in the ghetto." Poor black folk yearn for knowledge of God's relation to their suffering, joy, self-perception and quandary under the heel of American white racism. To construct an authentic black theology, therefore, one begins at the bottom with the "least of these" (Mt 25:31ff.). Likewise Desmond Tutu, the first contemporary black South African theologian to dialogue with black theologians in the United States offers a similar definitional and constructive project.

> Black theology is a gut level theology, relating to the real concerns, the life and death issues of the black man. . . . Black theology seeks

to make sense of black suffering at the hands of white racism and to understand this in the light of what God has said about himself, about man, and about the world.[6]

Continuing with other theological themes in common between BTUSA and BTSA, Wilmore and Cone touch on *Christology*. They present a thoroughly incarnational God in Christ who does not bring false tidings of neutrality or an impotent passivity. Rather, Jesus Christ, the "Incarnation of God," assumes an active role as the Oppressed One waging war for liberation. In Christ's revelation the poor witness God's doing justice and also the divine imperative to pick up their cross and follow Christ in the movement toward liberation. Furthermore, Cone and Wilmore link Christology to *anthropology*. If Christ manifests God's incarnation among the oppressed and black people represent the "least of these," then the presence of blacks symbolizes God's presence among the oppressed throughout the land. Thus black anthropology designates divine value. At this point, one detects Cone's precise insight and particular contribution in redefining the core of Christianity and anthropology as liberation.

Finally, Cone and Wilmore espouse the *sources* unique to black theology. With this theological dimension they elevate the centrality of BTUSA's foundation in traditional African religions,[7] the African-Christian syncretistic religion of black slaves yearning for freedom, and the black poor folk religion of the ghetto. In these formative factors of black theology one can surmise Wilmore's advocacy for the Christian and non-Christian ghetto religious sources as well as Africanisms in the doing of theology. In fact, the joint presentation by Cone and Wilmore exemplifies the unified strands of the political (Cone) and cultural (Wilmore) theological trends in black theology. Therefore, it is fitting that the first indirect contact between BTUSA and BTSA encompasses and unites the parameters that define the differentiation and commonality in the cross Atlantic dialogue.

The First Publication, 1972

The publication of *Essays on Black Theology*[8] occasioned the second opportunity for *indirect* discussion. As the first book on black theology in South Africa, this text represented a collection of papers submitted at various black theology seminars in South Africa throughout 1971. The essays by Manas Buthelezi, Bonganjalo Goba and James Cone will serve to highlight the dialogue.

Buthelezi argues for clarity and exactness as the starting point in black theological methodology. He contrasts the incorrect perspective of the "ethnographic" approach with his more appropriate "anthropological" departure point. Capsulizing his theological position, he writes:

It is possible to distinguish two approaches to indigenous theology in South Africa: the ethnographic and the anthropological. The distinction centres on whether the point of departure in our theological method should be an ethnographic reconstruction of the African past or a dialogue with the present-day anthropological realities in South Africa.[9]

For example, he decries certain black theologians' propensity for such terms as "the African mind" and the "African worldview." Buthelezi would probably characterize both Charles Long's history of religions' concern for myth, symbol and primordial impulses in black religious morphology, and Cecil Cone's reconnection to African religion in his black theology, as bordering on the ethnographic methodological starting point.

However, James Cone's "Black Theology and Black Liberation" in *Essays on Black Theology* would more likely satisfy Buthelezi's anthropological theological bent. Cone advocates the centrality of black folk's political liberation and weaves this liberation theme throughout his sources of black culture, history, black power and scripture. For him, like Buthelezi, black theology attacks the present-day, existential cauldron of being black in "a white racist society."

Goba's article, "Corporate Personality: Ancient Israel and Africa," would also unite with James Cone's contemporary black liberation thrust. But, more important from Goba's view, he would rather not move too quickly into the contemporary black theological challenge, for he values nurturing and drawing deeply from the ancestral instructions. Linking "African time" to corporate personality, he claims:

> For an African time is an ontological phenomenon and pertains to existence or being. An African experiences time partly through the society which goes back many generations before his birth. . . . It is important for us to understand this concept of time in Africa because it is bound up with the concept of corporate personality as it manifests itself in Africa.[10]

Corporate personality and African traditional religions bequeath a profound didactical faith-witness for the struggle for black liberation. And precisely because of this profundity, attests Goba, the intricacies of the religious past, for example, the faith of black foreparents, have to be carefully weighed and sorted out. At this point, where Buthelezi would agree more with James Cone in an anthropological slant, Goba would more readily join hands with the prominence of African religion in Cecil Cone's black theology. For example, Cecil Cone believes that the antebellum African slaves brought their African traditional religions and cultural values to the United States and regulated Christianity with these indigenous beliefs. The Almighty Sovereign God of Africa, in Cecil Cone's theology, completely permeates black Christianity. Similarly Goba situates the "Christian mythos" inside the "African cultural religious milieu." Thus black South Africans used the African cultural environment as a norm to appropriate Western Christianity.

In contrast to both Goba and Buthelezi, James Cone's assertion that black theology "puts black identity in a theological context, showing that Black Power is not only consistent with the gospel of Jesus Christ, but that it is the gospel of Jesus Christ"[11] draws a clear line of demarcation in the dialogue. In particular, Buthelezi's reading of the gospel as well as his black theology of racial fellowship forbid him to negotiate such an equivalency between the gospel and black power. Similarly, though Goba's African Christian theology's excavation of African traditional religions in the service of black liberation does permit a closer parallel with James Cone's stance than Buthelezi's black theological project, nonetheless Goba shies away from an exact equation.

An assessment of this (indirect) dialogue discloses Buthelezi's potential to pit falsely the ethnographic and anthropological methodologies in doing black theology. Granted that his essay assumes the most deleterious exemplars of ethnography as his foil, he fails to delineate the complementary potential of both dimensions in a black theology of liberation. At this point of discussion, James Cone and Goba perceive a more dynamic and integral relation between religious lineage and today's struggle against white racism. Nonetheless, taking all three essays together, the intensity of their silence on black theological perspectives of monopoly capitalism, sexism and penultimate socio-economic relations—that is, black theology's comprehensive social analysis and political economy—calls forth the need for more inclusive components in the cross-Atlantic encounter.

Ghana, 1974

The December 1974 Ghana conference, which focused primarily on black and African theologies, marks the third major context for *indirect* American-South African discussion.[12] However, in June of 1973, in preparation for Ghana, the Society for the Study of Black Religion and the All African Conference of Churches co-sponsored a preliminary exploratory consultation at Union Theological Seminary, New York. This conference was also sponsored by the World Council of Churches' Program to Combat Racism, which was then under the direction of Charles Spivey, an A.M.E. minister. Now an A.M.E. pastor in Chicago, Spivey was also head of the Black Theology Project of Theology in the Americas in 1977. Within this *indirect* preparatory context on black theology and African theology, Desmond Tutu met James Cone, Gayraud Wilmore, Charles Long and other United States' theologians for the first time.[13] Twelve black North Americans and six Africans attended the Union meeting. Differing from the 1971 Tanzania experience, which included participants from diverse professions and covered a wide spectrum of issues, the 1973 Union meeting included only professional theologians who discussed African and black theologies, emphasizing their Christian dimensions.[14]

The Union meeting identified the issues that became the focus for the 1974 Ghana conference. Therefore we will resume our theological chronology by examining the Ghana presentations by Charles Long, James Cone and Desmond Tutu.

We can ferret out several points of BTSA-BTUSA agreement in Tutu's paper: (a) Both theologies arose in reaction against Euro-American Christianity, which failed to distinguish between the Christian faith and Western civilization; (b) like black Americans, Tutu writes, South African blacks had their humanity defined in terms of the "white man"; and (c) both theologies provide trenchant critiques of the West's claim that it typifies "a universal theology." However, Tutu's assumptions about other general features of unity fail to recognize the shades of difference between his black theology and that of his American colleagues.

Specifically, Tutu submits that we "are united willy nilly by our blackness (of all shades). . . . Our blackness is an intractable ontological surd."[15] Yet black theology in the United States displays more subtleties in an understanding of blackness. James Cone, for instance, interrelates the particularity of the blackness of black Americans with the universality of blackness as symbolic of all the oppressed. And J. Deotis Roberts advocates blackness (more specifically a black Christology) for psychological medicinal purposes given the depths of black self-hatred and confusion. Furthermore, Tutu offers black American and African relatedness to "mother Africa" as another consensus point. But here again, he lacks a grasp of the nuances between the American cultural theological trend, which would suggest itself more as Tutu's direct soulmate, and the political theological trend, which demands clarity on the relation of "mother Africa" to current black liberation.

Finally, Tutu states the "third level of unity":

> The third level of unity comes through our baptism and through our membership in the Body of Christ which makes us all His ambassadors and partakers in the ministry of reconciliation. . . . We are compelled to help the white man to correct many of the distortions that have happened to the gospel to the detriment of all.[16]

Admittedly black Americans and black South African theologians come together in the body of Christ (except, of course, William R. Jones). But to declare reconciliation with "the white man" as a unifying dialogical point would have the impact of raising a red flag before a charging bull. Somewhat rephrased, a doctrine of black-white reconciliation pricks deeply at the theological dissonance in BTUSA. Perhaps J. Deotis Roberts would come closest to Tutu's assessment. Still, even Roberts establishes linkages between liberation-reconciliation in a two-pronged approach. Though James

Cone does not negate possible black-white reconciliation, resulting from potential creative changes in the "white oppressor," he stresses black-black reconciliation as a priority. Similarly, he would lean more to first establishing a reconciliation project between blacks and liberation theologies in Africa, Asia and Latin America.[17] In contrast, Albert Cleage is not in favor of any reconciliation with the white Gentile oppressors of the black nation.

In addition to Tutu's paper, Charles H. Long presented points of unity and divergence in the dialogue. Long cites, in my judgment, two important commonalities between his position and that of the cultural theological trend in South African black theology. First, he deciphers the religious structural mode of black American cosmology and attributes this to the African continent. His preoccupation with the indigenous cultural strands in black religious thought matches the South African cultural trend's tenacious pursuit of African cultural resources. Long writes that

> a characteristic mode of orienting and perceiving reality has probably existed [in black Americans descended from Africa]. . . . With the breakdown of the empirical forms of language and religion as determinant for the social group, this persisting structural mode and the common situation as slaves in America may be the basis for the persistence of an African style among the descendents of the Africans.[18]

In particular, Long's position on the specificity of the African worldview parallels Bonganjalo Goba's efforts at constructing a unique African Christian theology.[19] Second, like the South African cultural trend, Long argues for the sacredness of land for black Americans. He maintains that black Americans, despite lacking a conscious memory of Africa, are possessed with the image of Africa related to historical beginnings. This image constitutes highly significant "primordial religious images." Moreover, Long continues, the image of Africa in black America elucidates "the religious revalorization of land." Granting his unity with the South African cultural trend in their views toward land, Long does, at the same time, acknowledge differences.

> The image of Africa as it appears in the religion of Blacks in the United States is unique, for the Black community in America is a landless people . . . unlike Africans in South Africa . . . the land is not occupied by groups whom the Africans consider aliens.[20]

Besides the lingering image of the African land, Long adds the persistence of black America's involuntary presence in the United States as a religious meaning. His handling of this "opaqueness" (negativity) of black reality and the imperative to negate this classification by transforming it into a positive cultural resource echoes the methodology employed in Takatso A. Mofokeng's Christological project. In particular, Long describes the following situation:

> The slave had to come to terms with the opaqueness of his condition and at the same time oppose it. He had to experience the truth of his negativity and at the same time transform and create another reality. . . . Probably Africans in South Africa have some experience of this in a similar manner.[21]

In fact, Mofokeng elaborates a similar necessity for black South Africans to accept the negativity (opaqueness) of their situation, confront it and transform it into a positive weapon for liberation. But, unlike Mofokeng, Long seemingly desires the transformation to unfold in the realm of the religious consciousness; Mofokeng sees the converted negativity driving the black liberation movement forward in attempts to destroy the system of white supremacy.[22]

Finally, in Cone's 1974 presentation at Ghana we can construe an engagement with another South African black theologian, Itumeleng Mosala. But first, a synopsis of Cone's essay is in order. He advances an investigation of how theological conclusions relate to and depend on social contexts. Arguing against and, thereby, unmasking white American theology's affinity with theological idealism, in which systematic thoughts about God appear to fall from the sky without any influence from concrete human struggle, he states:

> Like white American theology, black thought on Christianity has been influenced by its social context. But unlike white theologians, who spoke to and for the culture of the ruling class, black people's religious ideas were shaped by the culture and political existence of the victims in North America.[23]

In my judgment, Cone's position correctly describes a materialist connection between theology and social location. One should not confuse the universal, liberating and normative activity of God with the socially conditioned and oppressive talk about God on the part of white racist theologians. Indeed, cultural and political existence does distinguish the theology of the black victims from that of the white "ruling class." What we do and where we do it in society enormously affect how we think.

Cone's dialectical juxtaposition of social location and imaging of God in large part mirrors Itumeleng J. Mosala's historical materialist black theology of liberation. Like Cone Mosala combats the status quo pathology of idealism in white theological discourse. Like Cone he also places his materialist endeavors in theological conclusions. And like Cone Mosala traces all theological statements to the social conflict between the poor and the rich internal to societies as opposed to doing theology abstractly in the realm of ideas. For instance, Mosala adamantly disavows any God-talk that falsely privileges so-called universal, neutral principles and the rule of ideas over material reality. In fact, Mosala posits, Western Christian theology serves as a religious cover for "capitalist ruling class ideology."[24]

Nonetheless, though Cone and Mosala share a commonality in theological hermeneutics, they radically depart in biblical exegesis. Cone maintains scripture as an unshakeable source in black theology and the black American slave experience. Slaves, Cone asserts with his materialist exegesis, successfully appropriated the liberation paradigm of the poor in the Bible from the exploitative teachings and misuse by the slavemasters, compared this new Christianity with their oppressed situation, and thus felt called to an ethic of black liberation. For Cone scripture is a witness of liberating faith whose central and dominant theme is divine liberation.[25]

More dubious, Mosala will concede that the Bible can be a tool of theological struggle. However, he expresses more diffidence in biblical exegesis because his historical materialist scalpel carves up scripture and at its marrow discovers a ruling-class god and the God of the poor. Furthermore, he hesitates in a blanket endorsement of and too generalized declaration for the inherent and automatic liberation core of the Bible. For Mosala, the Bible reveals class struggle over ascendancy of whose divinity; and the privileged advantage of the poor's God is not readily accessible or so manifestly evident.[26]

Ghana, 1977

In December 1977 the Ecumenical Association of Third World Theologians in connection with the Pan-African Conference of Third World Theologians sponsored a conference on African theology, the fourth *indirect* contact between BTSA and BTUSA.[27] Tutu, Boesak, Cone and Wilmore prepared papers for this international gathering.

Desmond Tutu's approach to black theodicy shows how William R. Jones' doctrine of suffering brings a theological discontinuity in the intercontinental dialogue. At the 1977 Ghana gathering, Tutu did place heavy emphases on theodicy and black theology.

> Liberation theology more than any other kind of theology issues out of the crucible of human suffering and anguish. It happens because people cry out "Oh, God, how long? Oh, God, but why?" And so liberation theology is in a sense really a theodicy.[28]

Tutu specified the theodicy predicament of black victims arising from systemic oppression and exploitation. He was writing immediately after the mass slaughter of blacks during the eighteen-month Soweto Rebellion and two months after South African police had murdered Steve Biko in prison. Hence the poor turn their scarred faces toward the divine and cry out for answers to their innocent victimization beneath apartheid's crushing force of organized and initiating violence.

Likewise, we have seen how theodicy is the cornerstone of William R. Jones' sobering query: Is God a white racist? In brief, Jones claims that if black theologians pursue a black theology of liberation, they have to commence with the sociopolitical-economic anatomy of white power and privilege in America. In this scheme white power automatically breeds black suffering. If divinity initiated black victimization, then God is a white racist. However, in Jones' black theology of humanism, if humanity created the wickedness and lethalness of racism, then a black theology of liberation summons the decisive responsibility of humanity for humanity's own liberation.

Precisely at this crossroad we sense Jones' fundamental discontinuity with Tutu's theodicy. Admittedly they both understand the centrality of suffering. Tutu states that "in a sense" black theology is theodicy. Similarly, Jones' entire black theological course, we noted, travels on this same route. But when Jones veers toward the decisive responsibility of humanity for humanity's own liberation, Tutu detours toward the work and person of Jesus Christ Liberator. In fact, continuing his Ghana paper, Tutu notes that those who suffer have not usually doubted God's omnipotence and righteousness. Quite the contrary, the oppressed start with divine liberating power and, from that point, ask God about suffering.

Allan Boesak's paper at Ghana offers a challenge to both BTSA and BTUSA. He chastizes both theologies for dereliction in critical systemic analysis of white supremacist, organized violence perpetrated for the economic benefit of the ruling class. He writes:

> We must make a proper social analysis. I believe that as real and as ugly as racism is in our country, it is not the only question nor is it the ultimate question. . . . But beyond the question of race lies the economic question. . . . If we do not take cognizance of the economic question, liberation theology will fizzle out.[29]

Boesak's call for critical social analysis around the issue of class, "the ultimate question" beyond the race question, injects the issue of political economy and its relation to black theology. Though in my estimation he does not properly negotiate the dialectical and mutual cause and effect between race and class in black theology, he nevertheless raises the problem of capitalist economics' impact on racial formations. In a word, a black theology of liberation centered solely on the sin of racial discrimination while permitting the survival of capitalism is a denial of the gospel.

James Cone's 1977 paper in Ghana closely parallels Tutu's earlier presentation at Ghana in 1974. Cone believes there are three important reasons for black Americans and Africans to dialogue. First, both emerge from the same African continent. Originally significant distinctions did not differentiate Africa's current ebony offspring in the diaspora. Resuming this initial rationale, Cone argues that historical interrelatedness surpasses mere academic interests. Indeed, such an historical accounting of African origins lays the basis for contemporary theological sharing. Though the motherland's progeny is scattered, Cone writes, "the Black world is one." And Tutu writes: "All of us are bound to mother Africa by invisible but tenacious bonds. . . . All of us have roots that go deep in the warm soil of Africa."[30] Thus no matter how traumatic and distant the separation, Tutu's "invisible bonds" and Cone's "historical origins" weld black and African theologians together.

Second, Cone contends that the particularity of blackness in relation to the politics and economics of white power suggests another basis for dialogue. "International and political arrangements," explains Cone:

> require a certain kind of African and Black nationalism if we are to liberate ourselves from European and White American domination. . . . Each of us can make a choice that establishes our solidarity with the liberation of the Black World from European and American domination.

Hence, the politics and economics of the unified "black world" over against white European-American control also delimit theological significance for discussion. Again Tutu echoes with his general rejoinder: "We are united willy nilly by our blackness." But here Cone ties his trans-Atlantic black solidarity more directly with the gospel's specific mandate of liberation. He defines blackness exactly as liberation.

Cone's third reason for dialogue cites mutual faith in Jesus Christ. Tutu, also, draws on a shared membership in Christ's body. Unlike Cone, however, Tutu concludes that baptism in Christ implies a ministry of reconciliation to "help the white man." On the other hand, Cone's faith and membership in Christ compels a joint black practice in the contemporary movement toward liberation against white European-American domination. Faith in the Liberator, for Cone, implies and accompanies the practice of black liberation.

Finally, Gayraud S. Wilmore's paper, prepared as reflection on the 1977 Ghana meeting, sets the broader historical framework for theological interaction between BTUSA and BTSA. Wilmore teaches both sides that the 1960s black theological tributaries in both countries flow from a larger historical current of dynamic interactions between black theologians in both contexts. Wilmore insightfully states:

> The leadership of both the [North American] A.M.E. and the A.M.E.Z. churches began to propagate black liberation in Southern and West Africa late in the nineteenth century. Their bishops participated in the first Pan-African Congress.[31]

Wilmore positions the 1960s black God-talk in a proper relation to its antecedents. For him the liberation motif and practice in contemporary black theology are caught up in the larger stream of black religious thought, flowing from the creative fountainhead of earlier black foreparents. More specifically he highlights the pioneering work of Henry M. Turner. Continuing his historical connection between BTUSA and BTSA, Wilmore asserts:

> Most notable among the early influences upon Ethiopianism, the anti-racist Christian radicalism that broke out in Africa in the 1880s, was the A.M.E. bishop Henry M. Turner, who was an implacable advocate of black nationalism and helped to establish African Methodism in South Africa.[32]

Just as another A.M.E. minister, James Cone, accelerated the emergence of the 1960s black theology in South Africa by providing a systematic hermeneutic of liberation, the A.M.E. bishop Turner influenced the "anti-racist Christian radicalism" in the 1880s black theological movement in South Africa. Wilmore's point warrants attentive deliberation—historical precedents of joint witnessing to a gospel for black liberation undergird the pursuance of BTUSA and BTSA dialogue today.

Farewell to Innocence, 1977

Allan A. Boesak's *Farewell to Innocence: A Socio-Ethical Study on Black Theology and Black Power* (1977) indicates the final *indirect* theological engagement between BTUSA and BTSA. In this text Boesak assesses the opinions of James Cone, Gayraud Wilmore, and Albert Cleage.

Boesak unites with Cone's general definition of black theology when he (Boesak) writes:

> Black Theology is a theology of liberation. . . . Liberation is not only "part of" the gospel, or "consistent with" the gospel; it is the content and framework of the gospel of Jesus Christ.[33]

The passion and tenacity with which Boesak asserts this claim equals the intent of Cone's first two books on black theology. Fundamentally Cone began his published career by equating the gospel of Jesus Christ with liberation of the poor.

But by assuming the inherent Christocentrism of black theology, Boesak departs from Wilmore. Wilmore would disagree with Boesak's faith stance that "Black Theology . . . [is] a Christological theology"; and, therefore, the passion moving black theologians "is essentially a Passio Jesu Christi."[34] Boesak's Word of God black theology or Black Christian theology of liberation would obscure Wilmore's vision for a liberating black religious thought inclusive of non-Christian and non-religious sources.

Boesak also differs with Cone. Though they both link arms in a general black theology definition, Boesak nonetheless cautions Cone against subsuming the Word of God beneath the momentary and transitory demands of Black Power. Black theology falls within the light of the Word of God, states Boesak. Hence all black action and reflection, in the final analysis, undergo the gospel's judgment. The black reality is the framework for God's revelation in Jesus Christ. Jesus Christ is not the framework for a revelation dictated by black people. At stake for Boesak is his fear that Cone attributes revelational significance to the black experience on par with the gospel of Christ in scripture.[35]

But has Boesak correctly read Cone? I do not think so. Unlike Boesak, Cone depicts a dynamic balance or dialectical interaction between scripture and the black poor's experience. In both Jesus Christ Liberator is normative. The truth of scripture and the black reality is not the book and black particularity in and of themselves. On the contrary, the liberating event of God's presence in Jesus Christ is the truth. Yet at the same time, Cone resumes, no truth of Jesus Christ arises independent of the poor and oppressed of the land. To know the Liberator is to know Jesus Christ meshed in the thick of the poor's movement toward freedom. In refutation of those who employ an abstract and mechanical Logos Christology, Cone expounds:

Jesus Christ is not a proposition, not a theological concept which exists merely in our heads. He is an event of liberation, a happening in the lives of oppressed people struggling for political freedom.[36]

In this dialogue over truth judgments and authority in black theological claims, Cone's position complements more the views of Takatso Mofokeng. For the latter, the normative light of Jesus Christ shines both ways. From scripture the light of Jesus Christ Liberator blankets the black experience; from the black experience the gospel of liberation (the event of Jesus Christ) questions scripture's adherence to the norm.

In this cross-Atlantic dialogue over God's liberating judgment and presence in black theology, Boesak has more affinity with Cecil Cone's claim that God, not Black Power, is the starting point in black theology. Similar to Boesak's cautioning James Cone against subsuming God's word beneath Black Power politics, Cecil Cone hopes to bring the black church's Christian identity to the forefront. But even within Boesak's and Cecil Cone's unity over God's sovereignty, we detect a distinction. Boesak pursues the radical path of the white Reformed tradition. Cecil Cone draws on black Africa's Almighty Sovereign God.

Lastly, Boesak engages Albert Cleage's theological viewpoint. He agrees with Cleage's affirmation of the Black Messiah. But beyond this commonality, Boesak pictures him as the black twin of the white, apartheid Dutch Reformed Church in South Africa. Boesak decries Cleage's "total identification of the gospel with his [Cleage's] particular brand of Christian nationalism." He then chastises Cleage for maintaining "theological exclusivism" and "genetic predestination of black people." In Cleage's theology, writes Boesak:

> He again has his counterpart in white Christian Nationalism with its belief in the "white chosen." . . . We for our part can no more accept Black Christian Nationalism than we can accept the Afrikaner's white, Christian Nationalism.[37]

Here Boesak fails to distinguish between the method of theological criticism and self-criticism *within* the oppressed community and attacks from *outside*. In other words, if Boesak places Cleage outside the black theological movement for liberation, then he is correct in making Cleage a bedfellow with the fascism of apartheid theology. Consequently, just as the South African people and theologians are waging a concerted effort to kill apartheid's theology (as representative of the devil on earth), then similar aim should be taken against the equally pernicious target of Cleage's Godtalk and religious practice. In my judgment, however, by no stretch of the imagination can Cleage's theology be equated with the brutal practice of white Christian Nationalism. First of all, Cleage operates *within* the black theological discourse and, therefore, criticisms of his religious work seeks to improve his practice, not destroy it. Second, unlike the Afrikaner theology, Cleage's theology does not actively pursue genocide against another race. And finally, Cleage does not have the practical theological power to dominate another race of people.

Boesak's negative overstatement against Cleage flows from the danger inherent in a Word of God theology. Recognizing Boesak's legitimate project to build on the Reformed tradition's radical wing, we still should caution against possible excesses. For instance, though operating within the black theology of liberation discourse, a Word of God theology can suffer from a deductive application of static deposits of "Truth." Not distinguishing the particularity of the faith community (whether Cleage or Afrikaners, oppressed or oppressor), a top-down theology can miss the complex mix within the poor community's liberation struggle. The gospel is not simply an application of easy precepts. As the Word of God, Jesus Christ does absolutely condemn apartheid's victimizing practices. But within the victim's faith community the Word criticizes in order to marshall forces against the external Devil.

Likewise, Vincent Harding would apparently take exception to the danger of a Word of God theology potentially imposing doctrine from above. A key aspect of his black theology of spirituality is its unschematized characterization of the masses' spontaneous spirituality. Harding seeks to avoid theological straitjackets on the people's "unself-consciousness" in religious experience. In fact, he contends, theology can serve as an oppressive, European-American enterprise, whereas the black masses' God-encounter bubbles up from below. Regarding this theological methodology, Frank Chikane is more a kindred spirit to Harding's project. Like Harding, Chikane stresses the unlettered masses struggling from below in contrast to the religiously trained elites. Chikane consistently and persistently argues that "the people themselves" do theology. Thus for Harding and Chikane there is no word of God absent from the struggling black masses in motion below.

DIRECT DIALOGUE: 1986

Union Theological Seminary, 1986

The first and only *direct* discussions between BTUSA and BTSA occurred at Union Theological Seminary, New York City, in December of 1986.[38] James Cone's presentation framed three of the major theological issues at the conference: sexuality; race and class social analysis; and the authority of scripture in the development of a black theology of liberation.

Concerning social analysis, Cornel West's speech asserted the necessity of dissecting the multilevel and multidimensional traits of power in society. Black theology needs to understand better, West stressed, the "Europeanization of the world." This phenomenon operates in a four-pronged fashion: exploitation, that is, the unequal distribution of wealth and power fostered by the capitalist mode of production; subjugation, that is, racism, sexism, and homophobia; repression by the state apparatus; and domination by hierarchical bureaucracies. In his critique of black theology's negligence in political economy, West, now a professor at Princeton University, has made a valuable contribution. Because he speaks within the black theological discourse, his critique pushes the dialogue to take seriously the positives of Marxism.

A dialogical partner similar to West, Simon Maimela is one of the few black South African theologians who openly name their use of Marxist analysis. The sin of broken fellowship, in Maimela's estimation, has created the twin political evils of race and class. Therefore he targets the structure of capitalism and its attendant entrapments of economic exploitation and racial subjugation. Here Marxism enables black theology to unravel the social web of demonic entanglements. Other black theologians attribute their radical systemic hermeneutic to scripture. West and Maimela do this and more; they specify the tools of Marxist analysis.

Regarding the authority of scripture in the development of a black theology of liberation, Itumeleng J. Mosala's paper questioned the inherent liberative nature of the Bible. He described how "the white man" came to South Africa with the Bible and, in exchange for scripture, stole black people's land. Mosala questions the possibility of a black liberation theology employing Christianity and the Bible in the movement to get the land back to the indigenous people. In my opinion Mosala needs to distinguish between the limits of biblical criticism and the existential faith situation of poor blacks. Biblical criticism facilitates the unpacking of the redacted Bible that we use today. Though essential in black theology, it alone is not sufficient. On the other hand, black American slaves and the origin of the African Independent Churches in South Africa in the late 1800s indicate that the Bible can be, in Mosala's terms, "a discursive weapon of struggle." Though white southern slavemasters and white imperialistic missionaries preached "slaves obey your masters," the black poor appropriated whatever scriptural texts facilitated their survival and resistance. It is not so much black people's strict adherence to the Bible that guides their lives. It is more their personal witness to Jesus Christ in their oppressed lives that guides their sifting of scripture. At times the black poor's relation to the Bible's authority can befuddle the scientific nature of a materialist biblical criticism.

So far we have not spoken of black women's participation in black theology. Our silence is caused by black women's "invisibility"[39] in critical reflection on North American and South African black faith. However, at the December 1986 conference, the reasons for this forced invisibility was dramatically capsulized when one of the prominent male theologians laughed at the *black female* identity of God. This laughter signified more than one individual. It uncovered all black male theologians' collusion in silencing the voices of over one-half the black community and sixty to seventy percent of the black church. It was a sound of insecure arrogance and frightened male power. This black male laughter at a black female God-image exposed the Achilles heel in black male theology. For black men to spout theological *liberation* rhetoric and simultaneously participate in causing black women's pain delegitimizes the entire theological enterprise.

Again, a male theologian did not question a trivial theological issue. Black men laughed, snickered and smiled at the one foundational basis for all of black theology: the question of God's liberation. Black men joked about (a) God's will to express God's liberation in God's feminine attributes, and (b) God's grace of God's divine liberation image in black women. Since the late 1960s white "learned" North American and South African theologians have laughed when black men have raised the Black Messiah. Now, having monopolized their own black theological market, "learned" black male theologians laugh at black women!

Despite such trivializing "humor" Roxanne Jordan (South Africa) and Kelly Brown (USA) presented black women's theological views at the December conference. The women gave two of the more creative papers. They developed theologies from black women's unique experiences in their respective countries. Politically Brown, currently professor at Howard Divinity School, pointed to black women's unrecognized sacrifices and political leadership in the initial founding of the Southern Christian Leadership Conference (SCLC) and the Student Non-Violent Coordinating Committee (SNCC). In this sense black women spearheaded the civil rights struggle (led by SCLC) and the Black Power era (initiated by SNCC). Culturally North American women have been evaluating black women's literature, prayers and personal experiences. Black women, Brown asserted, hope to create a black "womanist theology" — God's particular liberation practice in Jesus Christ as it affects black women's pain from and resistance against a total sex, race and class oppression.

Jordan, a Congregational Church pastor, described how black Christian women have stood shoulder to shoulder with men in combating apartheid's political violence in the townships. She noted women's crucial role in nurturing black families because men have been forced to work jobs in segregated, white areas. Jordan saw the forging of black feminist theology from South African women's personal experiences in the home, workplace, church, streets and the over-all black cultural life under apartheid. Both Jordan and Brown exemplified black women's discovery of God's and Christ's encounter with them in their political and cultural existence. Together they painted an integral black womanist-feminist theological process. Attacking gender, race and class, black women are devising a creative theology from the integrated use of political and cultural sources.

CONCLUSION

What can black theology in the United States and South Africa say to each other? As we have discovered, both theologies share commonalities and dissimilarities.

Both theologies arose in response to the racist and idolatrous claim of European-American theology. Such a claim unilaterally decreed itself as universal and normative. Hence it ascribed blasphemy to the specificity and value of a black political and cultural theology. In contrast, black theologians insisted vehemently that genuine and authentic knowledge of God comes through revelations in Black Power and Black Consciousness. They believe God intentionally created them in God's own image. And as God's children, their blackness bears beauty and acts as an essential datum for theological reflection. Moreover, BTUSA and BTSA experienced God's presence as liberator in the black community's efforts toward liberation.

Because blacks suffer oppression and cry out for liberation, and because Jesus Christ privileges the oppressed in the liberation struggle, Jesus Christ is black. Similarly for both theologies, scripture also depicts a prototype liberation movement with the exodus as an emancipatory symbol *par excellence*. Therefore, in the Bible and in blacks' lives, God sides with the poor. God calls the faithful, for example, the church, to fight alongside divinity in the movement to free the poor. Indeed, the poor are the subjects of their own history. Methodologically, this forces the theologian to start with a practical commitment to the poor and to listen attentively to their questions. Whether in the United States or South Africa, God-talk ensues as the second step. To exhibit a preference for the poor's plight, black theological method admittedly and invariably solicits the aid of social analysis. In analyzing the black poor's particularity, black theology expresses solidarity with the liberation of the world's poor. And in the liberation of the universal poor, the rich oppressor simultaneously attains liberation. Without black victims to oppress, the white victimizer would also enjoy the fruits of Jubilee.

But in the USA and South Africa, black womanist or black feminist theology has questioned the entire intercontinental dialogue. To speak honestly of God's presence among the poorest of the poor, black women submit, black male theology will have to re-evaluate its own "liberation" presuppositions of black male theology. To successfully serve the black church and community, black theology also has to critically assess God's feminine attributes.

In addition to these similarities, BTUSA and BTSA have different social contexts affecting the uniqueness of black theology in each country. In the United States blacks operate in a bourgeois democracy; South Africans lack a constitution and the vote. In the United States a black minority status produces the omnipresent dilemma of potential genocide. On the other hand, the black majority reality poses the problem of what to do with a white minority elite in South Africa.

Further differences over land, culture and foreparents' religion separate the black theological dialogue. Black Americans suffer from centuries of forced removal from their land and lack a precise lineage to their progenitors' culture. In contrast, black South Africans dwell close to their own land—the land of their ancestors, their cultural identity and their African traditions.

Black Americans have been stripped of a dominant consciousness of their ancestral religious mores. Relative to South Africans, they have successfully resolved their past indigenous African religions into their appropriation of Christianity. However South African blacks' closeness to African traditional religions has caused more complications, though creative, in resolving indigenous religions with Christianity. For example, how to maintain the practical reverence for ancestors and simultaneously confess the decisive revelatory nature of Jesus Christ?

Finally, resulting from the urban rebellions of the 1960s, North American blacks have been nominally accepted into the political mainstream. Consequently, a racist state offers them seductive "opportunities" and the capitalist glitter of full citizenship in the existing society. Apartheid, however, indiscriminately cracks down on any form of protest. As a result the black resistance movement has opted for armed struggle against the existing state and a vision of a new communal social relationship.

These disunities and unities between BTUSA and BTSA fill in the outlines of our investigation. Originally our study began by contrasting the political and cultural theological trends inside both countries. Next we constructed and assessed a dialogue across the Atlantic. Throughout, our single purpose has sought to answer one question: What is the common denominator between black theology in the United States and South African black theology? As a response, our study has verified that, in the main, the denominator common to the two theologies is a gospel of political and cultural liberation. Though black theologians are at variance regarding their shades of black theology, nevertheless all would agree that the gospel of Jesus Christ has the potential to bring political and cultural freedom to the black poor.[40]

Still the problem remains: How does black theology synthesize the black political and black cultural theological trends? How do we creatively integrate and thus forge one black political-cultural or cultural-political theology of liberation? The next chapter offers a framework to initiate the resolution of this challenge for wholeness in a full humanity.

CHAPTER SEVEN

Black Theology: The Culture of Politics and the Politics of Culture

This new vocation to which we are called is *political* in the sense that it seeks radically to change, by whatever means necessary, the racist structures which dominate our lives; *cultural* in the sense that it seeks to identify, recreate, unify and authenticate whatever traditions, values and styles of life are indigenous or distinctive to the black community; and *theological* in the sense that we believe that it is God ... who has chosen black humanity as a vanguard to resist the demonic powers of racism, capitalism and imperialism, and to so reform the structures of this world that they will more perfectly minister to the peace and power of all peoples as children of One God and brothers of one another.

> National Conference of Black Churchmen, 1969

Black theology as a theology of liberation has become part of the struggle of a people for their liberation. ... It has become part of the black consciousness movement, which is concerned with the evangelical aim of awakening in blacks a sense of their intrinsic worth as children of God. ... Liberation theology takes very seriously the socio-political dimensions of reality as those which, to a large extent, determine the quality not only of secular but also of religious life.

> Archbishop Desmond M. Tutu, 1979

How can black theology in the United States and black theology in South Africa come together into a unified political and cultural theological trend toward liberation? This final chapter charts an answer to this question. By way of four theses I explore the broad parameters in which BTUSA and BTSA can work together for a comprehensive emancipation.

167

THESIS ONE: HISTORICAL-CONTEMPORARY BASIS

A historical and contemporary basis exists for a mutual political-cultural theological effort between BTUSA and BTSA. In the late 1890s the A.M.E. bishop Henry McNeal Turner journeyed to South Africa to work with black Christian independent churches—the Separatist Church movement—that had already seceded from the demonic control of a white ecclesial power structure. Turner was an ardent advocate of the blackness of God. Not only did he contend that the divine exhibited the *cultural* attributes of blackness, but he also fought for the *political* self-determination and separateness of black church formations. For Turner, the black God contradicted and condemned the anti-Christ theology of white American churches.

Likewise the Separatist movement in South Africa, which had voted in 1896 to affiliate with the A.M.E. church, claimed an ebony God. Such a divinity demanded a radical break with white missionary exploitation of black South African Christians; hence the rise of the Separatist churches. For instance, Isaiah Shembe's independent church among the Zulus resonated with Turner's belief in a black God. An heir to Shembe asserted the following:

> You, my people, were once told of a God who has neither arms nor legs, who cannot see, who has neither love nor pity. But Isaiah Shembe showed you a God who walks on feet and who heals with his hands, and who can be known by men, a God who loves and who has compassion.[1]

Implicit in this veneration of Shembe by his religious progeny is the theological belief in Shembe as a Black Messiah. Here Shembe, a prophet in a Separatist black South African church, and Turner, a doyen in a separatist black American church, converge in their reimaging of the divine theological and Christological substance. In brief, the direct affiliation of the A.M.E. church and the Separatist church movement lays the historical basis for a contemporary BTUSA and BTSA collaboration. In their joint theological project the two black churches worked to establish the authenticity of black cultural resources and struggled for political social change from white racism.

Furthermore, the contemporary basis for joint theological efforts emerges out of parallel theodocies in the black American and black South African quagmires. Both peoples suffer the scars of white racism. White supremacy knows no boundaries and is all-inclusive in its destruction. It constrains both black political development and black cultural aspirations. Consequently, to be black in the United States or South Africa inherently entails dodging the destructive attempts of white racist politics and white supremacist culture. Whether racism is manifest in the overt Ku Klux Klan-

Afrikaner version or the subtle, northern, liberal, English-speaking type, the normative theological anthropology is white people: the mocking of God by the white power structure. Today black Americans and black South Africans confront an analogous problem that exhorts an analogous resolution.

THESIS TWO: THEOLOGICAL BASIS

A clear theological basis underscores a BTUSA and BTSA joint attempt to devise a cultural-political theology of liberation. Indeed, God's revelation in the Bible attests to a comprehensive emancipation. First, our knowledge of God results from what we have seen God do. "You shall know that I, the Lord, am your God, the God who releases you from your labors in Egypt" (Ex 6:7b). Knowledge of God does not arrive through irrelevant esoteric discourse, or through an isolated individualistic mystery. Rather, we know God because God releases us from burdensome labors caused by oppressive rulers. Among the black poor in the United States and South Africa God renders knowledge of God's self in the midst of their freedom movement from subjugation. To know God, then, is to experience with our own eyes God's act of total liberation. Knowledge is to be carried on God's "eagles' wings" into a new reality (Ex 19:4).

Second, God does not separate God's person and work. In scripture the phrase "I am who I am" simultaneously signifies God's being and action. In fact, because of how God renders knowledge of God's self, "I am" denotes divine privileging of the poor. More specifically, God's beingness and practice coalesce into one phenomenon. "I am the Lord" speaks to God's person. But the divinity proceeds immediately to give substance to the revelation of ultimate being, that is, God's work: "I will release you from your labours in Egypt. I will rescue you from slavery there." Divine ontology brings release and rescue from the painful clutches of servile existence. Hence "I am" (God's person) immediately does the work of liberation. Similarly, "I am" brings salvation or redemption to the poor and marginalized. "I will redeem you with arm outstretched and with mighty acts of judgment" (Ex 6:6). Thus the person and work of God, in the final analysis, judge against systems of total enslavement and for redemption into complete human wholeness.

Third, God displays definite and exact attributes. "And now I have heard the groaning of the Israelites, enslaved by the Egyptians" (Ex 6:5). Here God listens with divine *compassion* to those entrapped in systemic sin. Divine empathy also provides shelter and defense for the oppressed against the powerful. "The Lord is my refuge and my defense." God, therefore, is the *defender* and *protector* of the victims. God "has shown himself my deliverer. . . . The Lord is a warrior" (Ex 15:2-4). Not only does God display the characteristic of emotional affinity with the oppressed, God fights their battles like a "warrior." God does not passively weep at a distance. On the contrary, with the traits of a *warrior* God defends the victims from exploitation initiated by guilty perpetrators. Furthermore, God "will judge the world with justice and try the cause of the peoples fairly. So may the Lord be a tower of strength for the oppressed" (Ps 9:8-9). In this instance God is the cosmic *judge* sorting out right from wrong and adjudicating sentences in favor of God's chosen people, the poor and victimized. In the capacity of a judge, God thus offers the granitelike attribute of a *tower of strength* for the oppressed.

Finally, what marks the content of divine justice? God's justice is not neutral. It does not casually or senselessly weigh the evidence with "equal objectivity." Instead, divine judgment deals out "justice to the poor and suffering" (Ps 72:2). It admittedly opts for the poor and it will "crush the oppressor" (Ps. 72:4) in order to bestow comprehensive liberation on the victim. God's justice narrows the target and unabashedly and unashamedly names names. From whom shall God rescue the oppressed? God "shall rescue the needy from their rich oppressors" and "deliver the poor from death; may he redeem them from oppression and violence" (Ps 72:12-14).

Building on the Old Testament prophecy, the revelation of Jesus Christ brings an ultimate and a decisive manifestation of holistic liberation. Jesus' inaugural proclamation to the world indicates that God became human especially for the poor. Jesus entered the temple and, of all the scriptural passages, turned to Isaiah 61. The selection of Isaiah shows deliberate divine intent. In fact, God has "anointed" Jesus to "announce good news to the poor." Good News means release for prisoners, sight for the blind, emancipation for broken victims. Having delivered God's edict, Jesus folds up the scroll and sits down; "and all eyes in the synagogue were fixed on him" (Lk 4:18-20). This passage echoes Exodus 19:4, "You have seen with your own eyes what I did to Egypt"—and for the oppressed Israelites. Again, we know God and Jesus Christ through witnessing divine acts, that is, through the jubilation of Jubilee, the liberation year for all poor and oppressed people.

Magnifying the concrete earthly jubilation event is the eschatological Jubilee that Matthew 25:31-46 parabolically expresses. Like his initial public sermon, Jesus promises that his first order of business with the parousia will be the same theme, the privileging of the poor and oppressed. On Judgment Day, then, the literal line of demarcation as Jesus separates the sheep from the goats becomes one's practical earthly aid in the full liberation of the victims in society. Thus to avoid "eternal punishment" and to "enter eternal life" one must account for earthly activities against an all-inclusive systemic oppression.

In conclusion, in both the Old Testament and New Testament, black theology in the United States and South Africa discovers a theological basis for a comprehensive emancipation. If Yahweh and Jesus Christ privilege the total freedom of the victims of society, then the foundation exists for an integral political-cultural theology of liberation.

THESIS THREE: NORMATIVE BASIS

The normative basis for a black cultural-political theology of liberation is liberation. This norm expresses itself in a multifaceted manner in the entire black community, Christian and non-Christian. For instance, black Christians make this norm concrete in Jesus Christ Liberator. In short, the norm remains consistent but its manifestations vary. One has to understand this normative basis within the context of a new orientation toward black theology.

In my judgment, a redefined black theology represents the *entire* black community's struggle for ultimate liberation. Here we can learn a great deal from the theological insights of James Cone and Gayraud Wilmore. The latter stressed the liberative themes in non-Christian sources and the former pioneered the redefinition and reimaging of traditional systematic theology. Both tend toward their different political and cultural concerns. Yet, what is important and fundamental is their joint work on pursuing total liberation for the black community in particular and the poor universal. For example, Wilmore emphasizes the following:

Black faith as a folk religion continued to be utilized as the motivating power for revolutionary and nationalist movements in the mass-based community. . . . Folk religion is a constituent factor in every significant crisis in the black community. We ignore it only at the risk of being cut off from the real springs of action.[2]

By accenting the non-Christian emancipatory elements in the black community, Wilmore contributes toward my redefinition of black theology as an expression of the entire black community's ultimate yearning and movement for freedom from racism and all forms of dehumanization. This aspect of my definition of black theology removes the ecclesial circumscription from traditional systematic theological claims. The broadening of the theological definition is vitally important in order to account for the liberation motif and actual practices of strong non-Christian impulses in black history and black experience (such as Malcolm X and others). In God's freedom to liberate, God chooses non-Christian allies and human vessels. However, God's action does not contradict the particularization of the normative revelation for Christians. For those of us who are Christians within the black community, the over-all normative basis for liberation translates into Jesus Christ Liberator. At this juncture Cone's seminal work on plumbing an uncompromising liberation substance in Christianity comes vitally into play.

The norm of black theology must take seriously two realities, actually two aspects of a single reality: the liberation of blacks and the revelation of Jesus Christ. With these two realities before us, what is the norm of black theology? The norm of all God-talk which seeks to be black-talk is the manifestation of Jesus as the black Christ who provides the necessary soul for black liberation.[3]

Thus, to synthesize the best contributions of Cone and Wilmore to facilitate a reinterpretation of systematic theology's function does not force black Christians to renounce or hide their unique identity. On the contrary, the over-all black community's norm complements the person and work of Jesus Christ. Christ is the hoped-for event of liberation; the entire black community's ultimate concern is likewise for a real event of liberation. Black theology, then, reimages a theology consistent with scripture and the black community.

Accordingly, a redefined black theology radically separates itself from the dominant Western enterprise of systematic theology, that is, the construction that theology is only an arm of the Christian church. This dominant European-American theology or white theology seeks to resolve issues of belief and nonbelief, the status of faith in a rationalistic age, issues of the "absence" of God, and the dethroning and marginalization of religion on the boundary of the ascendancy of science and metaphysics. In sharp contrast the black church and the black community have historically focused on resistance and freedom. They simply denied white people's aggressive propaganda that white was normative. This denial manifested itself in a resistance through self-reliance on indigenous cultural resources and through organized political protest against racism. For the black church Jesus Christ motivated the practice of correct Christian witness. For the non-Christian participants, an ultimate concern for liberation powered their pursuits. In sum, a unified black political-cultural theology of liberation has to be accountable to God's diverse expressions in the over-all black community and to the particular revelation of Jesus Christ Liberator.

THESIS FOUR: SOURCE BASIS

A black theology of political-cultural liberation draws its sources from black resources. But at the same time these sources are not blindly accepted as liberative elements. Indeed, they undergo the critique and judgment of (a) the norm — Do they engender the over-all black community's liberation, and for black Christians, do indigenous sources contradict or complement Jesus Christ Liberator? There has to be a critical separation of the "sheep" from the "goats." Black resources that serve to maintain the status quo of racism, sexism and economic exploitation suffer condemnation and exclusion. In addition to the normative critique, black resources also undergo (b) the political-cultural dialectical critique. Specifically, any source that *prima facie* suggests itself as primarily a political or cultural resource has to be immediately re-examined for its equal cultural or political implications for liberation. In other words a unified black theology of political-cultural liberation would review the nuances raised in the political theological trend for cultural import and conversely for the cultural theological trend. Thus all black sources would have to weather both the *normative* and the political-cultural *dialectical* screening. Below are sources from which a black theology might arise today.

Black USA and South African Women as a Source

The invisibility of black women in black theology presents a sobering challenge to the authenticity, legitimacy and hypocrisy of black male theology of liberation.[4] For instance, fifty-two percent of the black community is female and sixty to seventy percent of the black church is female. Yet the silence of black women's experience in black theology is deafening. How can black theology in the United States and in South Africa proclaim liberation against all oppression as their guiding norm but continue to exclude black women? In fact, *poor* black women bear a triple burden from gender discrimination, racial oppression and economic exploitation. When poor women suffer, men suffer as well. No sector of the black community can attain the fullness of the *imago dei* if another sector languishes in multifarious enslavement.

In the United States black women's experiences present a fountainhead of sources toward the development of a political-cultural black theology of liberation. *Fictional* writers like Zora Neal Hurston, Alice Walker and Toni Morrison have provided abundant ingredients from women's stories. Likewise, female *slave autobiographies* and *slave narratives*, such as the autobiography of Harriet A. Jacobs, are available. The lives and theological thought of black women *protest leaders* such as Harriet Tubman, Sojourner Truth, and various Civil Rights and Black Power leaders offer more information. Black women *church and spiritual visionaries*, represented by Rebecca Jackson and Jarena Lee, provide additional theological sources.[5]

Finally, contemporary black North American *womanist theologians* are spearheading a fight to make black theology accountable to its liberation claims and thus qualitatively raise the over-all level of black theological discourse and practice. For example, Jacquelyn Grant has engaged feminist Christologies through a review of white and black women's religious experiences. Similarly, Delores Williams has critiqued white women for failing to openly name their theology as merely white women's God-talk and not that of poor black women. Moving beyond the theological narrowness and exclusivity of white women, Williams explores and ferrets out black women's oppression from their religious narratives. Furthermore, Katie Cannon has sought a constructive womanist ethic in the life and writings of Zora Neal Hurston. And Kelly D. Brown is scrutinizing the black Christ for Christ's faithful or unfaithful reflection of black women's faith.[6]

Like their sisters in the United States, black South African women's experiences will disclose fundamental sources for a cultural-political theology of liberation. In *religion and church*, the lives of Charlotte Manye and Nongqause signify two praiseworthy female role models. Manye was a black South African woman who studied at Wilberfore University in the United States. Due to her connections to the A.M.E. communion she played a key part in engineering the 1896 union between the A.M.E. church and the South African Separatist churches. Nongqause, a 16-year-old prophet and African nationalist, stated that the African ancestors visited her in 1856. From her vision she depicted the African sacred ancestors as the "eternal enemies of the white man, they announce themselves as having come from battlefields beyond the sea to aid the Xhosas with their invincible power in driving the English from the land."[7] Nongqause's faith in black ancestors compelled her to organize against white settlers and their god.

Black South African women have also occupied prominent positions in the *resistance* against white settlers and apartheid in their country. During the 1955-56 opposition to the imposition of pass books on women, waves of female protestors successfully blocked the execution of this dehumanizing law. Women defiantly stood before a local government building, thrust clenched fists into the air and joined in their now-famous song: "You have struck a rock once you have touched a woman; you have dislodged a boulder, you will be crushed."[8] Lilian Masediba Ngoji played a decisive role in this victorious incident as well as in other anti-apartheid actions. More recently, Sibongile Mkhabela distinguished herself as the primary female student leader in the 16 June 1976 Soweto uprisings against the language of Afrikaans in "Bantu" schools. The only woman leader of the Soweto Students' Representative Council placed on trial, and tortured during incarceration, she nonetheless organized other female prisoners to combat the cruder forms of abuse employed in jails.[9] In addition, Winnie Mandela's life and thought contain a wealth of resources for the development of a South African black theology.[10]

Besides the well-known women in resistance, the stories of female *workers* open up a new window to the sufferings and faith of everyday people. *Working Women*[11] records the simple but powerful testimonies of black women laborers in rural areas, industry, clerical jobs, nursing and teaching, and domestic labor. In their own words black women tell stories about twenty-one hour workdays and the inability to see their children except for two weeks out of the year.

The subjugated status of women further intensifies with the ordeal of *prison*. The apartheid government habitually detains South African blacks because of pass book irregularities or for routine interrogation. But the particularity of torture forced upon women brings out an added dimension to fortitude, hope and faith. Though the government accomplishes the "breaking" of some, nevertheless the faith of detained women in ultimate liberation lends a profound resource for a political-cultural black theology.[12]

Finally, *contemporary* black female theologians in South Africa are raising their voices in the theological arena. At a 1984 fall conference on feminist theology, black women theologians discussed three theological areas: the Bible and women; culture, tradition and women's oppression; and women's role in the South African liberation struggle. The conferees detected a four-fold subjugation of black women in South Africa.

> They are discriminated against and oppressed as black people (racial). They are oppressed as workers (class). They are oppressed as women (sex). They are oppressed by one another as women both as individuals and as a group. One can therefore say that black women are the most oppressed group of the oppressed.[13]

Furthermore, Bernadette I. Mosala reasons that an authentic black theology dictates a "moral imperative" to change women's secondary status in the black church. In her estimate the body of Christ suffers when "the variety of gifts of its body" are negated. Similarly, Bonita Bennett exegetes the New Testament and discovers a Christological paradigm favorable to black women. She states:

> What women are asking for is not a reversal of male-female roles. . . . Rather, it is to be recognized as full human beings, with equal intellectual and spiritual worth. Jesus did not glorify women: he acted naturally toward them.[14]

For the creation of a black political-cultural theology of liberation, black women's experiences in the United States and South Africa provide the first source.

The Black Church as a Source

In the United States the black church consists of blacks in predominantly white churches (Lutheran, Episcopalian, Presbyterian, Methodist, Catholic, and so on) and the historic black churches, that is, Baptist, African Methodist Episcopal, African Methodist Episcopal Zion, Christian Methodist Episcopal and Pentecostal churches. The latter grouping includes the overwhelming majority of black Christians. These historic black churches or black Independent Churches have undergone "invisible institution" and visible ecclesial phases. Out of this continuum of separate and independent Christian worship, we discover sources for a black political-cultural theology of liberation.

The invisible institution demarcates black religion under slavery from the visible, above-ground black independent churches. In the secrecy of slave quarters or the surreptitious gatherings in thickets, ravines, swamps, gullies, or woods, bondsmen and women had to "steal away to Jesus" from the watchful eye of the ever-suspecting slavemaster. There, invisible to slave authority but everpresent with the Holy Spirit, the very structure of black American religion was sculptured from an African worldview and thought-forms. The invisible institution carved out both a political and cultural theology. The slaves differed remarkably from the theology of the slave-master. Politically, they imagined the fires of hell scorching the white slave-master along with his nefarious slave system. Picturing the inhuman barbarity of a slavemaster, one bondsman exclaimed his own religious convictions in this manner:

> Yes, in them days it was hell without fires. This is one reason why I believe in a hell. I don't believe a just God is going to take no such [white] man as that into his kingdom.[15]

Furthermore, when slave bosses cried to God to preserve the "peculiar institution," slaves prayed passionately for an Old Testament deliverance. An ex-slave described the liberative substance of slaves' prayers. Contradicting their master's explicit forbiddance, when slaves illegally prayed at night, "They'd pray, 'Lord, deliver us from under bondage.' "[16] This non-systematic theology of liberation empowered the slave rebellions and resistance movements of Denmark Vesey, Nat Turner, David Walker and Harriet Tubman.

In addition to political opposition the invisible institution countered slavery culturally. The fact that slaves risked life and limb "to hold church" clandestinely in their own cultural language far away from "white folks" indicates another form of resistance. Blacks could not express themselves freely under the watchful blue eyes of slavers. Despite whippings, torture and the threat of being sold off far away from loved ones, slaves persisted in seeking refuge in swamps in order to give religious and theological vent to the uniqueness of their speech, worldview and way of life. An Alabama slave speaks succinctly and graphically: "Ya' see 'Niggers' lack to shout a whole lot an' wid de white fo'ks al' round 'em, dey couldn't shout jes' lack dey want to."[17] Blacks had to be themselves by themselves to preserve their way of shouting "jes' lack dey want to," to preserve black culture against white folks' perennial and unprovoked genocidal attacks. In a word, cultural preservation subverted racial extinction.

Upon emancipation the invisible institution merged into the visible institution, for example, the Independent black churches that had broken with white denominations. In fact, in Wilmore's words, the black Independent Church development was the first black freedom movement.[18] Specifically, African Baptist, A.M.E and A.M.E.Z. communions believed that the gospel did not sanction segregation or slavery and that blacks should control and determine their own ecclesial affairs; hence the separation from white churches. More recently the black church led the Civil Rights Movement and black theology positioned itself as the theological justification for the gospel's favorable connection to Black Power. In sum, no black theology of cultural-political liberation will be fruitful without recognizing the centrality of the invisible and visible church to the black community historically and today.

In South Africa the black church source comprises Africans in missionary churches (Methodists, Congregationals, Lutherans, Dutch Reformed, Anglicans, Presbyterians, and so on) and the African Independent Churches. As offspring of the Separatist church movement, Independent Churches seek to clothe Christianity in the garb of African traditional culture and religion. They are the fastest-growing black churches in South Africa. Some have classified them into Ethiopian and Messianism churches, which pursue "physical liberation," and Zionism churches, which long for psychological freedom. Still others have categorized them as Ethiopian Churches, Prophetic/Pentecostal Churches and Messianic Movements.[19]

Their strength lies in unswerving adherence to primal African culture and religious practices. Because they strongly emphasize conservation, however, they experience the danger of supporting the white Dutch Reformed Church's homeland, tribal theology. But, at the same time their indigenous cultural assertion can be an affront and obstacle to European absorption. Therefore, the question for the emergence of a South African black theology of political-cultural liberation is: how can the Independent Churches' efforts to dissociate from European culture be transformed into conscious steps against apartheid's white supremacist theology, policy and practice?

Black Culture as a Source

Black culture in the United States and South Africa is an endless well of cultural and political resources. In North America black theologians need to examine and re-examine the depths of black *folklore and folktales* for political and cultural ingredients. Br'er Rabbit, High John the Conqueror, the Monkey in the Jungle and Shine stories offer a fountain of material bubbling over with black thought-forms, resistance techniques, an independent way of life and ultimate concerns. Black *songs*—work tunes, blues, jazz, chain gang singing and pop/soul tunes—also depict black people's struggle with that which concerns their faith and life. Black *talk*, for example, the "dozens" and "signifying," and black *English* represent instances of cultural and political resistance. Likewise black *cultural writers'* expression of poetry, plays, novels, games, laughter and dance exhibit a complex mélange of revealing theological sources. And, of course, slave *narratives* and *autobiographies*, representing foundational planks in the construction of the Afro-American ontology, are an endless resource for the development of a systematic theology of political-cultural liberation.[20]

Similarly, South Africa's cultural well gushes forth a wealth of cultural sources. *Folktales and folklore* of the African traditional religions not only signal a religious dimension but also cultural habits. In addition the diverse African *languages* communicate cultural obstinacy against European encroachment as well as political resistance; witness the 16 June 1976 student rebellion against the imposition of Afrikaans as the official medium of speech. Moreover black South African *songs* — vocal music of the rural areas; popular music such as political mbaqanga tunes, crossover and marabi sheebeen sounds; and freedom songs — provide theological resources. Furthermore, black *cultural writers* of poetry, plays, short stories, autobiographies, critical essays and novels produced works in various journals: *Drum* in the 1950s; *Africa South, The Purple Renoster, The Classic* and other literary magazines in the 1960s; and *Donga, Staffrider* and Black Consciousness writings, anthologies and theater in the 1970s. In fact, as early as the 1880s South Africans Job Moteame and Azariele M. Sekese employed animal fables as protest and satire. Accordingly, black culture proffers a great deal of creative, indigenous material for a black theology of liberation.[21]

Black Political Thought as a Source

The lives and thought of major political thinkers in the United States and South Africa can also contribute to the emergence of a political-cultural theology. In the United States Martin Delaney, Frederick Douglass, Marcus Garvey, W.E.B. DuBois, Booker T. Washington and, of course, Martin Luther King, Jr., and Malcolm X stand out for their impact on the political, cultural and theological texture of black Americans. In South Africa a similar sampling includes Nelson Mandela, Steve Biko, Robert Subukwe, Sol Plaatje and Anton Lembede. Black political thinkers serve to make concrete and magnify the theological ramifications of the movements out of which the particular black thinker comes. Put differently, we would examine diverse political thinkers primarily for the *theological* implications of the political and cultural movements that gave birth to the specific black thinker.

Social Analysis and Vision as a Source

The final source involves the specification of the new society in which a black cultural-political theology of liberation could flourish uninhibited by the sinful and constraining aspects of race, gender and class. In a word, we need a social analysis and vision for the penultimate social relations.

At minimum a contemporary black theology of liberation has to account for the relation between black culture and political class relations. Amilcar Cabral unravels the vibrant dynamic between the two:

> The value of culture as an element of resistance to foreign domination lies in the fact that culture is the vigorous manifestation on the ideological or idealist plane of the physical and historical reality of the society that is dominated or to be dominated. Culture is simultaneously the fruit of a people's history and a determinant of history, by

the positive or negative influence which it exerts on the evolution of relationships between man and his environment, among men or groups of men within a society, as well as among different societies.[22]

Cabral correctly pictures culture as a "vigorous manifestation" of the oppressed, dominated community. It is vigorous precisely because it manifests a particular "physical and historical reality" (read, political and economic reality) that vibrates and changes. Culture is not static because the political and social connections of a real, historically defined community are in constant motion. Hence the first part of Cabral's definition devises two points. First, on the ideological plane culture reflects a physical and historical existence, for example, politics and economics. Second, culture breathes because that which it reflects is in motion. The last part of Cabral's definition stipulates culture's reciprocal imprint on politics, for example, the physical and the real relations between humans in society. In brief, culture arises from a people's political history and social relations and, simultaneously, occupies a determining capacity. Culture is in debt to political and economic exigencies and also determines these exigencies. The politics of culture and the culture of politics interpenetrate.

Furthermore, Cabral offers a normative axis around which his dependent-reciprocal and cultural-political analysis revolves. For oppressed peoples struggling for a holistic liberation, Cabral states that the "value of culture" is "as an element of resistance" on the part of oppressed people for their liberation. Therefore, for him, *resistance for liberation* judges, critiques and thus normalizes the effectiveness and radicality of culture (manifested on an ideological plane) and politics (manifested in a physical and historical reality, and people's history).

Cabral offers some helpful insights for a black theology of political-cultural liberation. His normative axis instructs black theology to maintain the liberation of the black working poor as its paramount interest, its means of judging and critiquing both culture and class. Thus white supremacist *cultural* attacks against the entire black community have to be negated based on the normative axis of the black working poor's liberation. Here "white supremacist" indicates both overt dismissals of black culture as below standard, that is, white standard, and the more subtle white "acceptance" of black culture based on white criteria. Likewise white supremacist *political* and economic attacks on the entire black community need to be negated; in particular, the insidious tentacles of capitalist exploitation of the poor.

Admittedly the entire black community remains a target of the dominant white cultural and political practices. Nevertheless the normative axis of the liberation of the black working poor pushes black theology to further undergo a critique internal to the black community. More specifically, one has to recognize that the beneficiaries of both the Black Power and Black Consciousness movements have been primarily the small elite strata with wealth in the black community. Consequently the black minority elite, utilizing its wealth and privileged position, has a tendency to assert its own black culture, political interests, class traits and lifestyle as normative for the entire community. Rephrased, a rallying of the entire black community around an amorphous "black" banner could subvert the liberation of the black poor in the interests of the black elite. Thus a banner signifying the cultural and political liberation of the black community's majority—the black working poor—should *lead* cultural and political class interests in the black community.

Finally, the normative axis of political-cultural liberation of the black working poor would also regulate our penultimate vision. Thus, in a new society the working poor in general and the black working poor in particular would communally or collectively own and control wealth and the distribution of wealth. Simultaneously the black community under the leadership of the black working poor, would have the right to determine for itself, as a group, how to bring its various cultural talents and pursuits to full creativity. For a black theology of liberation the culture of politics and the politics of culture go hand-in-hand. Only when the black poor has attained the fullest heights of its political and cultural emancipation, will a black theology of political-cultural liberation jointly created by black theology in the United States and black theology in South Africa fulfill its mission. Concomitantly, in such a penultimate society the freedom of the black poor hails the freedom of the poor universal, regardless of color, for ultimately, God sides with all the poor. And for us Christians, then we will hear the longed-for voice say, "Well done, my faithful servants, well done!"

Notes

INTRODUCTION

1. Between 1836 and 1840 the Afrikaners (i.e., the Boers) departed from the southern part of South Africa, which was under British rule. The Boers trekked north to take whatever land they felt necessary for their own race. During the process of colonizing indigenous Africans' land, these trekboers or Voortrekkers, as they were called, would pull their wagons into a circle called a *laager*. Since that time, whenever Afrikaners feel threatened, they draw on their frontier survivalist *laager* mentality.

2. Held at Union Theological Seminary, New York City, December 1-3, 1986, this conference was sponsored by the Institute for Contextual Theology (South Africa), the Ecumenical Program and the Theological Field and the Ecumenical Association of Third World Theologians (EATWOT). Under the leadership of Drs. James H. Cone and Simon S. Maimela, I organized the groundwork for the conference.

CHAPTER ONE

1. On the background and factors that gave rise to black theology, see J. Cone, *For My People: Black Theology and the Black Church* (Maryknoll, NY: Orbis Books, 1984; Johannesburg, South Africa: Skotaville Publishers, 1985), chap. 1; idem, *Speaking the Truth: Ecumenism, Liberation, and Black Theology* (Grand Rapids, MI: Eerdmans Publishing Co., 1986), pp. 83-111; and Gayraud S. Wilmore, *Black Religion and Black Radicalism: An Interpretation of the Religious History of Afro-American People*, 2d edition (Maryknoll, NY: Orbis Books, 1983), chaps. 7-9.

2. On the Civil Rights Movement, see Harvard Sitkoff, *The Struggle for Black Equality, 1954-1980* (New York: Hill and Wang, 1981); Robert H. Brisbane, *Black Activism: Racial Revolution in the United States, 1954-1970* (Valley Forge, PA: Judson Press, 1974), chaps. 1-4; Lerone Bennett, Jr., *Before the Mayflower: A History of Black America* (Chicago: Johnson Publishing Co., 1987); John Hope Franklin, *From Slavery to Freedom: A History of Negro Americans*, 5th ed. (New York: Alfred A. Knopf, 1980); and Juan Williams, *Eyes on the Prize: America's Civil Rights Years, 1954-1965* (New York: Viking, 1987).

3. Robert L. Allen, *Black Awakening in Capitalist America* (Garden City, NY: Anchor Books, 1970), pp. 26-27; Benjamin Quarles, *The Negro in the Making of America* (New York: Macmillan Co., 1969), p. 262 and pp. 272-73; Nathan Wright, Jr., "The Crisis Which Bred Black Power," in *The Black Power Revolt*, ed. Floyd B.

Barbour (Boston: Beacon Press, 1968), pp. 104-8; Franklin, pp. 479-80.

4. Allen J. Matusow, "From Civil Rights to Black Power: The Case of SNCC, 1960-1966," in *Twentieth Century America*, ed. Bernstein and Matusow (New York: Harcourt, Brace & World, 1969), p. 543. Also see, Clayborne Carson, *In Struggle: SNCC and the Black Awakening of the 1960s* (Cambridge, MA: Harvard University Press, 1982).

Commenting on white liberal betrayal at the convention, Harvard Sitkoff cited this event as completing "SNCC's alienation from the mainstream of the movement and its estrangement from the federal government and the Democratic Party" (pp. 184-85); also see, John Oliver Killens, *Black Man's Burden* (New York: Simon & Schuster, 1965), chap. 1; and Williams, pp. 243-249.

5. See Sitkoff, pp. 124, 114-17; also see, Brisbane, pp. 80-81; Matusow, p. 537.

6. See Julius Lester, "The Angry Children of Malcolm X," in *Black Protest Thought in the Twentieth Century*, ed. A. Meier, et al. (Indianapolis: Bobbs-Merrill, 1980), p. 470. (Lester's article originally appeared in 11 December 1966); also see, Sitkoff, pp. 117-24.

7. See Malcolm X, *The Autobiography of Malcolm X* (New York: Grove Press, 1966).

8. See Lester, pp. 476-77.

9. James Foreman, *The Making of Black Revolutionaries* (New York: Macmillan Co., 1972), p. 451.

10. Charles V. Hamilton, "An Advocate of Black Power Defines It," in *The Rhetoric of Black Power*, ed. R. L. Scott and W. Brockriede (New York: Harper and Row, 1969), p. 178.

11. On violence, see Stokely Carmichael, "Stokely Carmichael Interviewed by *Sucesos* Magazine," in *The Rhetoric of Black Americans*, ed. J. L. Golden and R. D. Rieke (Columbus, OH: C. E. Merrill Publishing Co., 1971), pp. 528, 530.

For a fuller view of black community control and political power for poor blacks, see Carmichael, "What We Want," in *Chronicles of Black Protest*, ed. B. Chambers (New York: New American Library, 1968), pp. 219, 211; idem, "Stokely Carmichael Explains Black Power to a Black Audience in Detroit," in Scott and Brockriede, p. 87; idem., "Stokely Carmichael Explains Black Power to a White Audience in Whitewater, Wisconsin," in Scott and Brockriede, p. 102; and idem., "Toward Black Liberation," in *Black Fire*, ed. LeRoi Jones and Larry Neal (New York: William Morrow & Co., 1968), p. 129.

For Carmichael's comments on South Africa, see "Stokely Carmichael Explains Black Power to a Black Audience in Detroit," p. 90.

12. His demarcation points to some of the friction in the political-cultural trends discussed in Chapters 2 and 3 below.

13. "Huey Newton Talks to the Movement," in *Roots of Rebellion, the Evolution of Black Politics and Protest Since World War II*, ed. Richard P. Young (New York: Harper and Row, 1970), pp. 370–71; also see, Huey P. Newton, "Functional Definition of Politics," in *The Black Panthers Speak*, ed. Philip S. Foner (Philadelphia: J. B. Lippincott, 1970), pp. 45-47.

14. Karenga's current name is Maulana Karenga and Jones' new name is Amiri Baraka. We should note that Jones/Baraka has moved from a strict cultural nationalism to the use of Marxism. See " 'Why I Changed My Ideology': Black Nationalism and Socialist Revolution," *Black World* (July 1975).

15. Quotations referring to Karenga are from "The Quotable Karenga," in Barbour, pp. 162-67.

16. Quotations referring to Jones are from "The Need For a Cultural Base to Civil Rites & Bpower Mooments," in Barbour, pp. 119-26.

17. Gayraud S. Wilmore, "Appendix D, The Theological Commission Project of the National Committee of Negro Churchmen, Fall 1968," in *Christian Faith in Black and White*, Warner R. Traynham, ed. (Massachusetts: Parameter Press, 1973), p. 84.

18. The following are useful references for the origin and concerns of NCNC-NCBC: *Black Theology: A Documentary History, 1966-1979*, ed. Gayraud S. Wilmore and James H. Cone (Maryknoll, NY: Orbis Books, 1979); Wilmore, *Black Religion and Black Radicalism*; Cone, *For My People*; Grant S. Shockley, "Ultimatum and Hope, the Black Churchmen's Convocation: An Interpretation," *The Christian Century* (12 February 1969), pp. 217-19; Leon W. Watts, II, "The National Committee of Black Churchmen," *Christianity and Crisis* (2 November 1970 and 16 November 1970), pp. 237-43; Alex Poinsett, "The Black Revolt in White Churches," *Ebony* (September 1968), pp. 63-68; *Time* (15 November 1968), p. 78; and *Look* (7 January 1969), pp. 84-85.

19. Quotations in the text come from my interviews with Rev. Dr. Calvin B. Marshall, 17 March 1987, and Rev. Leon W. Watts, II, 23 March 1987. Both Marshall and Watts are members of the African Methodist Episcopal Zion Church, one of the historic black denominations. In its origin not only did NCNC have to face the racist *theology* of the white church, but also the self-denigrating, conservative *theology* of the historic black churches. Marshall states: "Our church called itself an African Methodist Church. But our church wanted to be part of the establishment. Our church had bought blindly into integration. Our church was an American church. Our church believed in the American Dream. Our church saw its fulfillment in terms of (irregardless of the fact that we would talk about James Varick the founder of the Zion Church) . . . John Wesley."

A black minister, Varick was the first superintendent and a founder of the AMEZ church. (See Wilmore, *Black Religion and Black Radicalism*, p. 85.)

20. Nathan Wright, Jr., *Black Power and Urban Unrest* (New York: Hawthorn Books, 1967), p. 153.

21. Ibid., p. 78.

22. Other references helpful in analyzing early black theological themes are: "Statement by the National Committee of Negro Churchmen, July 31, 1966," in Wilmore and Cone, pp. 23-30; National Committee of Negro Churchmen, "Racism and the Elections: The American Dilemma, 1966," in Wilmore and Cone, pp. 31-34; Vincent Harding, "Black Power and the American Christ," in Wilmore and Cone, pp. 35-42 (originally published 4 January 1967, in *Christian Century*); Henry H. Mitchell, "Black Power and the Christian Church," *Foundations* 11 (April-June 1968):99-109; James Cone, "Christianity and Black Power," in *Is Anybody Listening to Black America?*, ed. C. Eric Lincoln (New York: Seabury Press, 1968), pp. 3-9; Gayraud S. Wilmore, "The Case for a New Black Church Style," *Church in Metropolis* (Fall 1968):19-22; Preston N. Williams, "Shifting Radical Perspectives," *Harvard Divinity Bulletin* (Fall 1968):12-15; Vincent Harding, "The Religion of Black Power," in *Religious Situation: 1968*, ed. Donald Cutler (Boston: Beacon Press, 1968), pp. 3-38; J. Deotis Roberts, "The Black Caucus and the Failure of Christian Theology," *The Journal of Religious Thought* (Summer Supplement 1969):15-25; Wil-

more, "Appendix D, The Theological Commission Project of the National Committee of Negro Churchmen, Fall 1968," pp. 83-96; James Baldwin, "White Racism or World Community?" *Ecumenical Review* 20 (October 1968):371-76; Shelby Rooks, "Implications of the Black Church for Theological Education," *Bulletin of Crozer Theological Seminary* 61 (January 1969):3-22; Shockley, pp. 217-19; Gilbert H. Caldwell, "Black Folk in White Churches," *Christian Century* (12 February 1969), pp. 209-11; Alex Poinsett, "The Quest for a Black Christ," *Ebony* (March 1969); "Black Theology. Statement by the National Committee of Black Churchmen, June 13, 1969," in Wilmore and Cone, pp. 100-102; "A Message to the Churches From Oakland, California. Statement by the National Committee of Black Churchmen, Third Annual Convocation, November 11-14, 1969," in Wilmore and Cone, pp. 103-7; Frank T. Wilson, "Critical Evaluation of the Theme—'The Black Revolution: Is There a Black Theology?' " *The Journal of Religious Thought* (Summer Supplement 1969):5-9; and Geddes Hanson, "Black Theology and Protestant Thought," *Social Progress* (September–October 1969):5-12.

23. On black resistance in the 1950s, see Gail Gerhart, *Black Power in South Africa: The Evolution of an Ideology* (Berkeley: University of California Press, 1979), chaps. 4-5; Edward Roux, *Time Longer Than Rope: The Black Man's Struggle for Freedom in South Africa* (Madison, WI: The University of Wisconsin Press, 1978), chaps. 32-35; and Tom Lodge, *Black Politics in South Africa Since 1945* (New York: Longman, 1984), chaps. 8-10.

24. For a fuller explanation of the events between Sharpeville 1960 and SASO 1969, see the following: *Steve Biko—I Write What I Like*, ed. Aelred Stubbs (San Francisco: Harper and Row, 1986), chaps. 2, 3, 5, 7, 8, 10, and 18, referred to hereafter as *Biko*; Steve Biko, "White Racism and Black Consciousness," in *Student Perspectives on South Africa*, ed. HWVD Merwe and D. Welsh (Cape Town, South Africa: David Philip Publisher, 1972), pp. 190-202; Ranwedzi Nengwekhulu, "The Meaning of Black Consciousness in the Struggle for Liberation in South Africa," in U.N. Center Against Apartheid, *Notes and Documents*, 16/76 (New York: United Nations, July 1976), pp. 5-7; Mokgethi Motlhabi, *The Theory and Practice of Black Resistance to Apartheid, a Social-Ethical Analysis* (Johannesburg, South Africa: Skotaville Publishers, 1986), pp. 106-10; Denis Herbstein, *White Man, We Want to Talk to You* (New York: Africana Publishing Co., 1979), chap. 3; Gerhart, chaps. 7–8; Robert Fatton, Jr., *Black Consciousness in South Africa* (Albany: State University of New York Press, 1986), chaps. 3-4; Roux, pp. 406-44; Lodge, chaps. 9, 10, 13; and Ernest Harsch, *South Africa: White Rule Black Revolt* (New York: Monad Press, 1983), chaps. 17-18.

For an excellent review of the BCM organizations, see Bennie A. Khoapa, ed., *Black Review 1972* (Durban, South Africa: Black Community Programmes, 1973), chaps. 1 and 2. Khoapa was former director of the Black Community Programmes.

Regarding the significance of the segregated housing at the 1967 NUSAS conference vis-à-vis black student aversion to white liberalism, Steve Biko wrote: "This [incident] is perhaps the turning point in the history of black support for NUSAS" (*Biko*, p. 11).

25. *SASO Newsletter* (Natal, South Africa: SASO, August 1971), p. 11.

26. *Biko*, pp. 144, 51; also see, Steve Biko, "I Write What I Like. Black Souls in White Skins?" *SASO Newsletter* (August 1970), p. 17; and N. C. Manganyi, *Being-Black-In-The-World* (Johannesburg, South Africa: Spro-Cas/Raven, 1973), p. 17.

27. *Biko*, p. 86; and Motlhabi, pp. 131-32.

28. *Biko*, p. 27.

29. For a well-integrated analysis of apartheid, white liberalism and BCM see Barney Pityana, "Power and Social Change in South Africa," in Merwe and Welsh, pp. 174-89. Pityana succeeded Biko as SASO's second president.

30. Ibid., pp. 28-29.

31. See Adam Small, "Blackness versus Nihilism: Black Racism Rejected," in *The Challenge of Black Theology in South Africa*, ed. Basil Moore (Atlanta: John Knox Press, 1973), p. 11; also see, *Biko*, pp. 29, 28, 103.

Ranwedzi Nengwekhulu, one of SASO's premier full-time organizers, commented on the same subject: "Black Consciousness therefore calls for a psychological revolution in the Black community; this will be a revolution which is directed towards the elimination of all stereotypes by Blacks about themselves and one which is directed towards the complete eradication of the slave-mentality. . . . Black Consciousness therefore forces Black people to see themselves as full human beings, complete, full and total in themselves and not as extensions of others" (p. 2).

32. Lodge, pp. 324-25.

33. See *Biko*, p. 69; Gerhart, pp. 272-73; Fatton, p. 75; and Harsch, p. 258.

34. *Biko*, p. 49; *SASO Newsletter*, "SASO Policy Manifesto" (August 1971), p. 10; also see, Motlhabi, pp. 132-37.

In December 1971 SASO and other BCM groups formed the Black Peoples' Convention (BPC) as a national "confederate black political organization." SASO and BPC became the two main BCM forces. In its Constitution BPC agreed "to preach, popularise and implement the philosophy of Black Consciousness and Black Solidarity" and "to unite the South African Blacks into a Black Political Movement which would seek to realise their liberation and emancipation from both psychological and physical oppression." See *The Black Peoples' Convention (BPC)—South Africa: Historical Background and Basic Documents*, ed. Sipho Buthelezi (Harlem, NY: Black Liberation Press, n.d.), p. 13. Buthelezi was a former secretary-general of the BPC.

35. Pityana, pp. 183, 185, 189.

36. Bennie A. Khoapa, "The New Black," in *Black Viewpoint*, ed. B. S. Biko (Durban, South Africa: Spro-Cas Black Community Programmes, 1972), pp. 62-63.

37. Regarding the transformation of the government and economic system, see *Biko*, pp. 49, 149; and Motlhabi, p. 123. Concerning socialism, see *Biko*, p. 149; and Buthelezi, p. 32.

38. In the "Cultural Themes" section below we will discover that the nomenclature for the new society shifts from *socialism* to *communalism*. This appellation does not replace or inevitably contradict *socialism*. However, the existence of these two descriptors in the BCM presage the non-racialism (as a universal aspect of the gospel) and black theology (with emphasis on the indigenousness of communalism) debates among black South African theologians in Chapters 4 and 5 below.

39. See Buthelezi, p. 29; and Motlhabi, pp. 116-17.

40. See *Biko*, pp. 149-50.

41. Regarding "one person one vote," see Motlhabi, p. 116. See *Biko*, pp. 123, 150-51; and Buthelezi, p. 29.

42. Motlhabi, pp. 139-41; also see, *Biko*, p. 123; Biko, "I Write What I Like. Black Souls in White Skins?" pp. 18-19, 20; Donald Woods, *Biko* (New York: Paddington Press, 1978), p. 51; and "SASO Policy Statement," p. 10.

43. See SASO's position paper, "SASO: Understanding SASO," in *African Per-*

spectives on South Africa: A Collection of Speeches, Articles and Documents, ed. HWVD Merwe, et al. (Cape Town, South Africa: David Philip Publisher, 1978), p. 104. In this position paper presented at a SASO "Formation School," SASO maintained: "A study of the history of South Africa shows that at almost all times whites have been involved in black struggles and in almost all instances led to the death or confusion of what they were involved in. . . . That blacks are deciding to go it alone is not an accident but a result of years of history behind black-white cooperation."

44. Ibid., p. 101.

45. Ibid.

46. Ibid. Though BCM looked inward at what I am calling cultural ontology and cultural anthropology, this inwardness translated back outwardly in a political manner, that is, in order to "ask about the conditions under which [black people] live[d]." If one saw oneself as a person (i.e., the cultural anthropology), then one ought to question and engage the surrounding oppresive conditions (i.e., the existential predicament).

47. Nengwekhulu, p. 3. Also see, Motlhabi, pp. 135-37; and Khoapa, *Black Review 1972*, pp. 21, 25-26.

Baasskap described the policy of English-speaking whites in their attempt to remain the "trustees" of blacks until the latter were "competent" enough to achieve integration into white civilization. See Gerhart, pp. 5, 6.

48. Biko, "White Racism and Black Consciousness," in Merwe and Welsh, pp. 198-99.

49. See "Policy Manifesto," p. 11. Also see, *Biko*, pp. 49, 52, 71, 92; Motlhabi, p. 112; and Nengwekhulu, p. 1, where he writes: "Black Consciousness also means Black people should be aware of the significance and importance of their own value systems, i.e., their socio-economic, political and cultural values. . . . The challenge of Black Consciousness . . . is the need for a new redefinition, reidentification and reappraisal of the Black totality."

50. See *Biko*, pp. 41-47. On the BCM's view toward communalism, see "Understanding SASO," p. 102; Motlhabi, p. 124; and Buthelezi, p. 22.

The BCM placed a very high priority on communalism derived from *indigenous African culture*. In fact, the Black Peoples Convention passed a resolution on "Black Communalism," which, in part, stated: "B.P.C. adopts Black communalism as its economic policy and Black Communalism can be defined as an economic system which is based on the principle of sharing, lays emphasis on community ownership of land and its wealth and riches; and which strikes a healthy balance between what may legitimately be owned by individuals and what ought to be owned by the community as a whole." Black communalism is "a modified version of the traditional African economic life-style which is being geared to meet the demand of a highly industrialised and modern economy." Cited in *Pro Veritate* (June 1976), p. 6.

51. See Manganyi, pp. 19-21, where he defines black consciousness and black solidarity in terms of being-black-in-the-world.

52. Unless otherwise cited, references to Bonganjalo Goba are from my interview with him on 2 March 1987.

53. See Ntwasa, "The Concept of God in Black Theology," in Moore, p. 22. Other helpful accounts of the theological origins of BTSA are found throughout Moore's book; Vic Mafungo, "Black Theology, a Reassessment of the Christ," in *SASO Newsletter* (September 1971), p. 8; Herbstein, p. 69; Gwinyai H. Muzorewa,

The Origins and Development of African Theology (Maryknoll, NY: Orbis Books, 1985), chap. 8; "My Understanding of Black Theology," *SASO Newsletter* (November/December 1975), p. 15; "The Commission on Black Theology," *SASO Newsletter* (August 1971), p. 17; "Black Theology Resolution," *Pro Veritate* (15 July 1971), p. 25; and Elliot K. Mgojo, "Prolegomenon to the Study of Black Theology," *Journal of Theology for Southern Africa* (December 1977):28-31.

The Challenge of Black Theology in South Africa, edited by Moore, was originally titled *Essays on Black Theology* (Johannesburg, South Africa: Black Theology Project of the University Christian Movement, 1972) and edited by M. Motlhabi. The book was immediately banned by the government.

54. Moore, p. 35. In "The Relevance of Black Theology," *South African Outlook* 104 (December 1974):199, Buthelezi cogently expressed the theological obstacles confronting blacks and the resulting necessity for a black theology: "The fact that Africans, Indians and Coloureds have been collectively referred to as 'non-whites' in official terminology suggests that they have the identity of non-persons who exist only as negative shadows of whites. In a theological sense this means that they were created in the image of the white man and not of God." Assigning substance to whites and shadows of substance to blacks, he continues: "Hence black people have not had a meaningful share in the substance of the power and wealth of the land; they were treated to the shadow of the substance." This warped substance-shadow encounter coupled with the false nonperson theology mandated a black theology. "There is therefore a need for the substitution of a 'non-white theology' with a 'black theology' or a theology of the image of God in order to put the question of human identity in a proper theological perspective."

55. See Ntwasa, p. 27; Simon Gqubule, "What Is Black Theology?" *Journal of Theology for Southern Africa* (September 1974):19, 21; D.D.L. Makhathini, "Black Theology (I)," in *Relevant Theology For Africa*, ed. H-J Becken (Durban, South Africa: Lutheran Publishing House, 1973), p. 12 (where Makhathini writes specifically of the relation between God and theodicy in South Africa); and Makhathini, "Black Theology (II)," in Becken, pp. 14-17.

56. See *Biko*, p. 31; Biko, "Black Consciousness and the Quest for a True Humanity," in Moore, p. 43; Ntwasa, "The Concept of the Church in Black Theology," in Moore, pp. 112-13; Moore, p. 8; Mafungo, p. 9; and Sigqibo Dwane, "Christianity in the Third World," *Journal of Theology for Southern Africa* (December 1977):8-12.

57. See *Biko*, p. 58; Ntwasa, "The Concept of Church in Black Theology," pp. 110, 114-16; and Buthelezi, "The Relevance of Black Theology," pp. 198-99.

58. Small, p. 15; and Ananias Mpunzi, "Black Theology as Liberation Theology," in Moore, p. 139.

59. See Mpunzi, pp. 137-38; Ntwasa, "The Training of Black Ministers Today," in Moore, p. 146; Mafungo, p. 7; and Gqubule, pp. 22-23.

60. Quotations by Motlhabi are from my interview with him on 20 March 1987. Motlhabi joined the Black Theology Project as an assistant editor in 1971. For views on the origin of black theology and the UCM Black Theology Project, see Buthelezi, "The Relevance of Black Theology"; Bonganjalo Goba, "The Black Consciousness Movement: Its Impact on Black Theology," in *The Unquestionable Right to Be Free*, ed. Mosala and Tlhagale (Maryknoll, NY: Orbis Books, 1986; Johannesburg, South Africa: Skotaville Publishers, 1987), p. 62; Motlhabi, p. 121; *Biko*, pp. 158-59; John W. de Gruchy, *The Church Struggle in South Africa* (Grand Rapids, MI: Eerdmans

Publishing Co., 1979), pp. 153-56; and Marjorie Hope and James Young, *The South African Churches in a Revolutionary Situation* (Maryknoll, NY: Orbis Books, 1981), pp. 78-79.

CHAPTER TWO

1. Albert B. Cleage, *The Black Messiah* (New York: Sheed and Ward, 1968), p. 197.

2. In *Black Christian Nationalism* (New York: William Morrow & Co., 1972), p. 133, Cleage speaks to one of his basic recurring themes: "No Black People in America are really trying to structure a Black Revolution except the Black Christian Nationalists." Also see, *The Black Messiah*, p. 6, where Cleage calls on the church to reinterpret its message for the needs of a "Black Revolution."

3. Cleage asserts: "The theological basis for the gospel of liberation can be found in the life and teachings of Jesus." *Black Christian Nationalism*, p. 188.

4. Quoted in Alex Poinsett, "The Quest for a Black Christ," p. 174.

5. Cleage, *The Black Messiah*, pp. 62, 72, 85, 91, 214.

6. For Cleage's doctrine of Jesus, see *Black Christian Nationalism*, p. 42; also see his statement: "Not in his death, but in his life and in his willingness to die for the Black Nation. To say that God was in Jesus reconciling the world unto Himself at a particular moment on Calvary when Jesus died upon the cross is not the same as saying that God reconciled men unto Himself in the life and teachings of Jesus, which gave men a new conception of human dignity and inspired them to fight to be men instead of slaves" (ibid., p. 188).

7. Cleage's views on liberation can be found in *Black Christian Nationalism*, pp. 183, 188, 230, 9, xvii, 203; and in *The Black Messiah*, pp. 11, 19, 272.

8. See *The Black Messiah*, p. 277, and *Black Christian Nationalism*, p. vii.

9. On Cleage's creed and liturgy, see *Black Christian Nationalism*, p. xiii, and *The Black Messiah*, p. 99.

10. See *The Black Messiah*, p. 37, and *Black Christian Nationalism*, p. 232.

11. *Black Christian Nationalism*, p. 196; also see, *The Black Messiah*, pp. 268-70 for other crimes of whites against blacks. On reconciliation, see *The Black Messiah*, pp. 95, 232, 268-69; and *Black Christian Nationalism*, pp. 13, 55-57, 196. On the Muslims, see *The Autobiography of Malcolm X*, and C. Eric Lincoln, *The Black Muslims in America* (Boston: Beacon Press, 1973). For Cleage's position on violence, see *The Black Messiah*, pp. 16, 95, 120, and *Black Christian Nationalism*, pp. 15, 240.

12. Cleage labels his "very good friend Dr. James H. Cone" black people's "apostle to the Gentiles," because Cone "drags white Christians as far as they are able to go (and then some) in interpreting Black theology within the established framework which they can accept and understand." Cleage, *Black Christian Nationalism*, p. xvii, footnote.

13. See James H. Cone, *My Soul Looks Back* (Nashville, TN: Abingdon Press, 1982; Maryknoll, N.Y., 1986), chap. 2.

14. James H. Cone, "Black Power, Black Theology, and the Study of Theology and Ethics," *Theological Education* (Spring 1970), p. 209.

15. From my 31 March 1987 interview with Dr. Cone.

16. Cone, *Black Theology and Black Power* (New York: Seabury Press, 1969), pp. 32, 38; idem, *My Soul Looks Back*, p. 53.

Cone's theological development has been greatly enhanced by other theological encounters as witnessed in *My Soul Looks Back* and *For My People.* Yet his profound appreciation and support of other liberation theologies complement the inner conviction he penned in his first published theological statement: "It is my thesis ... that Black Power, even in its most radical expression, is not an antithesis of Christianity. ... It is rather Christ's central message to 20th century America." See "Christianity and Black Power," p. 3. From 1968 to the present Cone's basic concerns, questions and theological system revolve around Jesus Christ's liberation vis-à-vis black people's liberation.

17. Regarding the "non-person" comment, see *Black Theology and Black Power*, p. 11. See pp. 40-41 for Cone's view on "white structure of this American society."

18. See Cone, "Freedom, History and Hope," *The Journal of the Interdenominational Theological Center*, vol. 1, no. 1 (Fall 1973):56; and *Black Theology and Black Power*, p. 43.

19. See Cone, "Black Theology and Black Liberation," *The Christian Century* (16 September 1970), pp. 1086-87; and *Black Theology and Black Power*, pp. 36-37.

20. See Cone's *Black Theology and Black Power*, pp. 35, 38, and 120; also see, Cone, *A Black Theology of Liberation*, 2d ed. (Maryknoll, NY: Orbis Books, 1986), pp. 120-21.

21. In 1974 Roberts stated: "For blacks, Jesus is understood in a psychocultural sense. He leads us to a new self-understanding. He helps us to overcome the identity crisis triggered by white oppression of blacks" (*A Black Political Theology* [Philadelphia: Westminster Press, 1974], p. 137).

22. In 1968, Cleage wrote: "We are convinced, upon the basis of our knowledge and historic study of all the facts, that Jesus was born to a black Mary, that Jesus, the Messiah, was a black man" (*The Black Messiah*, p. 85).

23. See Cone, *God of the Oppressed* (New York: Seabury Press, 1975), pp. 135-37. On page 136 he also opposes Roberts' notion of psychocultural. "Christ," Cone claimed, "is black, therefore, not because of some cultural or psychological need of black people, but because and only because Christ really enters into our world where the poor, the despised, and the black are." In *For My People* Cone attacks Cleage's "Black Messiah" christology for "distorting history and the Christian gospel" (p. 36).

24. Cone, *A Black Theology of Liberation*, pp. 110-24.

25. See Cone, *Black Theology and Black Power*, pp. 36, 42-43; see also, *A Black Theology of Liberation*, p. 6.

26. See the introduction to *Black Theology and Black Power*.

27. See Roberts' section on reconciliation below.

28. See Cone, *Black Theology and Black Power*, p. 145; idem, "Toward a Black Theology," *Ebony*, vol. 25, no. 10 (August 1970), p. 114. In his reconciliation position Cone combats (a) white people's seemingly inevitable practice of setting the terms in black-white encounters. By redistributing power, white inclination to abusive authority lacks the potency to implement itself; and (b) he fights for the right of the oppressed community to self-determination when dealing with oppressors.

29. See Cone, "Theological Reflections on Reconciliation," *Christianity and Crisis* (22 January 1973), pp. 307-8; *God of the Oppressed*, p. 245; and *Black Theology and Black Power*, pp. 150-51.

30. Two other members of the black political theology trend need mentioning: Major J. Jones and Preston N. Williams. Jones' theological concerns parallel Rob-

erts'. Theologically both originate from the Martin Luther King, Jr., period. While agreeing with all political theologians' liberation stance, Jones is more sensitive to the goal of integration. Referencing his role in black theology's development, Jones stated in a 20 February 1987 interview with this author: "I was more indigenous to the Civil Rights days. . . . Martin [Luther King, Jr.] and I were close friends and contemporaries at Boston University's doctoral programs. [Therefore] I was much more schooled in the tradition of non-violence."

Like Jones, Preston N. Williams is a black ethicist. Similar to Roberts and Jones, his theology strives to be included equally around the decision-making table with whites. In the same instance, he applauds the contributions of Black Power.

31. J. Deotis Roberts, *Liberation and Reconciliation* (Philadelphia: Westminster Press, 1971), p. 34. Also see, Roberts, *A Black Political Theology*, p. 26.

32. Roberts, *Liberation and Reconciliation*, p. 28.

33. See Roberts, *Liberation and Reconciliation*, p. 43; his "on both sides of the fence" comments are from my 19 March 1987 interview with him; for other references to his "balance" approach, see *Liberation and Reconciliation*, p. 13. For his definition of theology, see "Black Theology in the Making," *Review and Expositor*, vol. 70 (1973), p. 321. On his interpretation of "Christian," review his "Black Theology in Faith and Ethics," *Black Theology Today: Liberation and Contextualization* (New York: Mellen Press, 1983), p. 58; "Black Liberation Theism," *The Journal of Religious Thought*, vol. 33, no. 1 (Spring-Summer 1976):33; and "The Roots of Black Theology: An Historic Perspective," in *Black Theology Today*, p. 83. For black theology as "inner city" theology, examine his *A Black Political Theology*, p. 115.

34. Roberts, "Black Theology in Faith and Ethics," p. 65 and *Liberation and Reconciliation*, p. 26. He also writes: "I stand somewhere between the generations— that is, on the boundary between the black militants and the old-fashioned civil rights integrationists, and also between the 'by whatever means necessary' ethicists and the view that liberation and reconciliation must be considered at the same time and in relation to each other" (ibid., p. 13).

35. "Black Theology in Faith and Ethics," p. 67. Other references to his liberation and reconciliation connection are found in *Liberation and Reconciliation*, pp. 28 ("in the context of reconciliation" and "beyond liberation"), 32 ("the priority consideration"), and 117 ("proper precondition"); *A Black Political Theology*, pp. 16, 221 ("essence of good news"); "Black Theology in the Making," pp. 326 ("heart and center"), 327 ("more excellent way"); "Christian Liberation Ethics: The Black Experience," *Religion in Life*, vol. 48, no. 2 (Summer 1979), p. 234 ("human liberation"); and "Black Liberation Theism," *The Journal of Religious Thought* (Spring-Summer 1976):35 ("reconciliation . . . final goal").

36. For an account of his Christological claims, that is, black Messiah, colorless Christ, liberation and reconciliation, see Roberts, *Liberation and Reconciliation*, chap. 6, "The Black Messiah," and *A Black Political Theology*, chap. 5, "Jesus Means Freedom."

37. From my 5 November 1987 interview with Dr. Jones.

38. For a fuller grasp of Jones' treatment of theodicy and secular humanism/ humanocentric theism, see Jones, *Is God a White Racist? A Preamble to Black Theology* (Garden City, NY: Anchor Books, 1973); "Theodicy: The Controlling Category for Black Theology," *Journal of Religious Thought*, vol. 30, no. 1 (Spring-Summer 1973); and "Theodicy and Methodology in Black Theology: A Critique of Washington, Cone and Cleage," *Harvard Theological Review*, vol. 64 (October 1971).

Also view "Religious Humanism: Its Problems and Prospects in Black Religion and Culture," *The Journal of the ITC* (Spring 1980) for his apologetic approach to the existence of religious humanism in black religion.

39. See Roberts, *Black Theology Today*, pp. 43, 109; and idem, *Black Theology in Dialogue* (Philadelphia: Westminster Press, 1987), pp. 116-17.

40. The "comprehensive field" reference is found in Roberts, *Liberation and Reconciliation*, pp. 19-20. Tutu's quote comes from *Maryknoll* magazine (July 1987), back cover. For Roberts' "liberating experience of reconciliation," see *A Black Political Theology*, p. 222.

41. See Roberts' "Black Theology and the Theological Revolution," *The Journal of Religious Thought*, vol. 28, no. 1 (Spring-Summer 1971):15 for the "broad field of theology" quote. And refer to *Liberation and Reconciliation*, p. 23, in regard to the "too often subjective" statement.

42. See Cleage, *Black Christian Nationalism*, pp. 64-65, 137, 218, 239.

43. For reference to what I call his genetic determinism, see Cleage, *Black Christian Nationalism*, p. 62.

44. Concerning Cleage and Marxism, see *Black Christian Nationalism*, p. 91.

45. Cone, *Black Theology and Black Power*, p. 91. We should note that with *God of the Oppressed* and *The Spirituals and the Blues* (New York: Seabury Press, 1972), Dr. Cone demonstrated the vital connection among black culture, Africa and black theology.

46. See Chapter 3 below for Long's and Wilmore's insistence on the intimate relation between Africa and Afro-America. And see Young, *Black and African Theologies: Siblings or Distant Cousins?* (Maryknoll, NY: Orbis Books, 1986), p. 33.

47. See Cone, *God of the Oppressed*, p. 54; idem, *For My People*, p. 2; idem, *Speaking the Truth*, p. 43; and idem, *A Black Theology of Liberation*, p. 59.

In "Christian Theology and the Afro-American Revolution," *Christianity and Crisis* (8 June 1970), pp. 124-25, Cone calls for "new theological sources" in the doing of theology and includes Malcolm X (a black nationalist Muslim) and LeRoi Jones (a black nationalist secularist). Yet his call for new non-Christian theological sources in the doing of black theology does not seem to suggest to Cone that these non-Christian sources raise the question of exploring a non-Christian (i.e., non-Barthian and non-Tillichian) definition of theology that both encompasses and goes beyond the Christian church.

48. Cone, *Speaking the Truth*, p. 43.

49. Karl Barth believed: "As a theological discipline dogmatics is the scientific self-examination of the Christian Church with respect to the content of its distinctive talk about God. . . . Theology is a function of the Church" (*Church Dogmatics I.1, The Doctrine of the Word of God* [Edinburgh: T&T Clark, 1980], p. 3). Tillich believed: "Theology, as a function of the Christian church, must serve the needs of the church" (*Systematic Theology*, vol. 1 [Chicago: University of Chicago Press, 1951], p. 3). Both define and restrict theology to the Christian church, notwithstanding Tillich's claim to intertwine the two strands of "eternal faith" and "temporal situation." Both Barth and Tillich were white European males who have become pillars in the white Euro-North American theological establishments. Their definitions of theology arose from their social, political and cultural locations. On the other hand, the black community and black church (sacred and secular *together* possessing a liberation impulse) wrestle with another problematic—white racism.

Based on Cone's own theological project, the black community should therefore define its own black theological paradigm.

50. Cone, *A Black Theology of Liberation*, pp. 8-9.

51. For a historical account of black faith in black life, see Wilmore, *Black Religion and Black Radicalism*; and Vincent Harding, *There Is a River, the Black Struggle for Freedom in America* (New York: Harcourt Brace Jovanovich, 1981). David Garrow's Pulitzer Prize winning *Bearing the Cross, Martin Luther King, Jr., and the Southern Christian Leadership Conference* (New York: William Morrow & Co., 1986) reflects an account of black faith in the Civil Rights Movement. Black faith during the Black Power era is shown in Wilmore and Cone, *Black Theology: A Documentary History, 1966-1979*. Black faith in the Rainbow Coalition can be found in Sheila Collins, *The Rainbow Challenge, the Jackson Campaign and the Future of U.S. Politics* (New York: Monthly Review Press, 1986); Manning Marable, *Black American Politics, from the Washington Marches to Jesse Jackson* (London: Verso, 1985), particularly chap. 5, "Rainbow Rebellion"; and Roger D. Hatch, *Beyond Opportunity: Jesse Jackson's Vision for America* (Philadelphia: Fortress Press, 1988).

CHAPTER THREE

1. From my 19 February 1987 interview with Dr. Wilmore.

2. See Wilmore, *Black Religion and Black Radicalism*, pp. 218–19.

3. Wilmore, "Black Theology: Its Significance for Christian Mission Today," *International Review of Mission*, vol. 63, no. 250 (April 1974), p. 214.

4. Peter Paris, *The Social Teachings of the Black Churches* (Philadelphia: Fortress Press, 1985). In my 10 March 1987 interview, Dr. Paris described his work as considering "the black church more as a holistic thing, putting the radical tradition in its place, but showing that the main thrust of black theology is not simply in the radical tradition of the black church, but it is even present in the conservative tradition and in the moderate tradition."

5. Wilmore, *Black Religion and Black Radicalism*, p. 237.

6. The following quotations referring to Wilmore's first three sources can be found in Wilmore, *Black Religion and Black Radicalism*, pp. 234-41.

7. Ibid., p. 222.

8. Wilmore's views and quotes on Africanisms come from my 19 February 1987 interview with him; *Black Religion and Black Radicalism*, p. 239; and his "Reinterpretation in Black Church History," *The Chicago Theological Seminary Register* (Winter 1983), p. 29.

9. Wilmore, *Black Religion and Black Radicalism*, p. 219.

10. Wilmore, "Black Theology: Its Significance for Christian Mission Today," p. 215.

11. Wilmore, "Spirituality and Social Transformation as the Vocation of the Black Church," in *Churches in Struggle. Liberation Theologies and Social Transformation in North America*, ed. William Tabb (New York: Monthly Review Press, 1986), pp. 240–41.

12. From my 19 February 1987 interview with Gayraud S. Wilmore. In "Spirituality and Social Transformation as the Vocation of the Black Church," Wilmore writes: "To speak of the mission and strategy of the black church as the cultural rather than political is not to deny the political, but to subsume it in a larger context;

and it is precisely in such a context that we can see how the spiritual dimension of life impinges upon the problems and possibilities of social transformation. This means that we intend to encompass the entire scale of perceptions, meanings, values, behavioral patterns, etc., all integrated in that system of symbols we call culture . . . and take passionate actions on the basis of such conceptions" (p. 248).

13. Charles H. Long, "The West African High God: History and Religious Experience," *History of Religions*, vol. 3, no. 2 (Winter 1964), p. 331.

14. Along with Long, Carleton L. Lee fought for establishing a black theological structure not based on white resources. For instance, commenting on the black political theological trend, Lee states: "With few exceptions, the criteria for judging the effectiveness of Black religious institutional forms have been in terms of norms arising from sources either remote from or foreign to the internal dynamics of the Black community." Specifying James Cone's 1969 text, Lee writes: Cone "seems too greatly bound to traditional theological categories." Commenting on Albert Cleage (Cone's black political theological trend colleague), Lee continues: "There is very little in his approach which challenges either the assumptions or the substance of 'white' Christianity that a modest quantity of 'white paint' would accomplish the task." Dismissing the inadequacy of these "external" characterizations of what he calls "black religious experience," Lee believes that there "is sufficient substance and content in Black religious experience for an autonomous theological statement; a Black religious critique." See Carleton L. Lee, "Toward a Sociology of the Black Religious Experience," *The Journal of Religious Thought* (Autumn-Winter 1972).

15. Charles H. Long, *Significations* (Philadelphia: Fortress Press, 1986), p. 7. In my 21 February 1987 interview with him, Dr. Long commented: Out of religion "all the other languages come . . . all of it comes from this attempt to orient yourself in your time and space. . . . Religion is produced out of the culture. . . . Given all that, and for black theology to come along and then narrow [religious language] all down again."

16. Interview of 21 February 1987.

17. Interview of 21 February 1987; and Charles H. Long, "Freedom, Otherness and Religion: Theologies Opaque," *The Chicago Theological Seminary Register* (Winter 1983), pp. 20-22.

18. Interview of 21 February 1987 with Dr. Long.

19. See Charles H. Long, "Perspectives for a Study of Afro-American Religion in the United States," *History of Religions*, vol. 11, no. 1 (August 1971), p. 55.

20. Interview of 21 February 1987.

21. Review Long, "Perspectives for a Study of Afro-American Religion in the United States," pp. 59-62. From his three sections I deduce four sources. Unless otherwise indicated, quotations in this section come from this article.

22. For Long's view and suggestions on Africanism, see Charles H. Long, "A New Look at American Religion," *Anglican Theological Review* (July 1973), p. 122; and idem, "Perspectives for a Study of Afro-American Religion in the United States," pp. 57-59.

23. See Long, *Significations*, p. 170. Dr. Long also elaborated similar points in my interview with him.

24. Long, *Significations*, p. 106.

25. See Charles H. Long, "The Black Reality: Toward a Theology of Freedom," *Criterion*, vol. 8, no. 2 (Spring-Summer 1969), p. 6. Here Long points out the pos-

sibility of liberation for the larger humanity coming through the "otherness" in the black community.

26. Charles H. Long, "Structural Similarities and Dissimilarities in Black and African Theologies," *The Journal of Religious Thought*, vol. 32, no. 2 (Fall-Winter 1975):16-17.

27. Ibid., p. 24.

28. Cf. Charles H. Long, "New Space, New Time: Disjunctions and Context for New World Religions," *Criterion* (Winter 1985), p. 7.

In *Significations* Long writes: "The religion of [Afro-Americans] who have had to bear the weight of [cultural contact] in the modern world should generate forms of critical languages capable of creating the proper disjunctions for a restatement of the reality of the human in worlds to come" (p. 6). One can note at least two points. First, within his larger project of dialogue between diverse American religious traditions, the Afro-American religious tradition is particularly suited to make a big contribution to the new language of religious meaning. Second, Long believes Afro-American religious experience can generate new language to restate human reality.

29. Cecil W. Cone, *The Identity Crisis in Black Theology* (Nashville, TN.: AMEC, 1975), p. 6.

30. Interview of 11 March 1987 with Dr. Cone.

31. See C. Cone, *The Identity Crisis in Black Theology*, pp. 42–44; and C. Cone, "The Black Religious Experience," *The Journal of the Interdenominational Theological Seminary*, vol. 2, no. 2 (Spring 1975), p. 137.

32. C. Cone, *The Identity Crisis in Black Theology*, p. 23.

33. My understanding of Cone's sources comes from *The Identity Crisis in Black Theology*, pp. 26-39, and my interview with him.

34. Interview of 11 March 1987; also C. Cone, *The Identity Crisis in Black Theology*, pp. 28-29.

35. C. Cone, *The Identity Crisis in Black Theology*, p. 83.

36. In our interview Dr. Cecil Cone clarified the difference between the "earlier Jim Cone" and the "later Jim Cone." The earlier James Cone catered more toward black power, in Cecil Cone's view. Though still a strong advocate of black political liberation, the later James Cone has moved closer to black religious sources in black theology.

37. C. Cone, *The Identity Crisis in Black Theology*, p. 71.

38. On C. Cone's understanding of liberation, see: *The Identity Crisis in Black Theology*, pp. 71, 118; and "The Black Religious Experience," pp. 138-39.

39. Wilmore, *Black Religion and Black Radicalism*, p. xii.

40. Vincent Harding, "Black Power and the American Christ," *Christian Century* (4 January 1967); idem, "The Religion of Black Power," in *The Religious Situation: 1968*, ed. D. R. Cutler (Boston: Beacon Press, 1968); idem, "Religion and Resistance Among Antebellum Negroes, 1800-1860," in *The Making of Black America*, vol. 1, ed. Meier and Rudwick (New York: Atheneum, 1969).

41. My assessment of Dr. Harding's spirituality theology comes from an 18 March 1987 interview with him; also see "The Religion of Black Power," where he writes, concerning black folk, that "we are a spiritual people."

42. Interview of 18 March 1987.

43. Quotations on Harding's sources are from the 18 March 1987 interview.

44. Ibid.

45. Harding, *There Is a River*, p. xxiii.

46. Ibid., p. xxiv.

47. Interview of 18 March 1987.

48. Interview of 19 February 1987.

49. This Christological critique does not disparage Dr. Wilmore's knowledge of the liberating work and person of Jesus Christ. Wilmore is an ordained minister in the Presbyterian Church U.S.A. My point accentuates and questions, rather, the dialectical unity between the liberative elements in Christian and non-Christian religions and theologies and the function of Jesus Christ in that dialectic.

50. C. Cone, "Toward a New Introduction to Christian Theology: Telling the Story," *The Journal of the ITC*, vol. 3, no. 2 (Spring 1976):17.

51. C. Cone, *The Identity Crisis in Black Theology*, pp. 35-36.

52. In *Theology Today*, vol. 26, no. 3 (October 1969), Wilmore's article was titled, "Reparations: Don't Hang Up on a Word." He exposed white ministers for avoiding granting the black community reparations through the black church by "having a veritable orgy these days with the word *reparations*" (p. 284).

CHAPTER FOUR

1. Allan Boesak, "Coming in Out of the Wilderness," in *The Emergent Gospel*, ed. Sergio Torres and Virginia Fabella (Maryknoll, NY: Orbis Books, 1978), p. 80.

2. Mosala and Tlhagale, p. xviii.

3. Peter Walshe, *Church Versus State in South Africa: The Case of the Christian Institute* (Maryknoll, NY: Orbis Books, 1983), pp. 87-88.

4. See Motlhabi; Gerhart; Walshe; Hope and Young.

5. See Alan Brooks and Jeremy Brickhill, *Whirlwind Before the Storm: The Origins and Development of the Uprising in Soweto and the Rest of South Africa From June to December 1976* (London: International Defence and Aid Fund for Southern Africa, 1980); and Baruch Hirson, *Year of Fire and Year of Ash, the Soweto Revolt: Roots of a Revolution?* (London: Zed Press, 1979).

6. For the details on the Freedom Charter, see Motlhabi; Gerhart; *30 Years of the Freedom Charter*, ed. Raymond Suttner and Jeremy Cronin (Johannesburg, South Africa: Raven Press, 1986); Roux; Lodge; and T.R.H. Davenport, *South Africa: A Modern History*, 3d ed. (Toronto: University of Toronto Press, 1987).

7. "Prophetic" Christians, black and white, began the process of writing the *Kairos Document* in June 1985. South Africa was and still is under a state of emergency and the country, particularly evidenced by military occupation of the townships, was and still is in a civil war. See *The Kairos Document*, rev. 2d ed. (Johannesburg, South Africa: Skotaville Publishers, 1986).

For further analysis of apartheid theology, see Charles Villa-Vicencio, *The Theology of Apartheid* (Cape Town, South Africa: The Methodist Publishing House, n.d.).

8. Manas Buthelezi, "The Christian Institute and Black South Africa," *South African Outlook* (October 1974), p. 163.

9. See Buthelezi, "Christianity in South Africa," *Pro Veritate* (15 June 1973), p. 6.

10. Ibid., p. 4.

11. Buthelezi, "Black Theology in Bangkok," *South African Outlook* (September 1973), p. 156.

12. Buthelezi, "The Christian Challenge of Black Theology," in *Black Renaissance*, ed. Thoahlane Thoahlane (Johannesburg, South Africa: Raven Press, 1975), p. 23.

13. Buthelezi "Towards Indigenous Theology in South Africa," in Torres and Fabella, p. 68.

14. See Buthelezi, "Change in the Church," *South African Outlook* (August 1973), p. 130; idem, "Six Theses: Theological Problems of Evangelism in the South African Context," *Journal of Theology for Southern Africa* (June 1973):56; and idem, "Black Theology in Bangkok," *South African Outlook* (September 1973), p. 156.

15. Buthelezi, "Change in the Church," *South African Outlook*, (August 1973), p. 129; and idem, "Change in the Church," *Pro Veritate* (September 1973).

16. Buthelezi, "Christianity in South Africa," *Pro Veritate* (15 June 1973), p. 4; and idem, "Christianity in My World," *Katallagete*, vol. 5, no. 1 (Spring 1974).

17. Buthelezi "The Relevance of Theology," p. 198.

18. Buthelezi, "Christianity in South Africa," p. 4.

19. See Buthelezi, "Church Unity and Human Divisions of Racism," *International Review of Missions* (August 1984), pp. 424-25.

20. Buthelezi, "Giving Witness to the Heart of the Gospel," *International Review of Mission* (August 1984), p. 417.

21. Buthelezi, "Christianity in South Africa," p. 6.

22. Buthelezi, "The Relevance of Black Theology," p. 199.

23. Buthelezi, "Christianity in South Africa," pp. 5-6. Also see, idem, "Six Theses," p. 55.

24. Buthelezi, "Toward a Biblical Faith in South African Society," *Journal of Theology for Southern Africa* (June 1977):58.

25. See Charles Villa-Vicencio, "An All-Pervading Heresy: Racism and the English-speaking Churches," in *Apartheid Is a Heresy*, ed. John W. de Gruchy and Charles Villa-Vicencio (Grand Rapids, MI: Eerdmans Publishing Co., 1983), p. 59.

26. Boesak, "Theology for Justice" speech presented at Stony Point, NY, 2 March 1987.

27. See Boesak, "Wholeness Through Liberation," *Church and Society* (May/June 1981), p. 36; idem, "Annexure H: He Made Us All But . . ." in *Apartheid Change and the NGK*, ed. J.H.P. Serfontein (Pretoria, South Africa: Taurus, 1982), pp. 243-48; idem, "The Black Church and the Future," *South African Outlook* (July 1979), p. 102; and idem, *If This Is Treason, I Am Guilty* (Grand Rapids, MI: Eerdmans Publishing Co., 1987), p. 2.

28. See Boesak, "Civil Religion and the Black Community," *Journal of Theology for Southern Africa* (June 1977):36; and idem, *Farewell to Innocence* (Maryknoll, NY: Orbis Books, 1977), p. 25.

29. Boesak, *Black and Reformed* (Maryknoll, NY: Orbis Books, 1984), p. 87.

30. See Boesak, "Coming in Out of the Wilderness," in Torres and Fabella, pp. 82-83; idem, *Farewell to Innocence*, p. 143; idem, "Introduction: Relevant Preaching in a Black Context," in *The Finger of God* (Maryknoll, NY: Orbis Books, 1982); idem, "The Relationship Between Text and Situation, Reconciliation and Liberation in Black Theology," in *Voices of the Third World*, vol. 2, no. 1 (June 1979), p. 30; and idem, *If This Is Treason, I Am Guilty*, p. 14.

31. Boesak, *Farewell to Innocence*, p. 9.

32. Boesak, "Holding on to the Vision," *All African Council of Churches Magazine* (December 1983), p. 20; and idem, *Black and Reformed*, p. 65.

33. Boesak, *Farewell to Innocence*, pp. 148-49; also see, idem, "Courage to Be Black, Part 1," *South African Outlook* (October 1975), p. 153, and *Black and Reformed*, pp. 9-10, regarding black oppressors and bourgeois individualism.

34. Boesak, *Black and Reformed*, p. 118; idem, *If This Is Treason, I Am Guilty*, p. 36; idem, *Farewell to Innocence*, pp. 151-152; and idem, "Liberation Theology in South Africa," in *African Theology En Route*, ed. Appiah-Kubi and Torres (Maryknoll, NY: Orbis Books, 1981), p. 173.

35. Boesak, "The Black Church and the Future," *South African Outlook* (July 1979), p. 103; and idem, "The Law of Christ," in *The Finger of God*.

36. See Boesak, "Courage to Be Black, Part 1," p. 152; and idem, *Farewell to Innocence*, pp. 17-20, 93.

37. On the task of blacks in reconciliation, see Boesak, "Courage to Be Black, Part 2," *South African Outlook* (November 1975), p. 168; idem, " 'To Break Every Yoke . . .' Liberation and the Churches of Africa," *South African Outlook* (October 1981), p. 62; and idem, *Farewell to Innocence*, p. 139.

38. On the task of whites, see Boesak, "The Black Church and the Future," p. 101; idem, *EcuNews Bulletin* (3 August 1979); idem, *If This Is Treason, I Am Guilty*, p. 41.

39. Boesak, "The Relationship Between Text and Situation, Reconciliation and Liberation in Black Theology," p. 36.

40. Boesak, "Coming in Out of the Wilderness," p. 87; and idem, "Courage to Be Black, Part 2," p. 167.

41. Boesak, "The Black Church and the Future," *South African Outlook*, p. 103; idem, *If This Is Treason, I Am Guilty*, pp. 14–15; idem, *The Finger of God*, pp. 53-54; idem, " 'To Break Every Yoke . . .' Liberation and the Churches of Africa," p. 161; and idem, *Black and Reformed*, pp. 34, 74.

42. In our 3 December 1986 interview Dr. Maimela sighted four major theological themes in his black theology: a) a God of liberation "who is essentially for us and for our well-being" revealed in the scriptures; b) God gave humans authority to be "creative and meaningful and helpful beings who act in God's stead." "So anthropology is one key doctrine"; c) "awareness that life as it is structured in society today is not necessarily according to God's will. . . . It is within our power and we are agents of change"; and d) "the broadening of that concept [of salvation] to include the social and physical dimension of liberation." The essence of all four themes, in my opinion, hinges primarily on a theological anthropology of liberation.

43. Maimela, "Man in 'White' Theology," *Missionalia,* vol. 9, no. 1 (April 1981), pp. 68-69; idem, *Proclaim Freedom to My People* (Johannesburg, South Africa: Skotaville Publishers, 1987). For a longer version of this article, see his "Man in 'White' Theology," *Journal of Theology for Southern Africa* (September 1981).

44. Maimela, "Theology and Politics in South Africa," *Chicago Theological Seminary Register* (Spring 1979), p. 11.

45. Maimela, "Man in 'White' Theology," pp. 67-75; idem, "Theology and Politics in South Africa," pp. 22-23; and idem, "Towards a Theology of Humanization," *Journal of Theology for Southern Africa* (December 1982):58.

In "Theology and Politics in South Africa," Maimela writes: "God meets and involves us nowhere but in the sociocultural and political situation. . . . Politics can be defined broadly as humans' attempt to structure, construct and institutionalize their interpersonal and personal social relationships so that they can live humanely and justly. . . . Politics, in our usage of this term, embraces all spheres of life in which humans find themselves, whether this be the social, economic, political, cultural, judicial, racial, and historico-psychological situations" (p. 12).

46. Interview of 3 December 1986 with Dr. Maimela. Also see, Maimela, "Black Theology," *All African Conference of Churches Magazine* (May 1984), p. 3; idem, "The Atonement in the Context of Liberation," *Journal of Theology for Southern Africa* (June 1982); idem, "The Atonement in the Context of Liberation Theology," *South African Outlook* (December 1981), p. 185; idem, *Proclaim Freedom to My People* (Johannesburg, South Africa: Skotaville Publishers, 1987), p. 87ff.; and idem, "Current Themes and Emphases in Black Theology," in Mosala and Tlhagale.

47. Refer to Maimela, "Theology and Politics in South Africa," p. 23; idem, "Black Power and Black Theology in Southern Africa," *Scriptura* 12 (June 1984), p. 46.; idem, "Towards a Theology of Humanisation," *Journal of Theology for Southern Africa* (December 1982):60-63; and idem, "Black Theology," p. 6.

48. Maimela, "Man in 'White' Theology," pp. 71-76.

49. Ibid., p. 77.

50. Maimela, "Black Power and Black Theology In Southern Africa," p. 48.

51. Maimela, "Man in 'White' Theology, p. 77; idem, "An Anthropological Heresy: A Critique of White Theology," in de Gruchy and Villa-Vicencio, pp. 48-58.

52. Maimela, "The Atonement in the Context of Liberation Theology," *South African Outlook* (December 1981), pp. 184-85. Also see, idem, "Black Theology," p. 5.

53. See "What Is Contextual Theology?" *All African Conference of Churches Magazine* (December 1984), pp. 14-15. The specific author of this article is named "The Institute for Contextual Theology." However, I attribute the substance of the article's argument to Chikane since he was the general secretary. Moreover, my 1 December 1986 interview with Chikane confirms his penchant toward a Contextual People's Theology.

54. See Chikane, "Doing Theology in a Situation of Conflict," in *Resistance and Hope: South African Essays in Honour of Beyers Naude*, ed. C. Villa-Vicencio and J. W. de Gruchy (Grand Rapids, MI: Eerdmans Publishing Co., 1985), p. 101.

55. Interview of 1 December 1986.

56. Interview of 1 December 1986. Also see, Chikane, "Doing Theology in a Situation of Conflict," p. 99.

57. Interview of 1 December 1986. Also see, Chikane, "Bible Study and Theological Reflection," *South African Outlook* (May 1985), p. 77: "In our struggle we are not only fighting to replace colour, but much more."

58. Chikane, "The Incarnation in the Life of the People in Southern Africa," *Journal of Theology for Southern Africa* (June 1985):47: "In the incarnation we are called to abandon the old theology of reconciliation."

59. Ibid., pp. 44-46.

CHAPTER FIVE

1. For example, Dr. Maimela, a prominent member of the South African political theological trend, has also shown serious interest in indigenous African sources, a major concern of the cultural theological trend. See Maimela, "Salvation in African Traditional Religions," *Missionalia*, vol. 13, no. 2 (August 1985).

2. The 1949 Programme of Action represented the pan-Africanist, nationalist

impulse in the African National Congress. Anton Lembede symbolizes this movement. Later this trend (often called the Africanists) broke with the ANC over the Freedom Charter (among other things) and founded the Pan Africanist Congress of Azania in 1959. On the Freedom Charter-ANC and the Programme of Action-PAC, see footnote 6 in Chapter 4, and also Fatton.

3. See Goba, "An African Christian Theology," *Journal of Theology for Southern Africa* (March 1979):3.

4. Ibid., p. 4.

5. Ibid., pp. 3-4. See also, Goba, *An Agenda for Black Theology: Hermeneutics for Social Change* (Johannesburg, South Africa: Skotaville Publishers, 1988), pp. 13-16; idem, "The Role of the Black Church in the Process of Healing Human Brokenness," *Journal of Theology for Southern Africa* (September 1979):8-9.

6. Goba, "Doing Theology in South Africa: A Black Christian Perspective," *Journal of Theology for Southern Africa* (June 1980):24; idem, *An Agenda for Black Theology in South Africa*, pp. 3, 7.

7. See Goba, "Towards a 'Black' Ecclesiology," *Missionalia*, vol. 9, no. 2 (August 1981), p. 49.

8. Goba's views on pan-Africanism come from my 2 March 1987 interview with him. The black consciousness reference comes from Goba, "The Black Consciousness Movement: Its Impact on Black Theology," in Mosala and Tlhagale, pp. 66-67.

9. Goba, *An Agenda for Black Theology in South Africa*, p. 6.

10. Goba, "Corporate Personality: Ancient Israel and Africa," in Moore, pp. 67-69; idem, "The Task of Black Theological Education in South Africa," *Journal of Theology for Southern Africa* (March 1978):19-21; idem, "An African Christian Theology," p. 8.

11. Goba, *Agenda for Black Theology in South Africa*, pp. 53-55.

12. Goba, "Doing Theology in South Africa: A Black Christian Perspective," pp. 24, 28; and idem, "Towards a 'Black' Ecclesiology," p. 56.

13. Interview of 2 March 1987.

14. Goba, "Doing Theology in South Africa: A Black Christian Perspective," p. 32; idem, "The Way Through—1" *South African Outlook* (September 1980), p. 136.

15. The discussion on Dr. Goba's critical theory source and how it contrasts with the "vulgar Marxist approach" comes from our 2 March 1987 interview.

16. Goba, "Emerging Theological Perspectives in South Africa," in *Irruption of the Third World: Challenge to Theology*, ed. V. Fabella and S. Torres (Maryknoll, NY: Orbis Books, 1983), p. 21.

17. Goba, "The Problem of Racism Revisited: A Theological Critique," in *New Faces of Africa*, ed. J. W. Hofmeyr and W. S. Vorster (Pretoria, South Africa: University of South Africa, 1984), p. 97. Goba's full citation reads: "For as we all know, the fundamental problem that continues to haunt our lives is that of racism. Unfortunately there is a tendency amongst some of our young black radicals to underestimate this problem by emphasizing the problem of class." Also see, Goba, "The Task of Black Theological Education in South Africa," pp. 26-27.

18. Goba, "Emerging Theological Perspectives," p. 20; idem, "Doing Theology in South Africa: A Black Christian Perspective"; and idem, "Two Views on Black Theology," *Pro Veritate* (15 September 1971), p. 9.

19. Goba, "The Problem of Racism Revisited: A Theological Critique," pp. 98-100; and idem, "A Black South African Perspective," in *Doing Theology in a Divided*

World, ed. V. Fabella and S. Torres (Maryknoll, NY: Orbis Books, 1985), p. 58.

20. Goba, "Emerging Theological Perspectives in South Africa," p. 21; idem, "Doing Theology in South Africa: A Black Christian Perspective," p. 24. Dr. Goba also spoke about the new liberated South Africa and humanity in our interview.

21. Goba, "Doing Theology in South Africa: A Black Christian Perspective," pp. 30, 35; idem, "Corporate Personality: Ancient Israel and Africa," pp. 70-72; and idem, "Two Views on Black Theology," pp. 9-10.

22. Goba, "The Task of Black Theological Education in South Africa," p. 24; and idem, "Corporate Personality: Ancient Israel and Africa," p. 73.

23. Itumeleng J. Mosala, "African Independent Churches: A Study in Socio-Theological Protest," in *Resistance and Hope,* p. 107.

Historical materialism permeates Mosala's understanding of both the Bible and African traditional religions, as well as all religions. On the relation between the Bible and historical materialism, see Mosala, "The Use of the Bible in Black Theology," in Mosala and Tlhagale, pp. 186-97; idem, "The Biblical God from the Perspective of the Poor," in *God and Global Justice: Religion and Poverty in an Unequal World*, ed. F. Ferre and R. H. Mataragnon (New York: Paragon House, 1985), p. 166-67; and idem, "African Independent Churches, p. 108.

On the relation between African traditional religions (and all religions) and historical materialism, see Mosala, "African Traditional Beliefs and Christianity," *Journal of Theology for Southern Africa* (June 1983):17-19; and idem, "African Independent Churches," p. 106.

24. Ibid., p. 105.

25. Ibid., pp. 103-7. Unfortunately Mosala does not acknowledge the specific context in which "contextual" theologians do theology. These theologians call for the contextualization of theology over against European-North American theology's claims about its normalcy, universality and timelessness. In other words "contextual theology" critiques any theology that submits to an analysis out of context. On the contrary, all theologies are limited by time, place and condition, that is, by contexts.

26. Mosala, "The Use of the Bible in Black Theology," in Mosala and Tlhagale, p. 181.

27. Interview of 1 December 1986.

28. Mosala, "The Relevance of African Traditional Religions and Their Challenge to Black Theology," in Mosala and Tlhagale, pp. 93-98; and idem, "African Traditional Beliefs and Christianity," pp. 25, 22.

29. Interview of 1 December 1986.

30. Mosala, "The Use of the Bible in Black Theology," p. 185; idem, "African Independent Churches, p. 109; and idem, "Social Scientific Approaches to the Bible: One Step Forward, Two Steps Backward," *Journal of Theology for Southern Africa* (June 1986):30.

In "African Independent Churches," Mosala hammers away at the liberal idealist notion of culture. Idealism paints a picture of an abstract, value-free culture. On the other hand Mosala's historical materialism defines culture "in relation to its historical, material basis. . . . It can be either reactionary or revolutionary, depending on the configuration of social forces in society and their corresponding degree of politicisation" (p. 109).

31. Mosala, "Black Theology in South Africa and North America: Prospects for the Future; Building of Alliances," unpublished paper presented at the Black Theology Conference: Dialogue Between U.S.A. and South Africa, Union Theological

Seminary, New York (1-3 December 1986), p. 7; and idem, "African Independent Churches, pp. 110-11.

32. Mosala, "Ethics of the Economic Principles: Church and Secular Investments," in *Hammering Swords Into Ploughshares: Essays in Honour of Archbishop Mpilo Desmond Tutu*, ed. B. Tlhagale and I. Mosala (Johannesburg, South Africa: Skotaville Publishers, 1986), p. 120; and idem, "The Biblical God From the Perspective of the Poor," pp. 160-66.

33. Mosala, "The Use of the Bible in Black Theology," p. 178; idem, "Biblical Grounding for a Black South African Theology of Liberation," speech at the Society for Biblical Literature Semeia Seminar on the Bible and Apartheid, Atlanta, GA (23 November 1986), pp. 5-12; and idem, "The Biblical God From the Perspective of the Poor," pp. 166-67.

34. Mosala, "Black Theology in South Africa and North America: Prospects for the Future; Building of Alliances," pp. 3-7.

35. Mosala, "The Biblical God From the Perspective of the Poor," pp. 161-66; idem, "African Independent Churches," pp. 109-11; and idem, "Biblical Grounding for a Black South African Theology of Liberation," p. 1.

36. See Mosala, "The Meaning of Reconciliation: A Black Perspective," *Journal of Theology for Southern Africa* (July 1987):22. My understanding of his views on liberation also come from my interview with Dr. Mosala.

37. Mofokeng, *The Crucified Among The Crossbearers: Towards a Black Christology* (J. H. Kok, Uitgeversmaatschappij, 1983), p. ix. (Referred to hereafter as *The Crucified*.)

38. Ibid., p. x.

39. Ibid., pp. 23, 21, 27, 29.

40. Ibid., pp. 34-35, 39-43, 108-9.

41. Ibid., p. 3. Dr. Mofokeng's views on black theology and black consciousness were also confirmed in my 5 December 1986 interview with him.

42. *The Crucified*, p. 13; also see Mofokeng, "A Black Christology: A New Beginning," *Journal of Black Theology in South Africa* (Atteridgeville, South Africa: Black Theology Project, 1987), pp. 7-12.

43. On his black cultural analysis and opinion of black history, see *The Crucified*, pp. 13-14, 21-33; and his speech at the Black Theology Conference: Dialogue Between the U.S.A. and South Africa, Union Theological Seminary, New York (1-3 December 1986).

44. On Dr. Mofokeng's biblical views, see "The Evolution of the Black Struggle and the Role of Black Theology", in Mosala and Tlhagale, *The Unquestionable Right to Be Free*, p. 123; and his speech at the Black Theology Conference: Dialogue Between U.S.A. and South Africa, Union Theological Seminary, New York (1-3 December 1986). He also confirmed his biblical views in our 5 December 1986 interview.

45. *The Crucified*, p. 23. In my interview with Dr. Mofokeng he did not see a significant contribution from the African Independent Churches to the development of black theology. Contrasting the sources of Itumeleng Mosala, Mofokeng stated: "I've heard black theologians say that the [African] Independent Churches should serve as the sources in the doing of black theology and that African traditional religion should also serve as sources in the doing of black theology. I'm not too sure what the Independent Churches can contribute to the doing of black theology."

46. *The Crucified*, pp. 230-34, 239. For Mofokeng's position on theological and psychological liberation, see ibid. pp. 1ff., 11.

47. Ibid., pp. 234-35, 246, 24.

48. Ibid., p. 10; also Dr. Mofokeng's speech at the Black Theology Conference: Dialogue Between U.S.A. and South Africa, Union Theological Seminary, New York (1-3 December 1986).

49. See Tutu, "Some African Insights and the Old Testament" and "Viability" in Becken, pp. 40-42, 36; idem, "Whither Theological Education? An African Perspective," *Theological Education,* vol. 9, no. 4 (Summer 1973):270; idem, "Black Theology," *Frontier* (Summer 1974), p. 73; idem, *Crying in the Wilderness: The Struggle for Justice in South Africa* (Grand Rapids, MI: Eerdmans Publishing Co., 1985), p. 82; and idem, "Apartheid and Christianity," in de Gruchy and Villa-Vicencio, *Apartheid Is a Heresy,* p. 44.

50. Tutu, "Black Theology," p. 74; idem, "Whither African Theology?" in *Christianity in Independent Africa,* ed. Fashole-Luke, et al. (London: Collins, 1978), p. 367; and idem, "Church and Nation in the Perspective of Black Theology," *Journal of Theology for Southern Africa* (June 1976):6.

51. See Tutu, "The Theology of Liberation in Africa," in Appiah-Kubi and Torres, p. 163; idem, "Black Theology/African Theology—Soulmates or Antagonists?" in Wilmore and Cone, p. 490; and idem, "Whither African Theology?" p. 369.

52. Tutu, "The Theology of Liberation in Africa," p. 167; idem, "God-Given Dignity and the Quest for Liberation in the Light of the South African Dilemma," in *Liberation,* ed. D. Thomas (Johannesburg, South Africa: South African Council of Churches, 1976), pp. 58-59; idem, "God-Given Dignity and the Quest for Liberation," in *African Perspectives on Africa,* ed. HWVD Merwe, et al. (Stanford, CA: Hoover Institution Press, 1978); idem, *Crying in the Wilderness,* pp. 41, 87; idem, "God Intervening in Human Affairs," *Missionalia,* vol. 5, no. 1 (April 1977), p. 115; and idem, "Church and Nation in the Perspective of Black Theology," pp. 10-11.

53. Tutu, *Hope and Suffering,* p. 38; and idem, "Spirituality: Christian and African," in Villa-Vicencio and de Gruchy, *Resistance and Hope,* p. 164.

54. Tutu, "Tearing People Apart," *South African Outlook* (October 1980), pp. 153-55.

55. Tutu, *Crying in the Wilderness,* p. 89; idem, "Apartheid and Christianity," pp. 40ff.; and idem, "God-Given Dignity and the Quest for Liberation in the Light of the South African Dilemma," p. 57.

56. Tutu, "Black Theology," p. 75.

57. See S. Maimela, "Archbishop Desmond Tutu—A Revolutionary Political Priest or Man of Peace?" in Tlhagale and Mosala, *Hammering Swords Into Ploughshares,* p. 46; and B. Goba, "A Theological Tribute to Archbishop Tutu," in ibid. p. 63; also see Tutu, *Hope and Suffering,* pp. 49ff., 81-83; and Tutu, "Church and Nation in the Perspective of Black Theology," p. 9.

58. Tutu, "Whither Theological Education? An African Perspective," p. 271; idem, "Some African Insights and the Old Testament," p. 41; and idem, "Whither African Theology?" p. 366.

59. Tutu, *Crying in the Wilderness,* p. 100; idem, "Viability," p. 38; and idem, "Some African Insights and the Old Testament," pp. 41-44.

60. Tutu, "Whither African Theology?" p. 369; and idem, "Black Theology/African Theology—Soulmates or Antagonists?" p. 490.

61. Tutu, "South Africa's Blacks: Aliens in Their Own Land," *Christianity and Crisis* (26 November 1984), p. 441.

CHAPTER SIX

1. For a report on this conference, see the *Journal of Black Theology in South Africa*, vol. 1, no. 1 (Atteridgeville, South Africa: Black Theology Project, 1987).

2. For background information on this conference as well as texts of conference speeches, see *Black Faith and Black Solidarity*, ed. Priscilla Massie (New York: Friendship Press, 1973); and Cornish Rogers, "Pan-Africanism and the Black Church: A Search for Solidarity," *Christian Century* (17 November 1971). The conference was sponsored by the African Commission of the National Conference of Black Churchmen and the Christian Council of Tanzania.

3. Participants shared their respective experiences with economic self-help projects. In the United States, blacks stated, such economic development was sponsored by the black church, whereas *Ujamma* (e.g., government sponsored economic socialism) guided similar efforts in Tanzania. Regarding education, Africans emphasized the need for political education of their people from a colonial mentality legacy. Thus their education stressed the rediscovery of "Africanness." Like their African counterparts, North American blacks sought a new education that fostered black self-identity and the acquisition of skills for the black community. They also detailed the growth of black liberation schools and black curricula in white American schools. However, during the theological exchange black and African theologies clearly differentiated over a liberation-political thrust and an Africanization-cultural leaning. Africans constructed their theology in post-colonial, independent nations. Thus they were more "colorless" in God-talk. In addition, African churches were not related to African Independent Christian Church movements. Contrasting this cultural theological nuance, black Americans emphasized a black political theology. Still several conferees noted that both political and cultural theologies opposed the same "principalities and powers" on a deeper level.

4. "Black Theology and African Theology: Considerations for Dialogue, Critique, and Integration," in Wilmore and Cone, pp. 465-66.

5. Ibid.

6. Tutu, "Black Theology," p. 74.

7. Cone and Wilmore write regarding BTUSA's religious inheritance from African traditional religions: "For example: the deep sense of the pervasive reality of the spirit world; the blotting out of the line between the sacred and the profane; the practical use of religion in all of daily life; reverence for the ancestors and their presence with us; the corporateness of social life; locating evil in the consequences of an act rather than in the act itself; and using drums, singing, and dancing in the worship of God" (Wilmore and Cone, p. 469).

8. *Essays on Black Theology*, ed. Mokgethi Motlhabi (South Africa: Black Theology Project of the University Christian Movement, 1972). Motlhabi's edition was immediately banned by the South African government for "security" reasons. This book was later published in England under the title *Black Theology: The South African Voice*, ed. Basil Moore (London: Hurst and Co., 1973); and in the United States as *The Challenge of Black Theology in South Africa*, ed. Basil Moore (Atlanta: John Knox Press, 1974).

9. Buthelezi, "An African Theology or a Black Theology?" in Moore, *The Challenge of Black Theology in South Africa*, pp. 30–31.

10. Goba, in Moore, p. 67.

11. James Cone, in Moore, p. 48.

12. For a report on this conference and the critical issues discussed, see James Cone's "Report, Black and African Theologies: A Consultation," *Christianity and Crisis* (3 March 1975); and Gayraud Wilmore, "To Speak With One Voice? The Ghana Consultation on African and Black Theology," *The Christian Century* (19 February 1975). The essays from the 1974 Ghana consultation are published in *The Journal of Religious Thought*, vol. 32, no. 2 (Fall-Winter 1975). This journal edition has an introduction by C. Shelby Rooks and summary reports by G. S. Wilmore and J.N.K. Nugambi.

13. The second mutual exposure between BTUSA and BTSA ensued when Allan Boesak spent a year of study in 1974 at Colgate Rochester divinity school and Union Theological Seminary, New York City. The product of Boesak's efforts culminated in his *Farewell to Innocence*.

14. James H. Cone, "Introduction," in Wilmore and Cone, p. 448.

15. Tutu, "Black Theology/African Theology—Soul Mates or Antagonists?" in Wilmore and Cone, p. 483.

16. Ibid. p. 485.

17. Cone, *Black Theology and Black Power*, "Introduction." Cone's focus on building unity between black theology and liberation theologies in Africa, Asia and Latin America is reflected in various Orbis Books publications of the Ecumenical Association of Third World Theologians' annual conferences.

18. Long, "Structural Similarities and Dissimilarities in Black and African Theologies," p. 11.

19. See the section on Goba in Chapter 5 above.

20. Long, "Structural Similarities and Dissimilarities in Black and African Theologies," pp. 11-12.

21. Ibid., p. 14.

22. See the section on Mofokeng in Chapter 5 above.

23. James Cone, "The Content and Method of Black Theology," in *The Journal of Religious Thought,* vol. 32, no. 2 (Fall-Winter 1975):91-92.

24. See the section on Mosala in Chapter 5 above.

25. Cone, "Christian Theology and Scripture as the Expression of God's Liberating Activity for the Poor" and "Black Religious Thought in American History, Part 1: Origins," in *Speaking the Truth*, pp. 4ff. and pp. 83ff.

26. See Mosala, "Ethics of the Economic Principles: Church and Secular Investments;" in Tlhagale and Mosala, *Hammering Swords Into Ploughshares*; idem, "Black Theology Versus The Social Morality Of Settler Colonialism: Hermeneutical Reflections On Luke 1 And 2," *Journal of Black Theology in South Africa*, vol. 1, no. 1 (Atteridgeville, South Africa: Black Theology Project, 1987); and idem, *Biblical Hermeneutics and Black Theology,* (Grand Rapids, MI: Eerdmans, 1989), chap. 1. Dr. Mosala also confirmed these views in my December 1986 interview with him. We will revisit Mosala's arguments below in the direct dialogue section.

27. Presentations from this consultation are in Appiah-Kubi and Torres. Though Wilmore attended, he did not present his paper at the consultation. It was prepared for this book.

We should also note that in South Africa in December 1974 the Black Consciousness organizations held a major delegates' meeting of all black groups in a Black Renaissance Convention. The only black American presentation, in abstentia, was James H. Cone's "Black Consciousness and the Black Church," in Thoahlane, pp. 66-72. This is significant for our chronology of indirect dialogue between BTUSA and BTSA because it signifies the pervasiveness of the influence of BTUSA, or more specifically, of James Cone, in the actual overall black liberation struggle in South Africa. For explanations of the Black Renaissance Convention, see *Black Review 1974/75*, ed. Thoko Mbanjwa (South Africa: Black Community Programmes, 1975), pp. 133-34; and Gerhart, p. 294.

28. Tutu, "The Theology of Liberation in Africa," in Appiah-Kubi and Torres, p. 163.

29. Boesak, "Liberation Theology in South Africa," in Appiah-Kubi and Torres, p. 175.

30. Tutu, "Black Theology/African Theology—Soul Mates or Antagonists?" p. 484.

Cone's 1977 Ghana presentation comes from his "A Black American Perspective on the Future of African Theology," in Wilmore and Cone, pp. 492-502.

31. Wilmore, "The Role of Afro-America in the Rise of Third World Theology: A Historical Reappraisal," in Appiah-Kubi and Torres, pp. 197-201.

32. Ibid.

33. Boesak, *Farewell to Innocence*, p. 10.

34. Ibid. p. 13.

35. Ibid. pp. 12, 73.

36. J. Cone, "The Content and Method of Black Theology," p. 102.

37. Ibid. pp. 119-21.

38. The conference was sponsored by the Institute for Contextual Theology (South Africa), the Ecumenical Association of Third World Theologians (EATWOT) and Union Theological Seminary's Ecumenical Center and Theological Field. Representing black Americans were James Cone, James Washington, Cornel West, Kelly Brown and Josiah Young. For the black South Africans, Simon Maimela, Itumeleng Mosala, Takatso Mofokeng, Frank Chikane, Roxanne Jordan and Cecil Ngcokovane were in attendance. The idea for the conference originated from early contacts in EATWOT between Cone and Goba and was finalized during Cone's and West's visit to South Africa in July 1985.

39. See Jacquelyn Grant, "Black Theology and the Black Woman," in Wilmore and Cone, pp. 418ff.

40. I write "in the main" to note the particular objections of William R. Jones and Charles H. Long. Though Jones asks about the racism of God, he still would not disallow the liberative nature of Jesus Christ in the Bible. Likewise Long would not categorically deny the practical results of poor blacks' usage of the gospel in their liberation movements, despite Long's argument against the "imperialistic" predisposition of Christianity.

CHAPTER SEVEN

1. Quoted in B.G.M. Sundkler, *Bantu Prophets in South Africa*, 2d ed. (London: Oxford University Press, 1970), p. 278.

To understand the rise of the South African Separatist Christian Church Movement and its connection to the American A.M.E. church, see Clement T. Keto, "Black Americans and South Africa, 1890-1910," in *A Current Bibliography on African Affairs* (Westport, CT: Greenwood Press, 1972); Sundkler; Absolom Vilakazi with Bongani Mthethwa and Mthembeni Mpanza, *Shembe: The Revitalization of African Society* (Johannesburg, South Africa: Skotaville Publishers, 1986); and M. M. Ponton, *Life and Times of Henry M. Turner* (New York: Negro University Press, 1970 reprint).

2. Wilmore, *Black Religion and Black Radicalism*, p. 235.

3. J. Cone, *A Black Theology of Liberation*, p. 38.

4. See Grant, in Wilmore and Cone, pp. 418-33.

5. See Harriet A. Jacobs, *Incidents in the Life of a Slave Girl, Written by Herself*, ed. Jean F. Yellin (Cambridge, MA: Harvard University Press, 1987); Dorothy Sterling, *Black Foremothers, Three Lives* (New York: McGraw-Hill Book Co., 1979); William L. Andrews, ed., *Three Black Women's Autobiographies of the Nineteenth Century: Sisters of the Spirit* (Bloomington, IN: Indiana University Press, 1986); B. J. Loewenberg and R. Bogin, eds., *Black Women in Nineteenth-Century Life* (University Park, PA: The Pennsylvania State University Press, 1976); Alfreda M. Duster, ed., *Crusade for Justice: The Autobiography of Ida B. Wells* (Chicago: University of Chicago Press, 1972); Jean M. Humez, ed., *Gifts of Power: The Writings of Rebecca Jackson, Black Visionary, Shaker Eldress* (Massachusetts: The University of Massachusetts Press, 1981); Jacqueline Jones, *Labor of Love, Labor of Sorrow: Black Women, Work and the Family, From Slavery to the Present* (New York: Vintage Books, 1986); Paula Giddings, *When and Where I Enter: The Impact of Black Women on Race and Sex in America* (New York: Bantam Books, 1985); Sarah Bradford, *Harriet Tubman: The Moses of Her People* (Secaucus, NJ: Citadel Press, 1961); and Debrah Gray White, *Ar'n't I a Woman? Female Slaves in the Plantation South* (New York: W. W. Norton & Co., 1985).

6. Jacquelyn Grant, "The Development and Limitations of Feminist Christology: Toward an Engagement of White Women's and Black Women's Religious Experience," Ph.D. diss., Union Theological Seminary, New York City, 1985; Delores Williams, "Womanist Theology: Black Women's Voices," *Christianity and Crisis* (2 March 1987); Williams, "The Color of Feminism: Or Speaking the Black Woman's Tongue," *Journal of Religious Thought* (Spring-Summer 1986); Katie G. Cannon, "Resources for a Constructive Ethic for Black Women with Special Attention to the Life and Work of Zora Neale Hurston," Ph.D. diss., Union Theological Seminary, New York City, 1983; and Kelly D. Brown, "Who Is Jesus Christ for the Black Community? A Black Feminist Critique of Black Male Theologians," Ph.D. diss., Union Theological Seminary, New York City, 1988.

7. Quoted in Roux, p. 36. Also see page 81 for the Manye reference.

8. Quoted in Muff Anderson, *Music in the Mix: The Story of South African Popular Music* (Johannesburg, South Africa: Raven Press, 1981), p. 32.

9. "Interview with Sibongile Mkhabela," in *Women in Southern Africa*, ed. Christine Qunta (Johannesburg, South Africa: Skotaville Publishers, 1987), pp. 115ff. Regarding Lilian Ngoji, see pp. 112-13.

10. Winnie Mandela, *Part of My Soul Went With Him* (New York: W. W. Norton & Co., 1984).

11. Helene Perold, ed., *Working Women* (Johannesburg, South Africa: Sached/Raven Press, 1985).

12. See June Goodwin, *Cry Amandla!: South African Women and the Question*

of Power (New York: Africana Publishing Co., 1984); and Beata Lipman, *We Make Freedom: Women in South Africa* (Boston: Pandora Press, 1984).

13. Institute for Contextual Theology, "Report, Women's Struggle in South Africa, Feminist Theology Conference, 31 August-2 September 1984, Hammanskraal" (Johannesburg, South Africa: Institute for Contextual Theology, n.d.), p. 38.

14. Bonita Bennett, "A Critique on the Role of Women in the Church," in Mosala and Tlhagale, *The Unquestionable Right to Be Free*, p. 173. Also see Bernadette I. Mosala, "Black Theology and the Struggle of the Black Woman in Southern Africa," p. 132.

15. Cited in *God Struck Me Dead: Religious Conversion Experiences and Autobiographies of Ex-slaves,* ed. Clifton H. Johnson (Philadelphia, PA: Pilgrim Press, 1969), p. 161.

16. Quoted in *Lay My Burden Down: A Folk History of Slavery,* ed. B. A. Botkin (Chicago: University of Chicago Press, 1957), p. 27.

17. Cited in Albert J. Raboteau, *Slave Religion: The "Invisible Institution" in the Antebellum South* (Oxford: Oxford University Press, 1980), p. 226.

18. See Wilmore, *Black Religion and Black Radicalism,* pp. 78-98.

19. See V. M. Mayatula, "African Independent Churches' Contribution to a Relevant Theology," in Becken, p. 175; and A. R. Sprunger, "The Contribution of the African Independent Churches to a Relevant Theology for Africa," in Becken, p. 164. Also see, "The Church Crisis on Race Relations," *Pro Veritate* (February 1974); Rev. E. Maqina, "African Independent Churches—Social and Political Implications," *Pro Veritate*(15 June 1970), p. 7; "Part 3—African Theology, Morality in African Tradition and Social Ethics in South Africa," in Tlhagale and Mosala, *Hammering Swords Into Ploughshares,* pp. 73-129; J. B. Ngubane, "Theological Roots of the African Independent Churches and Their Challenge to Black Theology," in Mosala and Tlhagale, *The Unquestionable Right to Be Free,* pp. 71ff.; and I. J. Mosala, "The Relevance of African Traditional Religions and Their Challenge to Black Theology," in Mosala and Tlhagale, *The Unquestionable Right to Be Free,* pp. 91ff.

20. George P. Rawick, *From Sundown to Sunup: The Making of the Black Community* (Westport, CT: Greenwood Press, 1972); Lawrence W. Levine, *Black Culture and Black Consciousness: Afro-American Folk Thought From Slavery to Freedom* (Oxford: Oxford University Press, 1981); C. T. Davis and H. L. Gates, Jr., eds., *The Slave's Narrative* (Oxford: Oxford University Press, 1985); Paul D. Escott, *Slavery Remembered: A Record of Twentieth-Century Slave Narratives* (Chapel Hill, NC: University of North Carolina Press, 1979); J. W. Blassingame, *The Slave Community: Plantation Life in the Antebellum South* (New York: Oxford University Press, 1972); Langston Hughes and Arna Bontemps, eds., *The Book of Negro Folklore* (New York: Dodd, Mead & Co., 1983); Eileen Southern, *The Music of Black Americans: A History* (New York: W. W. Norton & Co., 1983); and J. A. Emanuel and T. L. Gross, eds., *Dark Symphony: Negro Literature in America* (New York: The Free Press, 1968).

21. Jacques Alvarez-Pereyre, *The Poetry of Commitment in South Africa* (London: Heinemann Educational Books, Inc., 1984); Robert Kavanagh, *Theatre and Cultural Struggle in South Africa* (London: Zed Press, 1985); and Ursula A. Barnett, *A Vision of Order: A Study of Black South African Literature in English (1914-1980)* (Amherst, MA: University of Massachusetts Press, 1983).

22. Cited in Africa Information Service, ed., *Return to the Source: Selected*

Speeches by Amilcar Cabral (New York: Monthly Review Press, 1973), p. 41.

Within the black theological discourse, James Cone, Cornel West, Itumeleng Mosala and Allan Boesak, among others, have engaged the connection of culture and class.

Bibliography

INTERVIEWS WITH THE AUTHOR

Black Theology USA

Cone, Cecil W. New York City, March 11, 1987.
Cone, James H. New York City, March 31, 1987.
Harding, Vincent. Philadelphia, PA, March 18, 1987.
Herzfeld, Will. Oakland, CA, August 6, 1987.
Jones, Major J. Atlanta, GA, February 20, 1987.
Jones, William R. Berkeley, CA, December 5, 1987.
Long, Charles H. Chapel Hill, NC, February 21, 1987.
Marshall, Calvin B. Brooklyn, NY, March 17, 1987.
Paris, Peter J. Princeton, NJ, March 10, 1987.
Roberts, J. Deotis. Silver Springs, MD, March 19, 1987.
Rooks, C. Shelby. New York City, April 21, 1987.
Watts, Leon W. Larchmont, NY, March 23, 1987.
Williams, Preston N. Cambridge, MA, February 27, 1987.
Wilmore, Gayraud S. Atlanta, GA, February 19, 1987.

Black Theology South Africa

Chikane, Frank. New York City, December 1, 1986.
Farisani, Tshenuwani S. Berkeley, CA, March 2, 1988.
Goba, Bonganjalo C. Stony Point, NY, March 2, 1987.
Maimela, Simon S. New York City, December 3, 1986.
Mofokeng, Takatso A. New York City, December 5, 1986.
Mosala, J. Itumeleng. New York City, December 1, 1986.
Motlhabi, Mokgethi. Cambridge, MA, March 20, 1987.
Ngcokovane, Cecil M. New York City, December 2, 1986.

BLACK THEOLOGY USA REFERENCES

Adams, John Hurst. "Black Power Situation—Judgement Summons." *The African Methodist Episcopal Review* 93, no. 235 (April-June 1968).
Alston, Jon P. "Religiosity and Black Militancy." *Journal for the Scientific Study of Religion* 11, no. 3 (September 1972).
"Artists Portray a Black Christ." *Ebony* 26, no. 6 (April 1971).

Balazar, Eulaio R. *The Dark Center: A Process Theology of Blackness*. Paramus, NJ: Paulist Press, 1973.

Banks, Walter R. "Two Impossible Revolutions? Black Power and Church Power." *Journal for the Scientific Study of Religion* 8, no. 2 (Fall 1969).

Banks, William L. "Reparations, Black Power, and 'Black Theology.' " *Moody Monthly* 72, no. 8 (April 1972).

Barrett, Leonard. *Soul Force: African Heritage in Afro-American Religion*. New York: Doubleday, 1974.

Bastide, Roger. "Color, Racism, and Christianity." *Daedalus*, no. 2 (Spring 1967).

Beale, Frances. "Double Jeopardy: To Be Black and Female." In *Black Theology: A Documentary History, 1966-1979*, edited by Gayraud S. Wilmore and James H. Cone. Maryknoll, NY: Orbis Books, 1979.

Becker, William H. "Black Power in Christological Perspective." *Religion In Life* 38, no. 3 (Autumn 1969).

Bennet, Robert A. "Africa and the Biblical Period." *Harvard Theological Review* 64 (October 1971).

———. "Black Experience and the Bible." *Theology Today* 27, no. 4 (1971).

———. "Biblical Theology and Black Theology." *Journal of the ITC* (Spring 1976).

Bentley, William H. *The Meaning of History for Black Americans*. Chicago: The National Black Evangelical Association, 1979.

———. *The National Black Evangelical Association: Reflections on the Evolution of a Concept of Ministry*. Chicago: William H. Bentley, 1979.

Birch, Bruce C. "Black Theology Means Liberation for All." *Christian Advocate* 18, no. 13 (21 June 1973).

Birt, Robert E. "An Examination of James Cone's Concept of God and Its Role in Black Liberation." *The Philosophical Forum* 9, nos. 2-3 (Winter-Spring 1977-1978).

"Bishop Shaw Urges New Direction for Churchmen." *Afro American* (12 November 1968).

"The Black Christian Nationalist Church." *Black World* 23, no. 3 (January 1974). (Press conference by Albert Cleage.)

"The Black Church Acts." *National Black Monitor* Pilot Issue, no. 1 (1972).

Bourguignon, Erika. "Afro-American Religions: Tradition and Transformation." In *Black America*, edited by John F. Szwed. New York: Basic Books, 1970.

Brooks, Evelyn. "The Women's Movement in the Black Baptist Church, 1880-1920." Ph.D. diss., University of Rochester, 1984.

Brown, Charles S. "Present Trends in Black Theology." *Journal of Religious Thought* 32, no. 2 (Fall-Winter 1975).

Brown, Hubert L. *Black and Mennonite*. Scottdale, PA: Herald Press, 1976.

———. "Black Theology and African Heritage." *Journal of the ITC* (International Theological Center) (Fall 1979).

Brown, Kelly D. "Who Is Jesus Christ for the Black Community?: A Black Feminist Critique of Black Male Theologians." Ph.D. diss., Union Theological Seminary, New York City, 1988.

Bruce, Calvin E. "Black Spirituality and Theological Method." *Journal of the ITC* (Spring 1976).

Bruce, Calvin E. and Jones, William R., eds. *Black Theology II: Essays on the Formation and Outreach of Contemporary Black Theology*. Cranbury, NJ: Associated University Press, 1978.

Caldwell, Gilbert H. "Black Folk in White Churches." *Christian Century* 86 (12 February 1969).

———. "Black Churchmen Find African, American Links." *Christian Advocate* 15, no. 17 (16 September 1971).

———. "The Black Church in White Structures." *The Black Church* 1, no. 2 (1972).

Campbell, Ernest. "The Case for Reparations." *Theology Today* 26, no. 3 (October 1969).

Campen, Henry C. "Black Theology: The Concept and Its Development." *The Lutheran Quarterly* 23, no. 4 (November 1971).

Cannon, Katie G. "Responses to Theological Education and Liberation Theology Symposium." *Theological Education* 16 (Fall 1979).

———. "Resources for a Constructive Ethic for Black Women with Special Attention to the Life and Work of Zora Neale Hurston." Ph.D. diss., Union Theological Seminary, New York City, 1983.

———. "Moral Wisdom in the Black Women's Literary Tradition." *The Annual of the Society of Christian Ethics*, edited by L. Rasmussen (1984): 171-92.

———. "Resources for a Constructive Ethic in the Life and Work of Zora Neale Hurston." *Journal of Feminist Studies in Religion* 1, no. 1 (Spring 1985): 37-51.

———. "The Emergence of Black Feminist Consciousness." In *Feminist Interpretation of the Bible*, edited by L. Russell. Philadelphia: Westminster Press, 1985.

———. "Hitting a Straight Lick With a Crooked Stick: The Womanist Dilemma in the Development of a Black Liberation Ethic." *The Annual of the Society of Christian Ethics* (1987).

———. "Surviving the Blight." In *Inheriting Our Mothers' Gardens: Feminist Theology in Third World Perspective*, edited by L. Russel, et al. Philadelphia: Westminster Press, 1988.

———. *Black Womanist Ethics*. Atlanta: Scholars Press, 1988.

Carey, John J. "Black Theology: An Appraisal of the Internal and External Issues." *Theological Studies* 33, no. 4 (December 1972).

———. "What Can We Learn from Black Theology?" *Theological Studies* 35, no. 3 (September 1974).

Carter, Harold A. *The Prayer Tradition of Black People*. Valley Forge, PA: Judson Press, 1976.

Carter, Harold A., Walker, Wyatt T., and Jones, William A. *The Black Church Looks at the Bicentennial: A Minority Report*. Elgin, IL: Progressive National Baptist Publishing House, 1976.

Chandler, Russell. "Church Militants Fashion a New Black Theology." *The Evening Star* (2 November 1968).

Chapman, G. Clarke, Jr. "American Theology in Black: James H. Cone." *Cross Currents* 22, no. 2 (Spring 1972).

———. "Black Theology and Theology of Hope: What Have They To Say to Each Other?" *Union Seminary Quarterly Review* 29, no. 2 (Winter 1974).

Cleage, Albert B. *The Black Messiah*. Kansas City: Sheed, Andrews and McMeel, 1968.

———. "Albert Cleage on Black Power." *United Church Herald* (February 1968).

———. "The Black Messiah and the Black Revolution." In *Quest for a Black Theology*, edited by James J. Gardiner and J. Deotis Roberts. Philadelphia: United Press, 1971.

—. "Black UCC Clergyman Organizes New Denomination." *United Church Herald* 1, no. 3 (November 1972).

—. *Black Christian Nationalism: New Directions for the Black Church*. New York: William Morrow, 1972.

Cliff, Michelle. " 'I Found God in Myself and I Loved Her/I Loved Her Fiercely': More Thoughts on the Work of Black Women Artists." *Journal of Feminist Studies in Religion* (Spring 1986).

Cone, Cecil W. "The Black Religious Experience." *Journal of the ITC* 2, no. 2 (Spring 1975).

—. *The Identity Crisis in Black Theology*. Nashville: AMEC, 1975.

—. "Toward a New Introduction to Christian Theology: Telling the Story." *Journal of the ITC* 3, no. 2 (Spring 1976).

Cone, James H. "Christianity and Black Power." In *Is Anybody Listening to Black America?*, edited by C. Eric Lincoln. New York: Seabury Press, 1968.

—. *Black Theology and Black Power*. New York: Seabury Press, 1969.

—. "Black Theology and Violence." *The Tower Alumni Magazine UTS* (Spring 1969).

—. "Failure of the Black Church." *Liberator* 9, no. 5 (May 1969).

—. "Toward a Constructive Definition of Black Power." *Student World* 62, nos. 3-4 (1969).

—. "Black Theology: We Were Not Created for Humiliation." *Ladies' Home Journal* (December 1969).

—. *A Black Theology of Liberation*. Philadelphia: J. B. Lippincott, 1970.

—. "Black Consciousness and the Black Church: A Historical-Theological Interpretation." *Annals* (January 1970), also in *Evangelische Kommentare* (March 1971).

—. "Toward a Black Theology." *Ebony* 25, no. 10 (August 1970).

—. "Black Theology and Black Liberation." *Christian Century* 87, no. 3 (16 September 1970); also in *Essays on Black Theology*, edited by Mokgethi Motlhabi. Johannesburg, South Africa: Black Theology Project of the University Christian Movement, 1972.

—. "Dialogue on Black Theology" (with William Hordern). *Christian Century* (15 September 1971).

—. "The Black Church and Black Power." In *The Black Church*, edited by Hart Nelson, Raytha Yokley and Anne Nelson. New York: Basic Books, 1971.

—. "La revolte des Noir Americains et la theologie de la liberation." (An interview.) *Reforme* (May 1972).

—. *The Spirituals and the Blues*. New York: Seabury Press, 1972.

—. "An Interview with James H. Cone. Black Theology." *Mission* 6, no. 10 (April 1973).

—. "La teologia nera." *Rocca* 32, no. 10 (1973).

—. "Warum schwarze Theologie?" *Evangelishce Theologie* (January/February 1974).

—. "White and Black." (An interview.) *The Other Side* (May/June 1974).

—. "Prise de Conscience des noirs et englise noire" and "le christ dans la theologie noire." *Lumiere et Vie* (November/December 1974).

—. "Negro Churches (in the U.S.)." *Encyclopaedia Britannica,* 15th ed. (1974).

—. "Black And African Theologies: A Consultation." *C&C* 35, no. 3 (March 3, 1975).

————. "Black Theologians: 'Our Conversations Must Continue.'" *Rockefeller Foundation Illustrated* 2, no. 3 (August 1975).

————. "Black Consciousness and the Black Church: A Historical-Theological Interpretation." In *Black Renaissance: Papers From the Black Renaissance Convention, December 1974*, edited by Thoahlane Thoahlane. Johannesburg, South Africa: Raven Press, 1975.

————. *God of the Oppressed*. New York: Seabury Press, 1975.

————. "An Interview With James H. Cone by Theo Witvliet and Hugh C. White." *Witness* (January 1976).

————. "Speaking the Truth." *Black Books Bulletin* 4, no. 1 (Spring 1976).

————. "Black Theology and the Black College Student." *Journal of Afro-American Issues* 4, nos. 3-4 (Summer-Fall 1976).

————. "Een Zwart Perspectief op Amerika: Zwarte Theologie en het Tweede Eeuwfeest." *Wending* (October 1976).

————. Review of *Roots*, by Alex Haley. *The New York Review of Books and Religion* 1, no. 4 (December 1976).

————. "What Does It Mean to Be Saved?" In *Preaching the Gospel*, edited by Henry Young. Philadelphia: Fortress Press, 1976.

————. "Glaube als Verpflichtung zum Kampf." *Evangelische Kommentare* (August 1978).

————. "Accuse paul, levez-vous." *Lumiere et Vie* 27, no. 139 (1978).

————. "A Black American Perspective on the Future of African Theology." *Bulletin of African Theology* 1, no. 1 (January-June 1979).

————. "Asian Theology: Searching for Definitions." *The Christian Century* (23 May 1979).

————. "The New Right, the Irrelevant Left, and the Black Church." (An interview.) *The Other Side* (June 1979).

————. "James Cone's Macedonian Call." (An interview.) *New World Outlook* 39, no. 11 (July-August 1979).

————. "A Black American Looks at African Theology." *Worldview* 22, no. 12 (December 1979).

————. "What Is Christian Theology?" Chap. 1 in *Toward a Theology in an Australian Context*, edited by Victor C. Hayes. Bedford Park, South Australia: Australian Association for the Study of Religion, 1979.

————. "The Meaning of Heaven in the Black Spirituals." In *Concilium*, edited by Iersel and Schillebeeckx. New York: Seabury Press, 1979.

————. "Capitalism Means Property Over Persons." In *Will Capitalism Survive?: A Challenge by Paul Johnson With Twelve Responses*, edited by Ernest W. Lefever. Washington, D.C.: Ethics and Public Policy Center, 1979.

————. "The Black Church and Marxism: What Do They Have to Say to Each Other?" An occasional paper from *The Institute for Democratic Socialism* (April 1980).

————. "Christian Faith and Political Praxis." *Bulletin of African Theology* 2, no. 4 (July-December 1980).

————. "A Black American Perspective on the Asian Search for a Full Humanity." In *Asia's Struggle for Full Humanity*, edited by Virginia Fabella. Maryknoll, NY: Orbis Books, 1980.

————. "Left Strategies Must Deal With Racism." *The Witness* 64, no. 1 (January 1981).

————. "One Lord." In *Proceedings of the 14th World Methodist Conference*, edited by Joe Hale. Lake Junaluska, NC: World Methodist Council, July 21-28, 1981.

————. "La relacion entre el evangelio y luchas de los Pobres." *Paginas*, no. 42 (December 1981).

————. "From Geneva to Sao Paulo: A Dialogue Between Black Theology and Latin American Liberation Theology." In *The Challenge of Basic Christian Communities*, edited by S. Torres and J. Eagleson. Maryknoll, NY: Orbis Books, 1981.

————. "Intervista con James Cone." (An interview.) *Testimonianze* (April 1982).

————. "James Cone Interview." *Radix* 12, no. 2 (September/October 1982).

————. "One Lord." In *Part II of Proceedings of the 14th World Methodist Conference*, edited by Joe Hale. Lake Junaluska, NC: World Methodist Press, 1982.

————. "What Is the Church?" *Bulletin of African Theology*, no. 9 (January-June 1983).

————. "Martin Luther King: The Source of His Courage to Face Death." *Concilium*, no. 183 (March 1983).

————. "Black Theology and Third World Theologies." *The Chicago Theological Seminary Register* 73, no. 1 (Winter 1983).

————. *For My People: Black Theology and the Black Church*. Maryknoll, NY: Orbis Books, 1984; Johannesburg, South Africa: Skotaville Publishers, 1985.

————. "Ecumenical Association of Third World Theologians." *Ecumenical Trend* 14, no. 8 (September 1985).

————. *Speaking the Truth: Ecumenism, Liberation, and Black Theology*. Grand Rapids, MI: Eerdmans, 1986.

————. "A Dream or a Nightmare? Martin Luther King, Jr. and Malcolm X." *Sojourners* 15, no. 1 (January 1986).

————. "EATWOT Visits China: Some Theological Implications." *China Notes* 24, no. 4 (Autumn 1986).

————. *A Black Theology of Liberation,* 2d ed. Maryknoll, NY: Orbis Books, 1986.

————. *My Soul Looks Back*. Maryknoll, NY: Orbis Books, 1986.

————. "Zud-Afrika in zwart Amerikaans perspectief." *Wereld en Zending*, no. 1 (1987).

————. "James Cone: Integracion y separatismo en el movimiento negro de liberacion." (An interview.) *Paginas* 12, no. 82 (March 1987).

————. "Martin Luther King and the Third World." *Journal of American History* (Fall 1987).

Cone, James H. and Hordern, William. "Dialogue on Black Theology." *The Christian Century* (5 September 1971).

————, and Wilmore, Gayraud S. "The Future and . . . African Theology." *Pro Veritate* 10, no. 9 (15 January 1972).

————, and Wilmore, Gayraud S. "African Theology 2." *Pro Veritate* (15 February 1972).

————, and Wilmore, Gayraud S. "Black Theology and African Theology." Chap. 8 in *Black Faith and Black Solidarity*, edited by Priscilla Massie. New York: Friendship Press, 1973.

Copeland, Shawn. "The Atlanta Statement: Some Background and Commentary." *Cross Currents* (Summer 1977).

Culverhouse, Patricia. "Black Religion: Folk or Christian?" *Foundations: A Baptist Journal of History and Theology* 13, no. 4 (October-December 1970).

Davis, A. S. "The Pentecostal Movement in Black Christianity." *The Black Church* 2, no. 1 (1972).

Dickinson, Richard. "Black Theology and Black Power." *Encounter* 3, no. 4 (Autumn 1970).

Dodson, Jualynne. "Nineteenth Century A.M.E. Preaching Women: The Cutting Edge of Women's Inclusion in Church Polity." In *Women in New Worlds*, edited by H. F. Thomas and R. S. Keller. Nashville: Abingdon Press, 1981.

————, ed. *"Origin and Future of the Black Theology Project: Some Reflections" and "Racism and Rumors of Racism": Two Papers Presented to the 10th Anniversary Convocation of the Black Theology Project*. New York: Black Theology Project, 1988.

Dote, Kenneth. "Pastor Sees 'Black Theology' in Militants." *Washington Post* (14 December 1968).

Dowey, Edward A., Jr. " 'The Black Manifesto': Revolution, Reparation, Separation." *Theology Today* 26, no. 3 (October 1969).

DuBois, W.E.B. *The Negro Church*. Atlanta: Atlanta University Press, 1903.

Duke, Robert W. "Black Theology—and the Experience of Blackness." *Journal of Religious Thought* 29, no. 1 (Spring-Summer 1972).

Dunston, Alfred G., Jr. *The Black Man in the Old Testament and Its World*. Philadelphia: Dorrance and Co., 1974.

Edwards, Herbert O. "Introduction." *Harvard Theological Review* 64, no. 4 (October 1971).

————. "Third World and the Problem of God-Talk." *Harvard Theological Review* 64, no. 4 (October 1971).

————. "Racism and Christian Ethics in America." *Katallegete* 3, no. 2 (Winter 1971).

————. "Race Relations and Reformation-Oriented Theological Ethics." *The Journal of the ITC* 2, no. 2 (Spring 1975).

————. "Black Theology and the Black Revolution." *Union Seminary Quarterly Review* 31, no. 1 (Fall 1975).

————. "Black Theology: Retrospect and Prospect." *Journal of Religious Thought* (Fall-Winter 1975).

Eichelberger, William L. *Reality in Black and White*. Philadelphia: Westminster Press, 1969.

————. "Reflections on the Person and Personality of the Black Messiah." *The Black Church* 2, no. 1 (1972).

————. "The Black Messiah." *The Black Church* 2, no. 2 (Fall 1974).

————. "A Mytho-Historical Approach to the Black Messiah." *Journal of Religious Thought* 33 (Spring-Summer 1976).

Eugene, Toinette. "While Love Is Unfashionable: An Exploration of Black Spirituality and Sexuality." In *Women's Consciousness, Women's Conscience*, edited by C. H. Andolsen, C. E. Gudorf and M. D. Pellaver. Minneapolis: Winston Press, 1985.

Evans, Anthony Tyrone. *Black Theology and the Black Experience: A Biblical Analysis of Black Theology*. Dallas: Black Evangelistic Enterprise, 1977.

————. "A Biblical Critique of Selected Issues in Black Theology." Th.D. diss., Dallas Theological Seminary, 1982.

Evans, James H. "Apartheid Is Idolatry." *C&C* 41, no. 20 (14 December 1981).

————, comp. *Black Theology: A Critical Assessment and Annotated Bibliography.* Westport, CT: Greenwood Press, 1987.

————. "Toward an Afro-American Theology." *Journal of Religious Thought* 40, no. 2 (Fall-Winter 1983-1984).

Felder, Cain. *Troubling Biblical Waters.* Maryknoll, NY: Orbis Books, 1989.

Fields, Bruce. "The Soteriology of James H. Cone: An Examination and Evaluation." Th.M. thesis, Trinity Evangelical Divinity School, 1983.

Fiske, Edward B. "The Messiah Is Black." *Tempo* 1, no. 4 (1 December 1968).

Garber, Paul R. "Black Theology: The Latter Day Legacy of Martin Luther King, Jr." *Journal of the ITC* 2, no. 2 (Spring 1975).

Gardiner, James J., and Roberts, J. Deotis, Sr. *Quest for a Black Theology.* Philadelphia: Pilgrim Press, 1971.

Gelzer, David G. "Random Notes on Black Theology and African Theology." *Christian Century* (16 September 1970).

Gilkes, Cheryl T. "Holding Back the Ocean With a Broom: Black Women and Community Work." In *The Black Woman,* edited by La Frances Rodgers-Rose. Beverly Hills, CA: SAGE Focus Editions, 1980.

————. "Black Church as a Therapeutic Community: Suggested Areas of Research in the Black Religious Experience." *Journal of the ITC* (Fall 1980).

————. "Going Up for the Oppressed: The Career Mobility of Black Women Community Workers." *Journal of Social Issues* (1983).

————. "From Slavery to Social Welfare: Racism and the Control of Black Women." In *Class, Race and Sex: The Dynamics of Control,* edited by H. Lessinger and A. Swerdlow. Boston: G. K. Hall, 1983.

————. " 'Together and in Harness': Women's Traditions in the Sanctified Church." *Signs* (Summer 1985).

————. "Claiming Our Community: Toward a New Feminist Scholarship." *Journal of Feminist Studies in Religion* (Fall 1985).

————. "The Roles of Church and Community Mothers: Ambivalent American Sexism or Fragmented African Familyhood?" *Journal of Feminist Studies in Religion* (Spring 1986).

————. "The Role of Women in the Sanctified Church." *Journal of Religious Thought* (Spring-Summer, 1986).

————. " 'Some Mother's Son and Some Father's Daughter': Gender and Biblical Language in Afro-Christian Worship Tradition." In *Shaping New Vision: Gender and Values in American Culture,* edited by C. Atkinson, C. H. Buchanan, and M. Miles. Ann Arbor, MI: UMI Research Press, 1987.

Gilkes, Cheryl T., and Dodson, Jualynne. "Something Within: Social Change and Collective Endurance in the Sacred World of Black Christian Women." In *Women and Religion In America: Volume Three—The Twentieth Century,* edited by R. R. Ruether and R. S. Keller. San Francisco: Harper & Row, 1986.

Grant, Jacquelyn. "Black Theology and the Black Woman." In *Black Theology: A Documentary History, 1966-1979,* edited by Wilmore and Cone. Maryknoll, NY: Orbis Books, 1979.

————. "The Development and Limitations of Feminist Christology: Toward an Engagement of White Women's and Black Women's Religious Experience." Ph.D. diss., Union Theological Seminary, New York City, 1985.

————. "Womanist Theology: Black Women's Experience as a Source for Doing

Theology With Special Reference to Christology." *The Journal of the ITC* (Spring 1986).

Grier, William, and Cobbs, Price, eds. *The Jesus Bag.* New York: McGraw-Hill Book Company, 1971.

Grigsby, Marshall. "The Black Religious Experience and Theological Education." *Theological Education* (Winter 1977).

Groves, Richard. "Black Power in the Church." *The Student: The Changing Church* 50, no. 3 (December 1970).

Hamilton, Charles V. *The Black Preacher in America.* New York: William Morrow, 1972.

Hanson, Geddes. "Black Theology in Protestant Thought." *Social Progress* (September-October 1969).

"Happening at St. Louis." Editorial. *Tempo* 1, no. 4 (1 December 1968).

Harding, Vincent. "Menno Simons and the Role of Baptism in the Christian Life." *Mennonite Quarterly Review* 33 (October 1959).

———. "Black Power and the American Christ." *Christian Century* (4 January 1967).

———. "The Gift of Blackness." *Katallagete* (Summer 1967).

———. "The Religion of Black Power." In *The Religious Situation: 1968,* edited by D. R. Cutler. Boston: Beacon Press, 1968.

———. "The Use of the Afro-American Past." In *The Religious Situation: 1969,* edited by D. R. Cutler. Boston: Beacon Press, 1969.

———. "Religion and Resistance Among Antebellum Negroes, 1800-1860." In *The Making of Black America* 1, edited by Meier and Rudwick. New York: Atheneum, 1969.

———. "Reflections and Meditations on the Training of Religious Leaders for the New Black Generation." *Theological Education* (Spring 1970).

———. "No Turning Back." *Renewal* (October-November 1970).

———. "The Acts of God and the Children of Africa." In *Shalom.* Philadelphia: United Church Press, 1973.

———. *Harvard Educational Review,* monograph number 2 (1974).

———. "Is America in Any Way Chosen: A Black Response." In *An Almost Chosen People,* edited by W. Nicgorski. Notre Dame, IN: University of Notre Dame Press, 1976.

———. "Out of the Cauldron of Struggle: Black Religion and the Search for a New America." *Sound* 61 (Fall 1978).

———. *The Other American Revolution.* Los Angeles: Center for Afro-American Studies, 1980.

———. "The Land Beyond: Reflections on King's Speech." *Sojourners* 12, no. 1 (January 1983).

———. "Never Too Desperate to Be Human: A Black Historian Wrestles With Issues of Race, Peace, and Faith." *Sojourners* 12, no. 2 (February 1983).

———. *There Is a River: The Black Struggle for Freedom in America.* New York: Vintage Books, 1983.

———. "Vincent Harding: A Black Historian (Autobiographical Testimony)." In *Peacemakers,* edited by J. Wallis. San Francisco: Harper & Row, 1983.

———. "Struggle and Transformation: The Challenge of Martin Luther King, Jr." *Sojourners* 13, no. 9 (October 1984).

———. "Black History and the Perils of Equal Opportunity." *The Peacemaking*

Struggle, edited by R. Stone and D. Wilbanks. Lanham, MD: University Press of America, 1985.

———. "Getting Ready for the Hero: Reflections on Martin Luther King, Jr. and Us." *Sojourners* 15, no. 1 (January 1986).

———. "Re-calling the Inconvenient Hero: Reflections on the Last Years of Martin Luther King, Jr." *Union Seminary Quarterly Review* 40, no. 4 (1986).

———. "We Must Keep Going: Martin Luther King, Jr. and the Future of America." *Fellowship* (January-February 1987).

———. "Toward a Darkly Radiant Vision of America's Truth." *Cross Currents* 37, no. 1 (Spring 1987).

———, and Harding, Rosemarie. "A Way of Faith, a Time for Courage (Black Church in America)." *The Other Side* 21, no. 7 (October 1985).

———, and Harding, Rosemarie. "Martin Luther King, Jr. and the Company of the Faithful." *Sojourners* (1986).

Hargraves, J. Archie. "Blackening Theological Education." *Christianity and Crisis* 29 (14 April 1969).

Harrison, Bob, and Montgomery, Jim. *When God Was Black*. Grand Rapids, MI: Zondervan Publishing House, 1971.

Harvey, Louis-Charles. "Black Theology and the Expanding Concept of Oppression." *Journal of Religious Thought* (Fall-Winter 1981–1982).

Haughley, J. "Black Theology." *America* 120, no. 20 (17 May 1969).

Hayes, Diana. "Historical Experience and Method in Black Theology: The Interpretation of Dr. James H. Cone." S.T.L. thesis, The Catholic University of America, 1985.

Herzfeld, Will. "Black Theology and White Theology." *Lutheran Quarterly Review* (August 1975).

Hilliard, Clarence. "Down With the Honkey Christ—Up With the Funky Jesus." *Christianity Today* 20 (1976).

Hoover, Theresa. "Black Women and the Churches: Triple Jeopardy." In *Black Theology: A Documentary History, 1966-1979*, edited by Wilmore and Cone. Maryknoll, NY: Orbis Books, 1979.

Jackson, Jesse L. "Black Power and White Churches." In *Black Viewpoints*, edited by Arthur C. Littleton and Mary W. Burger. New York: New American Library, 1964.

James, R. B. "Tillichian Analysis of James Cone's Black Theology." *Perspectives in Religious Studies* 1 (Spring 1974).

Jeffers, R. A. "Poor of God and the Black Christian in America." *Catholic World* 213 (June 1971).

Johnson, Joseph A., Jr. *The Soul of the Black Preacher*. Philadelphia: United Church Press, 1971.

———. "The Need for a Black Chrisitan Theology." *Journal of the ITC* 2, no. 1 (Fall 1974).

———. *Proclamation Theology*. Shreveport, LA: Fourth Episcopal District Press, 1977.

Johnson, William R., Jr. "A Black Prayer and Litany." *Theology Today* 26, no. 3 (October 1969).

Jones, Lawrence N. "Black Churches in Historical Perspective." *Christianity and Crisis* 30 (2 November 1970 and 16 November 1970).

———. "Black Churches. A New Agenda?" *The Christian Century* (18 April 1979).

———. *Black Religious Scholarship: Reflections and Promise; Addresses at the Tenth Anniversary.* The Society for the Study of Black Religion, New York City, 22-24 October 1981.

Jones, Major J. "Black Awareness: Theological Implications of the Concept." *Religion in Life* 38, no. 3 (Autumn 1969).

———. *Black Awareness: A Theology of Hope.* Nashville: Abingdon Press, 1971.

———. *Christian Ethics for Black Theology: The Politics of Liberation.* Nashville: Abingdon Press, 1974.

———. *The Color of God: The Concept of God in Afro-American Religious Thought.* Macon, GA: Mercer Press, 1987.

Jones, Miles J. "Toward a Theology of the Black Experience." *Christian Century* 867, no. 37 (16 September 1970).

Jones, Randolph. "The Holy Spirit, Black Liberation and Black Pentecostal." *The Other Side* (May-June 1974).

Jones, William A. *God in the Ghetto.* Elgin, IL: Progressive National Baptist Publishing House, 1979.

Jones, William R. "Theodicy and Methodology in Black Theology: A Critique of Washington, Cone, and Cleage." *The Harvard Theological Review* 64 (October 1971).

———. "Toward an Interim Assessment of Black Theology." *Reflection.* New Haven: Yale Divinity School and Berkeley Divinity School (January 1972).

———. "Reconciliation and Liberation in Black Theology: Some Implications for Religious Education." *Religious Education* 67 (September-October 1972).

———. "Theodicy: The Controlling Category for Black Theology." *Journal of Religious Thought* 30, no. 1 (Spring-Summer 1973).

———. *Is God a White Racist?: A Preamble to Black Theology.* New York: Anchor Press/Doubleday, 1973.

———. "Toward a Black Theology." *Midstream* (Fall-Winter 1973-1974).

———. "Theism and Religious Humanism: The Chasm Narrows." *The Christian Century* 92 (21 May 1975).

———. "Black Theology and Black Higher Education." *Journal of Ministries to Blacks in Higher Education* (1976).

———. "Religious Humanism: Its Problems and Prospects in Black Religion and Culture." In *Perspectives of Black Theology*, edited by Rosino Gibellini. Brescia, Italy: Queriniana, 1978.

———. "The Case for a New Black Humanism." In *Black Theology II, Essays on the Formation and Outreach of Contemporary Black Theology*, edited by Calvin R. Bruce and William R. Jones. Lewisburg, PA: Bucknell University Press, 1978.

———. "Ethical Perspectives in Black Theology: Mao, Martin and Malcolm." In *Philosophy Born of Struggle*, edited by Leonard Harris. Dubuque, IA: Kendall-Hunt Publishing Co., 1982.

Kelsey, George D. *Racism and the Christian Understanding of Man.* New York: Scribner, 1965.

Kennedy, Robert F. "Suppose God Is Black." *Look* (23 August 1966).

Lee, Carleton L. "Patterns of Leadership in Race Relations: A Study of Leadership Among Negro Americans." Doctoral diss., University of Chicago, 1951.

———. "Religious Roots of Negro Protest." In *Assuring Freedom to the Free*, edited by Arnold Rose. Detroit: Wayne State University Press, 1964.

————. Review of *Black Religion*, by Joseph R. Washington. *The Christian Scholar* 48 (Fall 1965):242-47.

————. "Toward a Sociology of the Black Religious Experience." *Journal of Religious Thought* (Autumn-Winter 1972).

LeMone, Archie. "The Afro-American Churches." *Ecumenical Review* 20, no. 1 (January 1968).

————. "When Traditional Theology Meets Black And Liberation Theology." *C&C* 33, no. 15 (17 September 1973).

Lincoln, C. Eric. "Black Nationalism and Christian Conscience." *Concern* 5 (15 September 1963).

————. "The Black Revolution in Cultural Perspective." *Union Seminary Quarterly Review* 23, no. 3 (Spring 1968).

————. *The Black Muslims in America.* Boston: Beacon Press, 1973.

————. *The Black Church Since Frazier.* New York: Schocken Books, 1974.

————. "A Perspective on James H. Cone's Black Theology." *Union Seminary Quarterly Review* 31, no. 1 (Fall 1975).

————. "The Black Church and a Decade of Change: Part II." *Tuesday at Home* (March 1976).

————. "The Social Cosmos of Black Ecumenism." *Journal of the ITC* 7, no. 1 (Fall 1979).

————. "Black Church in the American Society: A New Responsibility." *Journal of the ITC* (Spring 1979).

————. "Black Church and Christian Liberty." *A.M.E. Zion Quarterly Review* (October 1981).

————. *Race, Religion and the Continuing American Dilemma.* New York: Hill and Wang, 1984.

————, ed. *Is Anybody Listening to Black America?* New York: Seabury Press, 1968.

————, ed. *The Black Experience in Religion.* New York: Anchor Press/Doubleday, 1974.

Long, Charles H. "Religion and Mythology: A Critical Review of Some Recent Discussions." *History of Religions* 1, no. 2 (Winter 1961).

————. "Myth, Culture, and History: An Inquiry Into the Cultural History of West Africa." Ph.D. thesis, University of Chicago, 1962.

————. *Alpha: Myths of Creation.* New York: G. Braziller, 1963.

————. "The West African High God: History and Religious Experience." *History of Religions* 3, no. 2 (Winter 1964).

————. "Primitive Religion." In *A Reader's Guide to the Great Religions*, edited by Charles J. Adams. New York: The Free Press, 1965.

————. "The Death of God: Creativity of Decadence, a Modest Reflection." *Criterion* 7, no. 3 (Spring 1968).

————. "The Black Reality: Toward a Theology of Freedom." *Criterion* (Spring-Summer 1969).

————. "Perspectives for a Study of Afro-American Religion in the U.S." *History of Religions* 11, no. 1 (August 1971).

————. "Structural Similarities and Dissimilarities in Black and African Theologies." *Journal of Religious Thought* 32, no. 2 (Fall-Winter 1975).

————. "The Oppressive Elements in Religion and the Religions of the Oppressed." *Harvard Theological Review* 69, nos. 3-4 (1976).

————. "Assessment and New Departures for a Study of Black Religion in the

United States of America." *Black Religious Scholarship: Reflections and Promise.* Addresses at the Tenth Annual Meeting. The Society for the Study of Black Religion, New York City, 22-24 October 1981.

————. "Freedom, Otherness, and Religion: Theologies Opaque." *The Chicago Theological Seminary Register* 73, no. 1 (Winter 1983).

————. *Signification.* Philadelphia: Fortress Press, 1986.

Long, Jerome. Review of *Black Religion,* by Joseph R. Washington. *Foundations* 7, no. 4 (October 1964).

Lucas, Lawrence. *Black Priest! White Church!: Catholics and Racism.* New York: Random House, 1970.

Marshall, Calvin. B. "The Black Church—Its Mission Is Liberation." *The Black Scholar* 2, no. 4 (December 1970). Also in *The Black Experience in Religion,* edited by C. Eric Lincoln. New York: Anchor Press/Doubleday, 1974.

Massie, Priscilla, ed. *Black Faith and Black Solidarity.* New York: Friendship Press, 1973.

Maultsby, Hubert. "Paul, Black Theology and Hermeneutics." *Journal of the ITC* 32 (Spring 1976).

Mays, Benjamin E. *The Negro's God As Reflected in His Literature.* Westport, CT: Greenwood Press, 1969.

————, and Nicholson, J. W. *The Negro's Church.* New York: Institute of Social Religious Research, 1933.

McCall, Emmanuel. "Black Liberation Theology: A Politics of Freedom." *Review and Expositor* 73, no. 3 (Summer 1976).

McClain, William B. "The Genius of the Black Church." *Christian Century* 30 (2 November 1970 and 7 November 1970).

McGraw, James R., ed. "NCBC Speaks." *Renewal* 10, no. 7 (October-November 1970).

McKinney, Richard. "Reflections on the Concept 'Black Power.' " *Journal of Religious Thought* 26, no. 2 (Summer Supplement 1969).

————. "The Black Church—Its Development and Present Impact." *Harvard Theological Review* 64, no. 4 (October 1971).

McWilliam, Warrren. "Theodicy According to James Cone." *Journal of Religious Thought* (Fall-Winter 1979-1980).

"Miracle in Atlanta—A Black Christ." *Ebony* 24, no. 2 (December 1968).

Mitchell, Henry. "Black Power and the Christian Church." *Foundations* (April-July 1968).

————. "Two Streams of Tradition." In *The Black Experience in Religion,* edited by C. Eric Lincoln. New York: Anchor Books, 1974. Originally published as "Black Preaching," *Review and Expositor* (Summer 1973).

————. *Black Belief.* New York: Harper & Row, 1975.

————. "Some Preliminary Reflections on Authority in Black Religion." *Journal of the ITC* 3, no. 1 (Fall 1975).

————. "Theological Posits of Black Christianity." In *Black Theology II: Essays on the Formation and Outreach of Contemporary Black Theology,* edited by Calvin E. Bruce and William R. Jones. Lewisburg, PA: Bucknell University Press, 1978.

————. *Black Preaching.* San Francisco: Harper & Row, 1979.

Molla, Serge. "Etude Critique au pays de la Black Theology." *Revue de Theologie et de Philosophie* 114 (1982).

————. "James H. Cone, theologien noir americain." *Revue de Theologie et de Philosophie* 116 (1984).

Morrison, Roy D. II, "Black Philosophy: An Instrument for Cultural and Religious Liberation." *Journal of Religious Thought* 33, no. 1 (Spring-Summer 1976).

Mosley, William. *What Color Was Jesus?* Chicago: African American Images, 1987.

Moss, James A. "The Negro Church and Black Power." *Journal of Human Relations* 2 (Spring 1964).

Mottu, Henry. "Vers une theologie de la liberation (James Cone and Ruben Alves)." *Bulletin du Centre Protestant d'Etudes* 24 (1972).

————. "Le context historique et culturel de la theologie noire." *Lumiere et Vie* 23, no. 120 (1974).

Moyd, Olin P. *Redemption in Black Theology*. Valley Forge, PA: Judson Press, 1979.

Murray, Pauli. "Black Theology and Feminist Theology: A Comparative View." In *Black Theology: A Documentary History, 1966-1979*, edited by G. S. Wilmore and J. H. Cone. Maryknoll, NY: Orbis Books, 1979.

National Committee of Negro Churchmen. "Black Power—A Statement by the National Committee of Negro Churchmen." In *Black Theology: A Documentary History*, edited by G. S. Wilmore and J. H. Cone. Maryknoll, NY: Orbis Books, 1979. Originally published in the *New York Times* (31 July 1966).

National Conference of Black Christians. "Black Theology in 1976." *Journal of Religious Thought* 33, no. 1 (Spring-Summer 1976).

Nelsen, H. M, and Nelsen, A. K. *Black Church in the 60's*. Lexington, KY: University of Kentucky, 1975.

Newman, Richard. *Black Power and Black Religion*. West Cornwall, CT: Locust Hill Press, 1987.

Norman, Clarence. "A Constructive Study of the Concept of Liberation in Contemporary 'Black Religion' With Special Preference to the Thought of James Cone, Vincent Harding and James Deotis Roberts." Doctor of Religion Paper. School of Religion, Howard University, 1971.

Oglesby, Enoch H. "Reflections on Cultural Racism: The Theoretical Task of the Black Ethicist." *Journal of the ITC* 3, no. 1 (Fall 1975).

————. *Ethics and Theology from the Other Side: Sounds of Moral Struggle*. Washington, D.C.: University Press of America, 1979.

Oliver, Kenneth. "The History and Philosophy of Radical Black Theology. M. Div. thesis, Western Evangelical Seminary, 1973.

Opocensky, M. "Afro-American Revolution in Black Theology." *Communio Viatorum* 15, no. 1 (1972).

————. "Lessons From Black Theology." *Communio Viatorum* 17, nos. 1-2 (1974).

Osborn, Robert T. "White Need for Black Theology." *Journal of the ITC* (Fall 1976).

The Other Side. "Tenth Anniversary Issue. The New Evangelical" (July-August 1975).

Paris, Peter J. "The Bible and Black Churches." In *The Bible and Social Reform* 6, edited by Ernest R. Sandeen. Society of Biblical Literature, Centennial Publications. Philadelphia: Fortress Press, 1982.

————. *The Social Teachings of the Black Churches*. Philadelphia: Fortress Press, 1985.

————. "The Task of Religious Social Ethics in Light of Black Theology." In *Liberation and Ethics: Essays in Religious Social Ethics in Honor of Gibson Winter*, edited by Charles Amjad-Ali and W. Alvin Pitcher. Chicago: Center for the Scientific Study of Religion, 1985.

Payne, Larry. "Black Theology and Its Concept of Liberation." Th.M. thesis, Grace Theological Seminary, 1983.

Pero, Albert, and Moyo, Ambrose. *Theology and the Black Experience: The Lutheran Heritage Interpreted by African & African-American Theologians.* Minneapolis: Augsburg Publishing House, 1988.

Poinsett, Alex. "The Black Revolt in White Churches." *Ebony* (September 1968).

————. "The Quest for a Black Christ." *Ebony* (March 1969).

Powell, Adam Clayton. "Black Power in the Church." *The Black Scholar* 2, no. 4 (December 1970).

Roberts, J. Deotis. *Faith and Reason.* Boston: Christopher, 1962.

————. *From Puritanism to Platonism in Seventeenth Century England.* The Hague: Martinus Nijhoff, 1968.

————. "The Black Caucus and the Failure of Christian Theology." *Journal of Religious Thought* (Summer Supplement 1969).

————. "Folklore and Religion: The Black Experience." *Journal of Religious Thought* 27 (Summer Supplement 1970).

————. "Black Theology and the Theological Revolution." *Journal of Religious Thought* (Spring-Summer 1971).

————. *Liberation and Reconciliation: A Black Theology.* Philadelphia: Westminster Press, 1971.

————. "Africanisms and Spiritual Strivings." *Journal of Religious Thought* (Spring-Summer 1973).

————. "Religio-Ethical Reflections Upon the Experiential Components of a Philosophy of Black Liberation." *Journal of the ITC* 1, no. 1 (Fall 1973).

————. "Black Theology in the Making." *Review and Expositor* 70 (1973).

————. *A Black Political Theology.* Philadelphia: Westminster Press, 1974.

————. "A Critique of James H. Cone's *God of the Oppressed.*" *Journal of the ITC* (Fall 1975).

————. "Contextual Theology: Liberation and Indigenization." *Christian Century* 93 (28 January 1976).

————. "Editorial Comments. A White Critique of Black Theology: 'Is James Cone the Uncle Tom of Black Theology?'" *Journal of Religious Thought* (Fall-Winter 1979-1980).

————. "Ecumenical Concerns Among National Baptists." *Journal Ecumenical Studies* 17 (Spring 1980).

————. "A Black Theologian In Mexico." *Journal of Religious Thought* (Spring-Summer 1980).

————. *A Theological Commentary on the Sullivan Principles.* Philadelphia: International Council for Equality of Opportunity, 1980.

————. *Roots of a Black Future: Family and Church.* Philadelphia: Westminster Press, 1980.

————. "Liberation Theologies: A Critical Essay." *Journal of the ITC* 9 (Fall 1981).

————. "Black Theology in Historic Perspective." In *Religionen Geschichte Oekumene,* edited by R. Flasche and E. Geldbaach. Leiden: Brill, 1981.

————. *Black Theology Today, Liberation and Contextualization.* New York: Edwin Mellon Press, 1983.

————. *Black Theology in Dialogue.* Philadelphia: Westminster Press, 1987.

Robison, B. James. "A Tillichian Analysis of James Cone's Black Theology." *Religious Studies* 1, no.1 (Spring 1974).

Rogers, Cornish. "Black Religion Group Probes African Roots: Society for the Study of Black Religion." *Christian Century* 90 (7 November 1973).

———. "Pan Africanism and the Black Church: A Search for Solidarity." *Christian Century* 88, no. 46 (17 November 1971).

Rogers, Jefferson P. "Black Worship: Black Church." *The Black Church* 1, no. 1 (1972).

Rollins, Metz. "Revolution, Ecumenicity and the Black Church." *The Black Church* 1, no. 2 (1972).

Rooks, C. Shelby. "Crisis in Church Negro Leadership." *Theology Today* 22, no. 3 (October 1965).

———. "Implications of the Black Church for Theological Education." *The Voice, Bulletin of Crozer Theological Seminary* 61, no. 1 (January 1969).

———. "Theological Education and the Black Church." *Christian Century* (12 February 1969).

———. "Toward the Promised Land." *The Black Church* 2, no. 1 (1972).

———. "The First Dozen Years Are the Hardest." *Journal of the ITC* 1, no. 1 (Fall 1973).

———. "The State of Black Theological Education in 1980." *Black Religious Scholarship: Reflections and Promise*. Addresses at the Tenth Annual Meeting. The Society for the Study of Black Religion, New York City, 22-24 October 1981.

———. "Ten Years with Black Religion." *Black Religious Scholarship: Reflections and Promise*. Addresses at the Tenth Annual Meeting. The Society for the Study of Black Religion, New York City, 22-24 October 1981.

———. "Contemporary Horizons in Black Theology." *The Chicago Theological Seminary Register* 73, no. 1 (Winter 1983).

———. *Rainbows and Reality: Selected Writings of the Author*. Atlanta: The ITC Press, 1985.

Ruether, Rosemary. "Black Theology and Black Church." *Journal of Religious Thought* (Summer Supplement 1969).

———. "The Black Theology of James Cone." *Catholic World* (October 1971).

———. *Liberation Theology: Human Hope Confronts Christian History and American Power*. New York: Paulist Press, 1972.

———. "Crisis In Sex and Race: Black Theology vs. Feminist Theology." *Christianity and Crisis* 34, no. 6 (15 April 1974).

Sally, Columbus, and Behm, Ronald. *Your God Is Too White*. Downers Grove, IL: Inter-Varsity Press, 1970.

———, eds. *What Color Is Your God?: Black Consciousness and the Christian Faith*. Secaucus, NJ: Citadel Press, 1988.

Sawyer, Mary R. "Black Ecumenism: Cooperative Social Change Movements in the Black Church." Ph.D. diss., Duke University, 1986.

Schackern, Harold. "Toward a New Black Theology." *Tempo* (1 December 1968).

Serrin, William. "Cleage's Alternative." *Reporter* 38 (30 May 1968).

Shannon, David, and Wilmore, Gayraud, eds. *Black Witness to the Apostolic Faith*. Grand Rapids, MI: Eerdmans, 1985.

Sheares, Reuben A. "Beyond White Theology." *Christianity and Crisis* 30 (2 November 1970 and 16 November 1970).

Shockley, Grant S. "Ultimatum and Hope." *Christian Century* (12 February 1969).

———. "Religious Education and the Black Experience." *The Black Church* 2, no. 1 (1972).

Skinner, Tom. *How Black Is the Gospel?* Philadelphia: J. B. Lippincott, 1970.

Smith, Archie, Jr. "A Black Response to Sontag's 'Coconut Theology.' " *Journal of Religious Thought* (Fall-Winter 1979-1980).

Smith, Luther E., Jr. "Black Theology and Religious Experience." *Journal of the ITC* (Fall 1980).

Smith, Theophus H. "The Biblical Shape of Black Experience, An Essay In Philosophical Theology." Ph.D. diss., Graduate Theological Seminary, Berkeley, 1987.

Sontag, Frederick. "Coconut Theology: Is James Cone the 'Uncle Tom' of Black Theology?" *Journal of Religious Thought* (Fall-Winter 1979-1980).

Soulen, Richard N. "Black Worship and Hermeneutic." *Christian Century* 87 (11 February 1970).

Spivey, Charles S., Jr. "The Future of the Black Church." *The Chicago Theological Seminary Register* 73, no. 1 (Winter 1983).

Stewart, Carlyle Fielding III. "The Method of Correlation in the Theology of James H. Cone." *The Journal of Religious Thought* 40, no. 2 (Fall-Winter 1983-1984).

Thibodeaux, Mary Roger. *A Black Nun Looks at Black Power.* New York: Sheed and Ward, 1972.

Thomas, George B. "Black Theology of Liberation." *Journal of the ITC* 7, no. 1 (Fall 1979).

———. "Black Theology: Vanguard of Pan-African Christianity in America." *Journal of the ITC* 1 (Spring 1974).

Thurman, Howard. *Jesus and the Disinherited.* Richmond, IN: Friends United Press, 1981.

———. "Racial Roots and Religion: An Interview With Howard Thurman." *Christian Century* 90, no. 19 (9 May 1973).

Time. "Is God Black?" (November 15, 1968).

Traynham, Warner. *Christian Faith in Black and White: A Primer in Theology From the Black Perspective.* Wakefield, MA: Parameter, 1973.

Turner, Henry McNeil. "God Is a Negro." In *Black Nationalism in America*, edited by A. Meier and E. Rudwick. Indianapolis: Bobbs-Merrill Educational Publishing, 1980.

———. "Letter From South Africa." *Voices of Missions* (1 June 1898).

Wade, Charles Russell. "An Inquiry Into Black Theology: An Attempt at White Understanding." Th.D. diss., Southwestern Baptist Theological Seminary, 1975.

Ward, Hiley H. *Prophet of the Black Nation.* Philadelphia: Pilgrim Press, 1969.

Washington, Joseph R. Jr. "Are American Negro Churches Christian?" *Theology Today* (20 April 1963).

———. *Black Power and White Power Subreption.* Boston: Beacon Press, 1969.

———. *Marriage in Black And White.* Boston: Beacon Press, 1970.

———. *The Politics of God: The Future of Black Churches.* Boston: Beacon Press, 1970.

———. *Black Sects and Cults.* New York: Anchor Press/Doubleday, 1973.

———. "The Roots and Fruits and Black Theology." *Theology Today* 30 (1973-74).

———. "The Black Religious Crisis." *Christian Century* 91 (1 May 1974).

———. "Shafts of Light in Black Religious Awakening." *Religion and Life* 43 (Summer 1974).

————. *Black Religion: The Negro and Christianity in the United States.* Lanham, MD: University Press of America, 1984.

Watts, Leon. "Discussion: The Black Revolution." *Union Seminary Quarterly Review* 23, no. 3 (Spring 1968).

————. "The Black Church Yes! COCU No!" *Renewal* 10 (March 1970).

————. "The National Committee of Black Churchmen." *C&C* 30, no. 18 (2 November 1970 and 16 November 1970).

————. "Caucuses and Caucasians." In *The Black Experience in Religion*, edited by C. Eric Lincoln. New York: Anchor Books, 1974. Originally published in *Renewal* 10, no. 7 (October-December 1970).

————. "Transcendence and Mystery in Black Theology." *IDOC International Documentation* 71 (March-April 1976).

Weems, Renita. "'Hush. Mama's Gotta Go Bye Bye': A Personal Narrative." *Sage: A Scholarly Journal on Black Women* (Fall 1984).

————. "On Holy Ground." *Ms.* (December 1985).

————. "Home Again." *Essence* (December 1986).

————. *Just a Sister Away.* San Diego, CA: Lura Media, 1988.

West, Cornel. "Philosophy and the Afro-American Experience." *Philosophical Forum* (March 1979).

————. "Socialism and the Black Church." *New York Circus: A Center for Social Justice and International Awareness* (October-November 1979).

————. "Black Theology and Marxist Thought." In *Black Theology: A Documentary History, 1966-1979*, edited by G. S. Wilmore and J. H. Cone. Maryknoll, NY: Orbis Books, 1979.

————. "Black Theology and Socialist Thought." *The Witness* (April 1980).

————. *Prophesy Deliverance: An Afro-American Revolutionary Christianity.* Philadelphia: Westminster Press, 1982.

————. "Religion and the Left." In *Churches in Struggle: Liberation Theologies and Social Change in North America*, edited by William K. Tabb. New York: Monthly Review Press, 1986.

————. *Prophetic Fragments.* Grand Rapids, MI: Eerdmans, 1988.

White, Willie. "Separate Unto God." *Christian Century* 91 (13 February 1974).

Williams, A. R. "A Black Pastor Looks at Black Theology." *Harvard Theological Review* 64 (October 1971).

Williams, Delores. "The Black Women Portrayed in Selected Black Imaginative Literature and Some Questions For Black Theology." M.A. thesis, Union Theological Seminary, New York City, 1975.

————. "Black Theology's Contribution to Theological Methodology." *Reflection* 80, no. 2, New Haven: Yale Divinity School and Berkeley Divinity School (January 1983).

————. "Women as Makers of Literature." *Women's Spirit Bonding*, edited by J. Kalven and M. Buckley. New York: Pilgrim Press, 1984.

————. "Mud Flowers (Poem)." In *Women's Spirit Bonding*, edited by J. Kalven and M. Buckley. New York: Pilgrim Press, 1984.

————. "Black Women's Literature and the Task of Feminist Theology." In *Immaculate and Powerful*, edited by C. Atkinson, C. Buchanan and M. Miles. Boston: Beacon Press, 1985.

————. "The Color of Feminism." *Christianity and Crisis* 45 (April 29, 1985).

————. "Women's Oppression and Lifeline Politics in Black Women's Religious

Narratives." *Journal of Feminist Studies* 1, no. 2 (Fall 1985).

———. "Examining Two Shades of 'Purple.' " *Los Angeles Times* (15 March 1986).

———. "The Color of Feminism: Or Speaking the Black Woman's Tongue." *Journal of Religious Thought* (Spring-Summer 1986).

———. " 'The Color Purple': What Was Missed." *Christianity and Crisis* 46, no. 10 (14 July 1986).

———. "Roundtable Discussion: Lesbianism and Feminist Theology." *Journal of Feminist Theology in Religion* (Fall 1986).

———. "Womanist Theology: Black Women's Voices." *Christianity and Crisis* (2 March 1987).

Williams, Preston N. "Shifting Racial Perspectives." *Harvard Divinity Bulletin* (Fall 1968.)

———. "Black Church: Origin, History, Present Dilemmas." *Andover Newton Quarterly* 9, no. 2 (November 1968).

———. "Black Church: Origin, History, Present Dilemmas." *McCormick Quarterly* 22, no. 4 (May 1969).

———. "The Ethical Aspects of the 'Black Church/Black Theology' Phenomenon." *Journal of Religious Thought* 26, no. 2 (Summer Supplement 1969).

———. "Ethnic Pluralism or Black Separatism?" *Social Progress* (September-October 1969).

———. "The Atlanta Document: An Interpretation." *Christian Century* (15 October 1969).

———. "The Black Experience and Black Religion." *Theology Today* 26, no. 3 (October 1969).

———. "Ethics and Ethos in the Black Experience." *C&C* (31 May 1971).

———. "Black Theology." *Communion Viatorum* 14, nos. 2-3 (Summer 1971).

———. "Toward a Sociological Understanding of the Religious Community." *Soundings* (Fall 1971).

———. "The Ethics of Black Power." In *Quest for a Black Theology*, edited by James J. Gardiner and J. Deotis Roberts. Philadelphia: Pilgrim Press, 1971.

———. "The New Black Politics Needs Revision." *The Christian Century* 89, no. 33 (20 September 1972).

———. "James Cone and the Problem of a Black Ethic." *The Harvard Theological Review* 65, no. 4 (October 1972).

———. "The Price of Social Justice." *Christian Century* (9 May 1973).

———. "Criteria for Decision-Making for Social Ethics in the Black Community." *Journal of the ITC* 1, no. 1 (Fall 1973).

Williams, Robert C. "Moral Suasion and Militant Aggression in the Theological Perspective of Black Religion." *Journal of Religious Thought* (Fall-Winter 1973-74).

Wilmore, Gayraud S. "The White Church and the Search for Black Power." *Social Progress* 57 (1967).

———. "The Case for a New Black Church Style." *Church In Metropolis* (Fall 1968). Also in *The Black Church In America*, edited by Nelsen, Yokley and Nelsen. New York: Basic Books, 1971.

———. "Stalking the Wild Black Theologues." *Social Progress* 60, no. 1 (September-October 1969).

———. "Reparations: Don't Hang Up on a Word." *Theology Today* 26, no. 3 (October 1969).

————. "Africa and Afro-Americans: Report of Conversations Between NCBC Officials and Members of the All Africa Conference of Churches." *The Christian Century* 87, no. 22 (3 June 1970).

————. Review of *A Black Theology of Liberation*, by James H. Cone. *Union Seminary Quarterly Review* 26, no. 4 (Summer 1971).

————. "Ethics in Black and White." *Christian Century* 90, no. 32 (12 September 1973).

————. "Appendix D. The Theological Commission Project of the NCBC (Fall 1968)." In *Christian Faith in Black And White: A Primer in Theology from the Black Perspective*, edited by Warner R. Trayham. Wakefield, MA: Parameter, 1973.

————. "Black Theology: Its Significance for Christian Mission Today." *International Review of Mission* 63, no. 250 (Spring 1974.)

————. "Black Power, Black People, Theological Renewal." In *A Reader in Political Theology*, edited by Alistair Kee. Philadelphia: Westminster Press, 1974.

————. "Black Messiah: Revising the Color Symbolism of Western Christology." *Journal of the ITC* 2 (Fall 1974).

————. "To Speak With One Voice?" *Christian Century* 92, no. 6 (19 February 1975).

————. "The Religion and Philosophy of Black America." *The World Encyclopedia of Black Peoples* conspectus volume. St. Clair Shores, MI: Scholarly Press, 1975.

————. *Union Theological Seminary Review* 31, no. 1 (1976).

————. "Black Theology: Raising the Questions." *Christian Century* 94, no. 24 (20-27 July 1977).

————. "Steve Biko, Martyr." *Christian Century* 37 (17 October 1977).

————. "Blackness As Sign and Assignment." In *Black Preaching: Select Sermons in the Presbyterian Tradition*, edited by Robert T. Newbold, Jr. Philadelphia: Geneva Press, 1977.

————. "Theological Ferment in the Third World." *Christian Century* 95 (15 February 1978).

————. "New Context of Black Theology in the United States." *Occ. Bul. Miss. R.* 2 (October 1978).

————. "Fascism With a Friendly Face (South Africa's Denial of Visas to Genesee Ecumenical Ministries, Rochester, New York)." *Christian Century* 98 (26 August 1981).

————. *Last Things First*. Philadelphia: Westminster Press, 1982.

————. "The Path Toward Racial Justice." *Journal of Pres. H.* 61 (Spring 1983).

————. *Black Religion and Black Radicalism: An Interpretation of the Religious History of Afro-American People,* 2d ed. Maryknoll, NY: Orbis Books, 1983.

————. *Black and Presbyterian: The Heritage and the Hope*. Philadelphia: The Geneva Press, 1983.

————. "Toward a Common Expression of Faith: A Black North American Perspective." *AME Zion Quarterly Review* 97, no. 2 (July 1985).

————. "The Disturbing Ecumenism of the Black Church in America." *Ecumenical Trends* 14, no. 8 (September 1985).

————. "Black Christians, Church Unity and One Common Expression of Apostolic Faith." *Mid-Stream* 24 (October 1985).

————. "Black Americans In Mission: Setting the Record Straight." *International Bulletin of Missionary Review* 10, no. 3 (July 1986).

————. "Religion and American Politics: Beyond the Veil" and "Spirituality and

Social Transformation as the Vocation of the Black Church." In *Churches in Struggle: Liberation Theologies and Social Change in North America*, edited by William K. Tabb. New York: Monthly Review Press, 1986.

———. "Reflections on the Origin and Future of the Black Theology Project." Presented at the 10th Annual Convocation of the Black Theology Project, The ITC, February 18-20, 1987.

———. *African American Religious Studies*. Durham, NC: Duke University Press, 1989.

———, and Song, C. S. "Asians and Blacks—Theological Challenges". *Scottish Journal of Theology* 28, no. 3 (1975).

———, and Cone, J. H. *Black Theology: A Documentary History, 1966-1979*. Maryknoll, NY: Orbis Books, 1979.

Wilson, Frank T. "Guest Editorial. Critical Evaluation of the Theme 'The Black Revolution: Is There a Black Theology?' " *Journal of Religious Thought* (Summer Supplement 1969).

Wilson, Sandra. " 'Which Me Will Survive All These Liberations': On Being a Black Woman Episcopal Priest." In *Speaking of Faith: Global Perspectives on Women, Religion and Social Change*, edited by D.L. Eck and Devaki Jain. Philadelphia: New Society Publishers, 1987.

Witvliet, Theo. *The Way of the Black Messiah*. Oak Park, Illinois: Meyer Stone, 1987.

Woodson, Carter G. *The History of the Negro Church*. Washington, D.C.: The Associated Publishers, 1972.

Wright, Leon E. " 'Black Theology' or Black Experience?" *Journal of Religious Thought* (Summer Supplement 1969).

Wright, Nathan. "Black Power: A Creative Necessity." In *Black Viewpoints*, edited by Arthur C. Littleton and Mary W. Burger. New York: New American Library, 1964.

———. "Power and Reconciliation." *Concern* 9, no. 16 (October 1, 1967).

———. *Black Power and Urban Unrest: Creative Possibilities*. New York: Hawthorn Books, 1967.

———. "The Crisis Which Bred Black Power." In *The Black Power Revolt*, edited by Floyd B. Barbour. Boston: Porter Sargent, 1968.

———. "The Black Spiritual: A Testament of Hope for Our Times?" *Journal of Religious Thought* (Spring-Summer 1978).

Yancey, William Lee. "Hearing Means Death: James H. Cone's Black Theology As a Resource for Confronting the Modern Problem of Death." D.Th. diss., Lutheran School of Theology at Chicago, June 1986.

Young, Henry James. "Black Theology and the Work of William R. Jones." *Religion in Life* 44, no. 2 (Spring 1975).

———. "Black Theology: Providence and Evil." *Journal of the ITC* 40, no. 2 (Spring 1975).

Young, Josiah. *Black and African Theologies: Siblings or Distant Cousins?* Maryknoll, NY: Orbis Books, 1986.

———. "Exodus As a Paradigm for Black Theology." In *Exodus—A Lasting Paradigm*, edited by Bas van Iersel and Anton Weiler. Edinburgh: T & T Clark, 1987.

Zieglar, Jesse H., ed. "Black Religious Experience and Theological Education." *Theological Education* 6 (Spring 1970).

BLACK THEOLOGY SOUTH AFRICAN REFERENCES

African Independent Churches: Speaking For Ourselves. Braamfontein, South Africa: Institute for Contextual Theology, 1985.
"Allan Boesak." *African Report* (July-August 1983).
Baartman, Ernest. "The Black and the Church." *Pro Veritate* 10, no. 3 (July 1971).
———. "The Significance of the Development of Black Consciousness for the Church." *SASO Newsletter* (November-December 1972).
———. "The Significance of the Development of Black Consciousness for the Church." *Journal of Theology for Southern Africa,* no. 2 (March 1973).
———. "Black Consciousness." *Pro Veritate* (March 1973).
———. "The Black Man and the Church." *Pro Veritate* (April 1973).
———. "Response: The Rev. Ernest Baartman." In *Liberation,* edited by David Thomas. Johannesburg, South Africa: South African Council of Churches, 1976.
———. "The Black Man and the Church." In *African Perspectives on South Africa,* edited by HWVD Merwe, et al. Stanford, CA: Hoover Institution Press, 1978.
———. "Education as an Instrument for Liberation." In *African Perspectives on South Africa,* edited by HWVD Merwe, et al. Stanford, CA: Hoover Institution Press, 1978.
Bax, Douglas. "The Tower of Babel in South Africa Today." *Journal of Theology for Southern Africa* 42 (1983).
"Black Caucus of the S.A. Council of Churches: The Soweto Disturbances." In *African Perspectives on South Africa,* edited by HWVD Merwe, et al. Stanford, CA: Hoover Institution Press, 1978.
"Black Ministers of the Dutch Reformed Church." In *African Perspectives on South Africa,* edited by HWVD Merwe, et al. Stanford, CA: Hoover Institution Press, 1978.
"Black Religion in South Africa." *African Studies* 33, no. 2 (1974).
Becken, H-J., ed. *Relevant Theology for Africa.* Durban, South Africa: Lutheran Publishing House, 1973.
Bennett, Bonita. "A Critique on the Role of Women in the Church." In *The Unquestionable Right to Be Free,* edited by I. J. Mosala and B. Tlhagale. Johannesburg, South Africa: Skotaville Publishers, 1986; Maryknoll, NY: Orbis Books, 1986.
Beyerhaus, P. "An Approach to the African Independent Church Movement." *Ministry* 9 (1969).
"Black Caucus of the South African Council of Churches: The Soweto Disturbances." In *African Perspectives on South Africa,* edited by HWVD Merwe, et al. Stanford, CA: Hoover Institution Press, 1978.
"Black Ministers of the Dutch Reformed Church: Statement on Apartheid." In *African Perspectives on South Africa,* edited by HWVD Merwe, et. al. Stanford, CA: Hoover Institution Press, 1978.
"Black Theology Resolution." *Pro Veritate* (July 15, 1971).
Boesak, Allan A. "Courage to Be Black, Part 1." *South African Outlook,* no. 1253 (October 1975).
———. "Courage to Be Black, Part 2." *South African Outlook,* no. 1254 (November 1975).

———. "Black Consciousness, Black Power and Coloured Politics." *Pro Veritate* (February 1977).

———. "Civil Religion and the Black Community." *Journal of Theology for Southern Africa* (June 1977).

———. "The Challenge for Christians in South Africa." *Pro Veritate* (September 1977).

———. "Coming in out of the Wilderness." In *The Emergent Gospel*, edited by V. Fabella and S. Torres. Maryknoll, NY: Orbis Books, 1978.

———. "The Relationship Between Text and Situation, Reconciliation and Liberation in Black Theology." *Voices of the Third World* 2, no. 1 (June 1979).

———. "What Belongs to Caesar? Once Again Romans 13." In *Voices of the Third World* 2, no. 1 (June 1979).

———. "The Black Church and the Future." *South African Outlook* (July 1979).

———. "The Black Church and the Future." *EcuNews Bulletin* 24 (3 August 1979).

———. "The Black Church and the Struggle in South Africa." *The Ecumenical Review* (January 1980).

———. "The Way Through – II. Interview With Allan Boesak." *South African Outlook* (September 1980).

———. "Wholeness Through Liberation." *Church and Society* (May 1981).

———. " 'To Break Every Yoke . . .' Liberation and the Churches of Africa." *South African Outlook* (October 1981).

———. *Farewell to Innocence.* Maryknoll, NY: Orbis Books, 1981.

———. "Suffer the Children to Come: To Whom Does the Kingdom of God Belong." *Otherside* (May 1982).

———. "The Heresy of Apartheid." In *Apartheid Change and the NGK*, edited by JHP Serfontein. Pretoria, South Africa: Taurus, 1982.

———. "He Made Us All But . . . Racism and the WARC." In *Apartheid Change and the NGK*, edited by JHP Serfontein. Pretoria, South Africa: Taurus, 1982.

———. *The Finger of God.* Maryknoll, NY: Orbis Books, 1982.

———. "Falling Out of Step With a World of Wonders." *One World* (June 1983).

———. "Jesus Christ the Life of the World." *Reformed World* (September 1983).

———. "Jesus Christ – Life of the World." *South African Outlook* (September 1983).

———. "In His Life, Death and Resurrection Lies the Future of the World." *International Review of Mission* (October 1983).

———. "The Hour Comes and It Is Now." *The Ecumenical Review* (October 1983).

———. "Holding on to the Vision." *AACC Magazine* (December 1983).

———. "Relevant Preaching in Black Situation." *All African Conference of Churches Magazine* (August 1984).

———. "Tensions Are Deepening, Anger Is Rising." *C&C* 44, no. 19 (26 November 26 1984).

———. *Black and Reformed.* Maryknoll, NY: Orbis Books, 1984.

———. *Walking on Thorns.* Geneva: World Council of Churches, 1984.

———. "Called to Witness to the Gospel Today: Report for South Africa." *Reformed World* 38, no. 2 (1984).

———. "And Even His Own Life. . . " *Voices From the Third World* (January 1985).

———. "Sermon: In the Name of Jesus, Acts 4:12." *Journal of Theology for Southern Africa* (September 1985).

———. "In the Name of Jesus: A Sermon for 16 June." In *When Prayer Makes*

News, edited by A. A. Boesak and C. Villa-Vicencio. Philadelphia: Westminster Press, 1986.

———. *Comfort and Protest*. Philadelphia: Westminster Press, 1987.

———. *If This Is Treason, I Am Guilty*. Grand Rapids, MI: Eerdmans, 1987.

———, and Brews, Alan. "The Black Struggle for Liberation: A Reluctant Road to Revolution." In *Theology and Violence, The South African Debate*, edited by Charles Villa-Vicencio. Johannesburg, South Africa: Skotaville Publishers, 1987.

Bolink, Peter. "God in Traditional African Religion: A *Deus Otiosus*?" *Journal of Theology for Southern Africa* no. 5 (December 1973).

Bosch, D. J. "Currents and Crosscurrents in South African Black Theology." In *Black Theology: A Documentary History, 1966-1979*, edited by Gayraud S. Wilmore and James H. Cone. Maryknoll, NY: Orbis Books, 1979.

———. "Church Unity Amidst Cultural Diversity." *Missionalia* (April 1982).

Boshoff, Carel. "Christ in Black Theology." *Missionalia* 9, no. 3 (November 1981). Publication of the South African Missiological Society, Pretoria, South Africa.

Boulay, Shirley du. *Tutu: Voice of the Voiceless*. Grand Rapids, MI: Eerdmans, 1988.

Burnet, Amos. "Ethiopianism." *Church Missionary Review* 73 (1922).

Butelezi, Peter John. "Black Theology in South Africa." In *African Perspectives on South Africa*, edited by HWVD Merwe, et al. Stanford, CA: Hoover Institution Press, 1978.

Buthelezi, Manas. "Christianity in South Africa." *Pro Veritate* 12, no. 2 (June 1973).

———. "Six Theses: Theological Problems of Evangelism in the South African Context." *Journal of Theology for Southern Africa* (June 1973).

———. "Change in the Church." *South African Outlook* (August 1973).

———. "The Christian Institute and Black South Africa." *South African Outlook* (September 1973).

———. "Change in the Church." *Pro Veritate* (September 1973).

———. "African Theology and Black Theology: A Search for a Theological Method." In *Relevant Theology for Africa*, edited by Hans-Jurgen Becken. Durban, South Africa: Lutheran Publishing House, 1973.

———. "Christianity in My World." *Katallagete* 5, no. 1 (Spring 1974).

———. "The Relevance of Black Theology." *South African Outlook* 104, no. 1243 (December 1974).

———. "Black Renaissance Convention, Hammanskrall, December 12, 1974. The Christian Challenge of Black Theology." Mimeo.

———. "Theological Grounds for an Ethic of Hope." In *The Challenge of Black Theology in South Africa*, edited by Basil Moore. Atlanta: John Knox Press, 1974.

———. "An African Theology or a Black Theology?" In *The Challenge of Black Theology in South Africa*, edited by Basil Moore. Atlanta: John Knox Press, 1974.

———. "The Theological Meaning of True Humanity." In *The Challenge of Black Theology in South Africa*, edited by Basil Moore. Atlanta: John Knox Press, 1974.

———. "The Meaning of the Christian Institute for Black South Africa." *Lutheran World Federation* (June 1975).

———. "Daring to Live for Christ: By Being Human and by Suffering for Others." *Journal of Theology for Southern Africa* (July 1975).

———. "Black Theology and the Le Grange-Schlebush Commission." *Pro Veritate* (October 1975).

———. "The Ethical Questions Raised by Nationalism." In *Church and Nationalism in South Africa*, edited by Theo Sundermeier. Johannesburg, South Africa: Raven Press, 1975.

———. "The Christian Challenge of Black Theology." In *Black Renaissance*, edited by Thoahlane Thoahlane. Johannesburg, South Africa: Raven Press, 1975.

———. "Black Creativity as a Process of Liberation." *Pro Veritate* (June 1976).

———. "The Christian Presence in South Africa." *Journal of Theology for Southern Africa* (16 September 1976).

———. "The Relevance of Black Theology." *All African Council of Churches Bulletin* 9 (1976).

———. "Daring to Live for Christ." In *Missions Trends No. 3*, edited by G. H. Anderson and T. F. Stransky. New York: Paulist Press, 1976.

———. "The Proclamation of the Gospel and Marks of the Church." *Lutheran World* 23, no. 1 (1976).

———. "Service to the Down-Trodden." *Pro Veritate* (January 1977).

———. "Towards a Biblical Faith in South African Society." *Journal of Theology for Southern Africa* (June 1977).

———. "In Christ: One New Community." *AFER: African Ecclesial Review* (December 1977).

———. "L'Apartheid dans l'Eglise est une heresie condamnable." *Bulletin de la CETA* (1977).

———. "Being With Christ In His Suffering People." *Diakonia News* (May 1978).

———. "Mutual Acceptance from a Black Perspective." *Journal of Theology for Southern Africa* (June 1978).

———. "Black Theology: A Quest for the Liberation of Christian Truth." In *All African Lutheran Consultation on Christian Theology and Christian Education in the African Context*, edited by Lutheran World Federation. Geneva: 1978.

———. "How to Promote Peace in South Africa." In *African Perspectives on South Africa*, edited by HWVD Merwe, et al. Stanford, CA: Hoover Institution Press, 1978.

———. "Toward Indigenous Theology in South Africa." In *The Emergent Gospel*, edited by S. Torres and V. Fabella. Maryknoll, NY: Orbis Books, 1978.

———. "In Christ: One Community in the Spirit." *Africa Theological Journal* 7, no. 1 (1978).

———. "Extracts from an Address by Dr. Manas Buthelezi at the South African Christian Leadership Conference, July 11, 1979—Violence and the Cross in South Africa Today." *EcuNews Bulletin* 22 (20 July 1979).

———. "Violence and the Cross in South Africa Today." *Journal of Theology for Southern Africa* (December 1979).

———. *Power Is Ours*. New York: Books in Focus, 1979.

———. "Giving Witness to the Heart of the Gospel." *International Review of Mission* (October 1984).

———. "Church Unity and Human Divisons of Racism." In *International Review of Mission* (October 1984).

———. "An Ethic of Hope." In *Cry Justice*, edited by John de Gruchy. Maryknoll, NY: Orbis Books, 1986.

———. "Power Beyond Words." In *Cry Justice*, edited by John de Gruchy. Maryknoll, NY: Orbis Books, 1986.

———. "In Times of Crisis Can We Remain in our Chairs?" *EcuNews* (August 1987).

Buti, S. *EcuNews* (17 June 1975).

————. "The Acid Test." *South African Outlook* (August 1978).

————. "What Is Black Theology?" and "Race Conflict." In *Facing the New Challenge: The Message of PACLA (Pan African Christian Leadership Assembly)*, edited by Michael Cassidy and Luc Verlinden. Kisumu, Kenya: Evangel Publishing House, 1978.

————. "Shadows of Death and the Future of South Africa." In *The Church and the Alternative Society: Papers and Resolutions of the Eleventh Conference of the SACC*, edited by M. Nash, South Africa.

————. "Crosscurrents and Crossroads in the South African Scene and the Kingdom of God." In *Your Kingdom Come (SACC 1980)*, edited by M. Nash.

Chikane, Frank. "Bible Study and Theological Reflection." *South African Outlook* (May 1985).

————. "The Incarnation in the Life of the People in Southern Africa." *Journal of Theology for Southern Africa* (June 1985).

————. "Progressive Theological Education." *South African Outlook* (November 1985).

————. "Doing Theology in a Situation of Conflict." In *Resistance and Hope: South African Essays in Honour of Beyers Naude*, edited by Charles Villa-Vicencio and John deGruchy. Grand Rapids, MI: Eerdmans, 1985.

————. Opening Worship at the Kairos Convocation sponsored by the National Council of Churches of Christ. Held in Chicago (19 November 1986).

————. "God's Option for the Poor." In *Cry Justice*, edited by John de Gruchy. Maryknoll, NY: Orbis Books, 1986.

————. "Where the Debate Ends." In *Theology and Violence: The South African Debate*, edited by Charles Villa-Vicencio. Johannesburg, South Africa: Skotaville Publishers, 1987.

————. *No Life of My Own: An Autobiography by Frank Chikane*. Johannesburg, South Africa: Skotaville Publishers, 1988; Maryknoll, NY: Orbis Books, 1989.

"Church and Black Theology in South Africa. (Yaounde, Cameroon, January 1984)." *Bulletin of African Theology* 6, no. 12 (July-December 1984).

Cragg, D.G.L. "The State of Ecumene in South Africa." *Missionalia* 10, no. 1 (April 1982).

Daneel, M. L. "The Missionary Outreach of African Independent Churches." *Missionalia* 8 (1980). Pretoria, South Africa: Journal of the South African Missiological Society.

————. "Towards A Theological Africana? The Contribution of Independent Churches to African Theology." *Missionalia* 12, no. 2 (1984).

de Gruchy, John. *The Church Struggle in South Africa*. Grand Rapids, MI: Eerdmans, 1979.

————. *Bonhoeffer and South Africa*. Grand Rapids, MI: Eerdmans, 1984.

————. *Theology and Ministry in the Context of Crisis*. Grand Rapids, MI: Eerdmans, 1987.

Dwane, Siqibo. "Christology in the Third World." *Journal of Theology for Southern Africa* (December 1977).

————. "Black Christianity in Kingdom Perspective. In *Your Kingdom Come (SACC Papers 1980)*, edited by M. Nash.

————. "Christology and Liberation." *Journal of Theology for Southern Africa*, no. 21 (June 1981).

———. "In Search of an African Contribution to a Contemporary Confession of Christian Faith. *Journal of Theology for Southern Africa* (March 1982).

———. "Part II: The Task of Theology Today: Investigating God's Liberating Love." *Journal of Theology for Southern Africa* (December 1982).

———. "Archbishop Tutu, A Personal Tribute." In *Hammering Swords Into Ploughshares: Essays in Honour of Archbishop Mpilo Desmond Tutu*, edited by B. Tlhagale and I. Mosala. Johannesburg, South Africa: Skotaville Publishers, 1986.

———. "Gospel and Culture." *Journal of Black Theology in South Africa* 1, no. 1 (1987). Atteridgeville, South Africa.

Evangelical Witness in South Africa. Dobsonville, South Africa: Concerned Evangelicals, 1986.

Farisani, T. S. *Diary From a South African Prison*. Philadelphia: Fortress Press, 1987.

Goba, Bonganjalo. "Two Views on Black Theology." *Pro Veritate* (September 1971).

———. "The Task of Black Theological Education in South Africa." *Journal of Theology for Southern Africa* (March 1978).

———. "Doing Theology in South Africa: A Black Christian Perspective." Ph.D. diss., Chicago Theological Seminary, 1978.

———. "Personnalité Collective En Israel et En Afrique." In *Chretiens D'Afrique du Sud Face A L'Apartheid*, edited by Anne Marie Goguel and Pierre Buis. Paris: Editions L'Harmattan, 1978.

———. "An African Christian Theology: Towards a Tentative Methodology From a South African Perspective." *Journal of Theology for Southern Africa* (March 1979).

———. "The Role of the Black Church in the Process of Healing Human Brokenness: A Perspective in Pastoral Theology." *Journal of Theology for Southern Africa* (September 1979).

———. "Doing Theology in South Africa." *Journal of Theology for Southern Africa* (June 1980).

———. "The Way Through." *South African Outlook* 10, no. 1311 (September 1980).

———. "The Urban Church: A Black South African Perspective." *The South African Outlook* (March 1981).

———. "Towards A 'Black' Ecclesiology." *Missionalia* 9, no. 2 (1981).

———. "The Role of the Urban Church: A Black South African Perspective." *Journal of Theology for Southern Africa* (March 1982).

———. "Three Christological Models in Third World Theology." *Theologia Evangelica* (November 1982).

———. "Theology and Existential Commitment." *Journal of Theology for Southern Africa* (December 1982).

———. "Emerging Theological Perspectives in South Africa." In *Irruption of the Third World*, edited by V. Fabella and S. Torres. Maryknoll, NY: Orbis Books, 1983.

———. "Role of the Urban Church." *Evangelical Review of Theology* (April 1984).

———. "The Problem of Racism Revisited." In *New Faces of Africa*, edited by J. Hofmeyr and W. Vorster. Pretoria, South Africa: University of South Africa (UNISA), 1984.

———. "Response." In *Sexism and Feminism in Theological Perspective*, edited by W. S. Vorster. Pretoria, South Africa: UNISA, 1984.

———. "A Black South African Perspective." In *Doing Theology in a Divided World*, edited by V. Fabella and S. Torres. Maryknoll, NY: Orbis Books, 1985.

———. "Contextual Understanding: The Problem in South Africa of Differing Perceptions and Analyses." *Transformations* 3, no. 2 (April/June 1986).

———. "The Use of Scripture in the Kairos Document: A Biblical Ethical Perspective." *Journal of Theology for Southern Africa* (September 1986).

———. "Healing Means Social and Personal Conversion." In *Cry Justice*, edited by John de Gruchy. Maryknoll, NY: Orbis Books, 1986.

———. "The Black Consciousness Movement: Its Impact on Black Theology." In *The Unquestionable Right to Be Free*, edited by I. J. Mosala and B. Tlhagale. Johannesburg, South Africa: Skotaville Publishers, 1986; Maryknoll, NY: Orbis Books, 1986.

———. "A Theological Tribute to Archbishop Tutu." In *Hammering Swords Into Ploughshares*, edited by B. Tlhagale and I. Mosala. Johannesburg, South Africa: Skotaville Publishers, 1986.

———. *An Agenda for Black Theology in South Africa: Hermeneutics for Social Change*. Johannesburg, South Africa: Skotaville Publishers, 1988.

———. "Toward a Quest for Christian Identity." *Journal of Black Theology in South Africa* (November 1988).

Hodgson, Janet. *Ntsikana's 'Great Hymn,' A Xhosa Expression of Christianity in the Early 19th Century Eastern Cape*. Cape Town, South Africa: Centre for African Studies, University of Cape Town, 1980.

———. "The Faith-Healer of Cancele. Some Problems in Analysing Religious Experience Among Black People." Paper presented to the Fourth Conference of A.H.R.S.A. University of Natal, Pietermaritzburg, South Africa. 29-30 June 1982.

Institute for Contextual Theology. "Report. Women's Struggle in South Africa. Feminist Theology Conference. 31 August-2 September 1984. Hammanskrall."

———. "What Is Contextual Theology? (parts one and two)." *AACC Magazine* (December 1984).

Jordan, Roxanne. "Black Feminist Theology." Presentation at the Black Theology in South Africa and North America Conference held at Union Theological Seminary, New York. 1-3 December 1986.

Kairos Theologians. *The Kairos Document: A Theological Comment on the Political Crisis in South Africa, Revised Second Edition. Challenge to the Church*. Johannesburg, South Africa: Skotaville Publishers, 1986.

Kameeta, Z. "A Black Theology of Liberation." *Lutheran World* 22, no. 4 (1975).

———. "The Cross in the World." *Pro Veritate* (July 1976).

Kretzschmar, Louise. *The Voice of Black Theology in South Africa*. Johannesburg, South Africa: Raven Press, 1986.

Kritzinger, J.N.J. "Black Eschatology and Christian Mission." *Missionalia* 15, no. 1 (April 1987).

Kurewa, Z.J.W. "The Meaning of African Theology." *Journal of Theology for Southern Africa* 11 (1975).

Legida, S. P. "A Relevant Theology." In *A Relevant Theology for Africa*, edited by H-J Becken. Durban, South Africa: Lutheran Publishing House, 1973.

Logan, Willis, ed. *The Kairos Covenant: Standing With South African Christians*. Oak Park, IL: Meyer-Stone Books, 1988.

Loram, C. T. "The Separatist Church Movement." *International Review of Missions* 15 (July 1926).

Louw, Lionel. "From Streets, Lanes, Highways, and Hedges . . . They Came." In

When Prayer Makes News, edited by A. A. Boesak and C. Villa-Vicencio. Philadelphia: Westminster Press, 1986.

Mabona, A. D. "Africanisation of the Church." *Pro Veritate* (15 March 1970).

———. "White Worship and Black People." *Pro Veritate* (15 May 1971).

Mafungo, Vic. "Black Theology, A Re-assessment of the Christ." *SASO Newsletter* (September 1971).

Maimela, Simon. "Theology and Politics in South Africa." *Chicago Theological Seminary Register* (Spring 1979).

———. "Man In 'White' Theology." *Missionalia* 9, no. 1 (April 1981).

———. "Man in 'White' Theology." *Journal of Theology for Southern Africa* no. 36 (September 1981).

———. "The Atonement in the Context of Liberation Theology." *South African Outlook* (December 1981).

———. "Hermeneutics As a Truth-revealing Praxis: The Theory-praxis in Theology Revisited." *Theologia Evangelica* 14, no. 3 (December 1981).

———. "Religious Pluralism in South Africa—Response." In *Christianity Among Religions*, edited by W. S. Vorster. Pretoria, South Africa: UNISA, 1981.

———. "The Atonement in the Context of Liberation Theology." *Journal of Theology for Southern Africa* (June 1982).

———. "Towards a Theology of Humanization." *Journal of Theology for Southern Africa* (December 1982).

———. "Denominationalism—An Embarrassment for the Church." In *Denominationalism—Its Sources and Implications*, edited by W. S. Vorster. Pretoria, South Africa: UNISA, 1982.

———. "The New Testament Forms of Ministry and the Lutheran Concept of Ministry." *Africa Theological Journal* 2, no. 1 (1982).

———. "An Anthropological Heresy: A Critique of White Theology." In *Apartheid Is a Heresy*, edited by John W. de Gruchy and Charles Villa-Vicencio. Grand Rapids, MI: Eerdmans, 1983.

———. "Black Theology." *All African Conference of Churches Magazine* (May 1984).

———. "The Annual Theological Seminar: Hammanskrall." *Theologia Evangelica* 17, no. 3 (September 1984).

———. "Black Power and Black Theology in Southern Africa." *Scriptura* 12 (June 1984).

———. "The Categories of Power and Truth." *Africa Theological Journal* 13, no. 2 (1984).

———. *God's Creativity Through the Law*. Pretoria, South Africa: UNISA, 1984.

———. "The Philosophical-Phenomenological Presuppositions in the Theology of Karl Barth." *Theologia Evangelica* 18, no. 2 (June 1985).

———. "Salvation in African Traditional Religions." *Missionalia* 13, no. 2 (August 1985).

———. Review of *The Crucified Among the Crossbearers*, by Takatso Mofokeng. *Missionalia* 13, no. 2 (August 1985).

———. "The Implications for Theology of the Contemporary South African Understanding of War and Peace." *Africa Theological Journal* 14, no. 3 (1985).

———. "Archbishop Desmond Tutu—A Revolutionary Political Priest Or Man of Peace?" In *Hammering Swords Into Ploughshares: Essays in Honour of Archbishop Mpilo Desmond Tutu*, edited by B. Tlhagale and I. Mosala. Johannesburg, South Africa: Skotaville Publishers, 1986.

――――. "The Concept 'Israel' in White Theology." *Africa Theological Journal* 15, no. 2 (1986).

――――. "Current Themes and Emphases in Black Theology." In *The Unquestionable Right to Be Free*, edited by I. J. Mosala and B. Tlhagale. Johannesburg: Skotaville Publishers, 1986; Maryknoll, NY: Orbis Books, 1986.

――――. "Present Socio-politico-economic Movements for Change." Presentation given at the Black Theology South Africa and North America Conference held at Union Theological Seminary, New York. 1-3 December 1986.

――――. "Law and Faith in Barth's Theology." *Journal of Theology for Southern Africa* (March 1987).

――――. "What Do The Churches Want and Expect From Religious Education in Schools?" *Journal of Black Theology in South Africa* 1, no. 1 (1987).

――――. *Proclaim Freedom to My People*. Johannesburg, South Africa: Skotaville Publishers, 1987.

Makhathini, Douglas. "Black Theology." In *Relevant Theology for Africa*, edited by H-J Becken. Durban, South Africa: Lutheran Publishing House, 1973.

Maqina, E. "African Independent Churches—Social and Political Implications." *Pro Veritate* (15 June 1970).

Mayatula, Victor. "African Independent Churches' Contribution to a Relevant Theology." In *A Relevant Theology for Africa*, edited by H-J Becken. Durban, South Africa: Lutheran Publishing House, 1973.

Mayson, Cedric. "The Gospel According to Blackness." *Pro Veritate* (May 1977).

Mazibuko, Sophie. "Archbishop Desmond Tutu—The Man." In *Hammering Swords Into Ploughshares: Essays in Honour of Archbishop Mpilo Desmond Tutu*, edited by B. Tlhagale and I. Mosala. Johannesburg, South Africa: Skotaville Publishers, 1986.

Mgogo, Elliott. "Prolegomenon to the Study of Black Theology." *Journal of Theology for Southern Africa*, no. 21 (December 1977).

Mgojo, K.E.M. "Church and Africanization." In *Hammering Swords Into Ploughshares: Essays in Honour of Archbishop Mpilo Desmond Tutu*, edited by B. Tlhagale and I. Mosala. Johannesburg, South Africa: Skotaville Publishers, 1986.

Mofokeng, Takatso A. *"The Possibilities of Reconciliation for Blacks and Whites in South Africa Today."* Presented at the Christian Academy of Southern Africa Conference. October 1975.

――――. *The Crucified Among the Crossbearers: Towards a Black Christology*. Uitgeversmaatschappij: J. J. Kok, 1983.

――――. Review of *Theology in Africa*, by Kwesi Dickson. *International Bulletin of Missionary Research* (July 1986).

――――. "Theological Reflections." Presented at the Black Theology South Africa and North America Conference held at Union Theological Seminary, New York. 1-3 December 1986.

――――. "Reconciliation and Liberation." In *Cry Justice*, edited by John de Gruchy. Maryknoll, NY: Orbis Books, 1986.

――――. "Evolution of the Black Struggle and the Role of Black Theology." In *The Unquestionable Right to Be Free,* edited by I. J. Mosala and B. Tlhagale. Johannesburg, South Africa: Skotaville Publishers, 1986; Maryknoll, NY: Orbis Books, 1986.

――――. "A Black Christology: A New Beginning." *Journal of Black Theology in South Africa* 1, no. 1 (1987).

Mogoba, Mmutlanyanes Stanley. "Theological Education in Africa." *Missionalia* 8 (1980).

————. "Christianity in a Southern African Context." *Journal of Theology for Southern Africa* (September 1985).

————. "From Munsieville To Oslo." In *Hammering Swords Into Ploughshares: Essays in Honour of Archbishop Mpilo Desmond Tutu*, edited by B. Tlhagale and I. Mosala. Johannesburg, South Africa: Skotaville Publishers, 1986.

Mokoka, Gobi C. "Black Experience In Black Theology." Ph.D. diss., Catholic University of Nijmegen.

Moore, Basil, ed. *The Challenge of Black Theology in South Africa.* Atlanta: John Knox Press, 1974.

Mosala, Bernadette. "Black Theology and the Struggle of the Black Women in Southern Africa." In *The Unquestionable Right to Be Free,* edited by I. J. Mosala and B. Tlhagale. Johannesburg, South Africa: Skotaville Publishers, 1986; Maryknoll, NY: Orbis Books, 1986.

Mosala, Itumeleng J. "African Traditional Beliefs and Christianity." *Journal of Theology for Southern Africa* (June 1983).

————. "Liberation Theology." *LINK (TEEC) News* 14 (August 1983).

————. "Black Theology Revisited." Presented at the Congress of the Azanian Peoples' Organization (AZAPO). 1984.

————. "African Independent Churches: A Study in Socio-Theological Protest." In *Resistance and Hope: South African Essays in Honour of Beyers Naude,* edited by Charles Villa-Vicencio and John deGruchy. Grand Rapids, MI: Eerdmans, 1985.

————. "The Biblical God From the Perspective of the Poor." In *God and Global Justice, Religion and Poverty in an Unequal World,* edited by Frederick Ferre and Rita H. Mataragnon. New York: Paragon House, 1985.

————. "Social Scientific Approaches to the Bible: One Step Forward, Two Steps Backward." *Journal of Theology for Southern Africa* (June 1986).

————. "Biblical Grounding for a Black South African Theology of Liberation." Presented at the Society of Biblical Literature Special Semeia Seminar on the Bible and Apartheid, Atlanta, Georgia, 23 November 1986.

————. "Black Theology in South Africa: Prospects for the Future; Building of Alliances." Presented at the Black Theology South Africa and North America Conference held at Union Theological Seminary, New York. 1-3 December 1986.

————. "The Relevance of African Traditional Religions and their Challenge to Black Theology" and "The Use of the Bible in Black Theology." In *The Unquestionable Right to Be Free,* edited by I. J. Mosala and B. Tlhagale. Johannesburg, South Africa: Skotaville Publishers, 1986; Maryknoll, NY: Orbis Books, 1986.

————. "Ethics of the Economic Principles: Church and Secular Investments." In *Hammering Swords Into Ploughshares: Essays in Honour of Archbishop Mpilo Desmond Tutu,* edited by B. Tlhagale and I. Mosala. Johannesburg, South Africa: Skotaville Publishers, 1986.

————. "Biblical Hermeneutics of Black Theology in South Africa." Ph.D. diss., University of Cape Town, South Africa, February 1987.

————. "The Meaning of Reconciliation: A Black Perspective." *Journal of Theology for Southern Africa* (July 1987).

————. "Black Theology Versus the Social Morality of Settler Colonialism: Hermeneutical Reflections on Luke 1 and 2." *Journal of Black Theology for Southern Africa* 1, no. 1 (1987).

———. "The Implications of the Text of Esther for African Women's Struggle for Liberation." *Journal of Black Theology in South Africa* (November 1988).

———. *Biblical Hermeneutics and Black Theology in South Africa.* Grand Rapids, MI: Eerdmans, 1989.

———. "Violence and the Prophets." In *Theology and Violence:The South African Debate*, edited by Charles Villa-Vicencio. Johannesburg, South Africa: Skotaville Publishers, 1987.

Mosothoane, E. K. "The Message of the New Testament Seen in African Perspective." In *A Relevant Theology for Africa*, edited by H-J Becken. Durban, South Africa: Lutheran Publishing House, 1973.

———. "Communion Sanctorum in Africa." *Missionalia* 1 (1973).

———. "The Liberation of Peoples in the New Testament?" *Missionalia* 5, no. 1 (April 1977).

———. "The Use of Scripture in Black Theology." In *Scripture and the Use of Scripture*, edited by W. S. Vorster. Pretoria, South Africa: UNISA, 1979.

———. "Toward a Theology for South Africa." *Missionalia* 9, no. 3 (1981).

Motlhabi, Mokgethi. "Black Theology: A Personal View" and "Black Theology and Authority." In *The Challenge of Black Theology in South Africa*, edited by Basil Moore. Atlanta: John Knox Press, 1974.

———. "The Historic Origin of Black Theology." *Bulletin De Theologie Africaine* 6, no. 12 (July-December 1984).

———. *The Theory and Practice of Black Resistance to Apartheid: A Social-Ethical Analysis.* Johannesburg, South Africa: Skotaville Publishers, 1985.

———. "The Historical Origins of Black Theology." In *The Unquestionable Right to Be Free*, edited by I. J. Mosala and B. Tlhagale. Johannesburg, South Africa: Skotaville Publishers, 1986; Maryknoll, NY: Orbis Books, 1986.

———. "The Concept of Morality in African Tradition." In *Hammering Swords Into Ploughshares: Essays in Honour of Archbishop Mpilo Desmond Tutu*, edited by B. Tlhagale and I. Mosala. Johannesburg, South Africa: Skotaville Publishers, 1986.

———. *Challenge to Apartheid: Toward A Moral National Resistance.* Grand Rapids, MI: Eerdmans, 1988.

Mpunzi, Ananias. "Black Theology as Liberation Theology." In *A Reader in Political Theology*, edited by Alistair Kee. Philadelphia: Westminster Press, 1974.

Mutloatse, Mothobi, ed. *Africa South: Contemporary Writings.* London: Heinemann, 1981.

———. *Reconstruction: Ninety Years of Black South African Literature.* Johannesburg, South Africa: Raven Press, 1981.

———. "Seminar on Black Theology at Wilgerspruit." *EcuNews* (November 1983). News Service of the South African Council of Churches, Johannesburg.

Muzorewa, Gwinyai H. *The Origins and Development of African Theology.* Maryknoll, NY: Orbis Books, 1985.

———. "A Quest for an African Christology." *Journal of Black Theology in South Africa* (November 1988).

Mzimela, Sipo E. *Apartheid: South African Naziism.* New York: Vantage Press, 1983.

Ngcokovane, Cecil M. *Apartheid in South Africa: Challenge to Christian Churches.* New York: Vantage Press, 1984.

———. "Historical, Social and Cultural Origins." Presentation given at the Black

Theology South Africa and U.S.A. Conference at Union Theological Seminary, New York. 1-3 December 1986.

———. "The Church and the Politics of Our Time." In *Hammering Swords Into Ploughshares: Essays in Honour of Archbishop Mpilo Desmond Tutu*, edited by B. Tlhagale and I. Mosala. Johannesburg, South Africa: Skotaville Publishers, 1986.

Ngubane, J. B. "Theological Roots of the African Independent Churches and Their Challenge to Black Theology." In *The Unquestionable Right to Be Free,* edited by I. J. Mosala and B. Tlhagale. Johannesburg, South Africa: Skotaville Publishers, 1986; Maryknoll, NY: Orbis Books, 1986.

Noko, Ishmael. "The Concept of God in Black Theology: An Appreciation of God As Liberator and Reconciler." Ph.D. diss., McGill University, Canada, 1977.

Nolan, Albert. *God in South Africa; The Challenge of the Gospel.* Cape Town, South Africa: David Philip, 1988.

Ntintili, Prince Vuyani. "An Analysis, Comparison, and Evaluation of the Doctrine of God in Black Theology of Liberation and African Christian Theology." Th.M. thesis, Dallas Theological Seminary, 1984.

Nurnberger, K. "Comment (on a Relevant Theology for Africa: An Examination of Black Theology—African Theology)." *Journal of Theology for Southern Africa* (December 1972).

Nxumalo, Jabulani A. "Christ and Ancestors in the African World." *Journal of Theology for Southern Africa* (September 1980).

———. "The Church From a Black Perspective: A Response to Bonganjalo Goba." *Missionalia* 9, no. 1 (April 1981).

Odoki, Sabino. "Presentation and Evaluation of T. A. Mofokeng's Black Christology." *African Christian Studies* 3, no. 1 (March 1987).

Oosthuizen, G. C. *Theological Battleground in Africa and Asia.* London: Billing and Sons, 1971.

———. "Black Theology in Historical Perspective." *The South African Journal of African Affairs* 3 (1973).

Pro Veritate. "Black Theology Resolution" (of the Hammanskrall Seminar, 1971) 10, no. 3 (July 1971).

Qqubule, Simon. "What Is Black Theology?" *Journal of Theology for Southern Africa* 8 (September 1974).

———. "Pastoral Problems of the Migratory Labor System." In *African Perspectives on South Africa*, edited by HWVD Merwe, et al. Stanford, CA: Hoover Institution Press, 1978.

———. "Can Each Church Remain United?" In *The Church and the Alternative Society (SACC Papers 1979)*, edited by M. Nash, South Africa.

———. "They Hate Him Without A Cause." In *Hammering Swords Into Ploughshares: Essays in Honour of Archbishop Mpilo Desmond Tutu*, edited by B. Tlhagale and I. Mosala. Johannesburg, South Africa: Skotaville Publishers, 1986.

SASO Newsletter. "My Understanding of Black Theology" (November/December 1975).

Sebidi, L. J. "Encounter of African Religion with Christianity." *Pro Veritate* (May 1977).

———. "The Dynamics of the Black Struggle and Its Implications For Black Theology." In *The Unquestionable Right To Be Free,* edited by I. J. Mosala and B. Tlhagale. Johannesburg, South Africa: Skotaville Publishers, 1986; Maryknoll, NY: Orbis Books, 1986.

———. "Toward an Understanding of the Current Unrest in South Africa." In *Hammering Swords Into Ploughshares: Essays in Honour of Archbishop Mpilo Desmond Tutu*, edited by B. Tlhagale and I. Mosala. Johannesburg, South Africa: Skotaville Publishers, 1986.

Setiloane, Gabriel. "God of My Fathers and My God." *South African Outlook* (October 1970).

———. "Racism and Us—The Church's Calling." *Pro Veritate* (15 November 1970).

———. "I Am An African—Poem." *Pro Veritate* (15 December 1970).

———. "Black Theology." *South African Outlook* (February 1971).

———. "Modimo: God Among the Sotho-Tswana." *Journal of Theology for Southern Africa* (September 1973).

———. "Confessing Christ Today From an African Perspective, Man and Community." *Journal of Theology for Southern Africa* (September 1975).

———. *The Image of God Among the Sotho-Tswana*. Balkema, Rotterdam, 1976.

———. "I Am an African." In *Missions Trends*, no. 3, edited by G. H. Anderson and T. F. Stransky. Grand Rapids, MI: Eerdmans Publishing Co., 1976.

———. "How the Traditional Worldview Persists in the Christianity of the Sotho-Tswana." In *Christianity and Independent Africa*, edited by Edward Fasholé-Luke, et al. London: Rex Collins, 1978.

———. "Theological Trends in Africa." *Missionalia* 8, no. 2 (August 1980).

———. "Where Are We in African Theology?" In *African Theology En Route*, edited by K. Appiah-Kubi and S. Torres. Maryknoll, NY: Orbis Books, 1981.

———. "The Ecumenical Movement in Africa: From Mission Church to Moratorium." In *Resistance and Hope: South African Essays in Honour of Beyers Naude*, edited by Charles Villa-Vicencio and John deGruchy. Grand Rapids, MI: Eerdmans, 1985.

———. *African Theology: An Introduction*. Johannesburg, South Africa: Skotaville Publishers, 1986.

———. "On Which Side Is God?" In *When Prayer Makes News*, edited by A. A. Boesak and C. Villa-Vicencio. Philadelphia: Westminster Press, 1986.

———. "Salvation and the Secular." In *Hammering Swords Into Ploughshares: Essays in Honour of Archbishop Mpilo Desmond Tutu*, edited by B. Tlhagale and I. Mosala. Johannesburg, South Africa: Skotaville Publishers, 1986.

———. "Civil Authority—From the Perspective of African Theology." *Journal of Black Theology in South Africa* (November 1988).

Shuuya, T. K. "An Encounter Between the New Testament and African Traditional Concepts." In *A Relevant Theology for Africa*, edited by H-J Becken. Durban, South Africa: Lutheran Publishing House, 1973.

Sikakane, Enos. "The Need for Black Theology." *Pro Veritate* 12, no. 12 (April 1974).

———. "The African's Spiritual Concepts. In *African Perspectives on South Africa*, edited by HWVD Merwe, et al. Stanford, CA: Hoover Institution Press, 1978.

Simpson, Theodore. "Black Theology—and White." *Pro Veritate* (March 1974).

South African Council of Churches. "June 16 Memorial Service—A Theological Rationale and a Call to Prayer for the End to Unjust Rule." (16 June 1985).

South African Delegation. "The Role of the Church in Southern Africa." *Bulletin De Theologie Africaine* 6, 12 (July-December 1984).

Sprunger, A. R. "The Contribution of the African Independent Churches to a Relevant Theology for Africa." In *Relevant Theology for Africa*, edited by Hans-

Jurgen Becken. Durban, South Africa: Lutheran Publishing House, 1973.

Tlhagale, Buti. "Towards a Black Theology of Labor." *Voices from the Third World* (December 1983).

———. "Towards a Black Theology of Labor." In *Resistance and Hope: South African Essays in Honour of Beyers Naude,* edited by Charles Villa-Vicencio and John deGruchy. Grand Rapids, MI: Eerdmans, 1985.

———. "Culture in an Apartheid Society." *Journal of Theology for Southern Africa* (June 1985).

———. "On Violence: A Township Perspective." In *The Unquestionable Right to Be Free,* edited by I. J. Mosala and B. Tlhagale. Johannesburg, South Africa: Skotaville Publishers, 1986; Maryknoll, NY: Orbis Books, 1986.

———. "Nazism, Stalinist Russia and Apartheid—A Comparison." In *Hammering Swords Into Ploughshares: Essays in Honour of Archbishop Mpilo Desmond Tutu,* edited by B. Tlhagale and I. Mosala. Johannesburg, South Africa: Skotaville Publishers, 1986.

Tshenkeng, I. D. "A Theology for the People." *Pro Veritate* (February 1977).

———. "Jesus the Liberator." *Pro Veritate* (September 1977).

Tutu, Desmond. "God—Black or White?" *Ministry* 11, no. 4 (1971).

———. "South African Insights and the Old Testament." *Journal of Theology for Southern Africa* (1972).

———. "Whither Theological Education? An African Perspective." *Theological Education* (Summer 1973).

———. "Some African Insights and the Old Testament" and "Viability." In *Relevant Theology for Africa,* edited by Hans Jurgen Becken. Durban, South Africa: Lutheran Publishing House, 1973.

———. "Black Theology." *Frontier* 17 (Summer 1974).

———. "African Theology and Black Theology." In *African Challenge,* edited by K. Best. Nairobi: Transafrica, 1975.

———. "Church and Nation in the Perspective of Black Theology." *Journal of Theology for Southern Africa,* no. 15 (June 1976).

———. "Theologie Africaine et theologie noire. La quête de l'authenticité et la lutte pour la liberation." *Flambeau* (1976).

———. "God-Given Dignity and the Quest for Liberation in the Light of the South African Dilemma." In *Liberation,* edited by David Thomas. Johannesburg, South Africa: South African Council of Churches, 1976.

———. "God Intervening in Human Affairs." *Missionalia* 5, no. 2 (1977).

———. "Whither African Theology?" In *Christianity and Independent Africa,* edited by Fashole-Luke et al. London: Rex Collins, 1978.

———. "God-Given Dignity and the Quest for Liberation." In *African Perspectives on South Africa,* edited by HWVD Merwe, et al. Stanford, CA: Hoover Institutional Press, 1978.

———. "Black Theology/African Theology—Soul Mates or Antagonists?" In *Black Theology: A Documentary History, 1966–1979,* edited by G. S. Wilmore and J. H. Cone. Maryknoll, NY: Orbis Books, 1979.

———. "Mission in the 1980s." *Occ Bul Miss R* 4 (January 1980).

———. "Tearing People Apart." *South African Outlook* (October 1980).

———. "The Theology of Liberation in South Africa." In *African Theology En Route,* edited by Kofi Appiah-Kubi and S. Torres. Maryknoll, NY: Orbis Books, 1981.

————. "The South African Council of Churches on Namibia." *IDOC Bul* (1982).

————. "The Blasphemy That Is Apartheid." *Africa Report* (July-August 1983).

————. "Christianity and Apartheid." In *Apartheid Is a Heresy*, edited by John W. de Gruchy and Charles Villa-Vicencio. Grand Rapids, MI: Eerdmans, 1983.

————. "Persecution. Suffering: Biblical Teaching." In *Martyrdom Today*, edited by J-B. Metz and E. Schillebeeckx. New York: Seabury Press, 1983.

————. "Barmen and Apartheid." *Journal of Theology for Southern Africa* (June 1984).

————. "South Africa's Blacks: Aliens in Their Own Land." *C&C* 44, no. 19 (26 November 1984).

————. "The Bishop and South Africa: An Interview With Desmond Tutu." *Worldview* (December 1984).

————. "Bishop Tutu Speaks Out: Excerpts From the Nobel Prize Winner's Addresses." *Witness* (December 1984).

————. "Desmond Tutu, Tracing the Roots." *Otherside* (January-February 1985).

————. "Desmond Tutu, One Who Speaks Truth to Power." *Sojourners* (February 1985).

————. "Wall of Fire." *Trinity Seminary Review* (Spring 1985).

————. "Christian Witness in South Africa." *Ref J* 35 (October 1985).

————. "How Can You Say You Love God Whom You Have Not Seen When You Hate Your Brother Whom You Have Seen?" *E-SA* 13 (December 1985).

————. *Hope and Suffering*. Grand Rapids, MI: Eerdmans, 1985.

————. *Crying in the Wilderness*. Grand Rapids, MI: Eerdmans, 1985.

————. "Spirituality: Christian and African." In *Resistance and Hope: South African Essays in Honour of Beyers Naude*, edited by Charles Villa-Vicencio and John deGruchy. Grand Rapids, MI: Eerdmans, 1985.

————. "Bishop Desmond Tutu, Interview." *Africa Report* 31 (March-April 1986).

————. "The Process of Reconciliation and the Demand of Obedience." *Transformation* 3 (April-June 1986).

————. "What Jesus Means to Me." In *Cry Justice*, edited by John de Gruchy. Maryknoll, NY: Orbis Books, 1986.

————. "Freedom Fighters or Terrorists?" In *Theology and Violence: The South African Debate*. Johannesburg, South Africa: Skotaville Publishers, 1987.

Van Rooy, J. A. "The Image of Man in White Theology: Calvinist, Biblical, or Self-Centered? A Response to Simon Maimela." *Missionalia* 9, no. 1 (April 1981).

Villa-Vicencio, Charles. *The Theology of Apartheid*. Cape Town, South Africa: The Methodist Publishing House, circa 1982.

————. "South Africa's Theologized Nationalism." *Ecumenical Review*.

————, ed. *On Reading Karl Barth in South Africa*. Grand Rapids, MI: Eerdmans, 1988.

Vorster, W. S., ed. *Sexism and Feminism in Theological Perspective*. Pretoria, South Africa: UNISA, 1984.

Zulu, Alphaeus. "Whither Black Theology?" *Pro Veritate* 11, no. 11 (March 1973).

————. "The Church Confronts South Africa." In *African Perspectives on South Africa*, edited by HWVD Merwe, et al. Stanford, CA: Hoover Institution Press, 1978.

Index